THE GOOD GIRLS

THE GOOD GIRLS

An Ordinary Killing

SONIA FALEIRO

BLOOMSBURY CIRCUS
LONDON · OXFORD · NEW YORK · NEW DELHI · SYDNEY

UM
IFM and ZFM

BLOOMSBURY CIRCUS
Bloomsbury Publishing Plc
50 Bedford Square, London, WC1B 3DP, UK
29 Earlsfort Terrace, Dublin 2, Ireland

BLOOMSBURY, BLOOMSBURY CIRCUS and the Bloomsbury Circus logo are
trademarks of Bloomsbury Publishing Plc

First published in Great Britain 2021

A catalogue record for this book is available from the British Library

ISBN: HB: 978-1-4088-7672-5; TPB: 978-1-4088-7673-2; EBOOK: 978-1-4088-7674-9

2 4 6 8 10 9 7 5 3 1

Typeset by Newgen KnowledgeWorks Pvt. Ltd., Chennai, India
Printed and bound in Great Britain by CPI Group (UK) Ltd, Croydon CRO 4YY

To find out more about our authors and books visit www.bloomsbury.com
and sign up for our newsletters

'Women must particularly be guarded against evil inclinations, however trifling [they may appear]; for, if they are not guarded, they will bring sorrow on two families.'

—*The Laws of Manu*

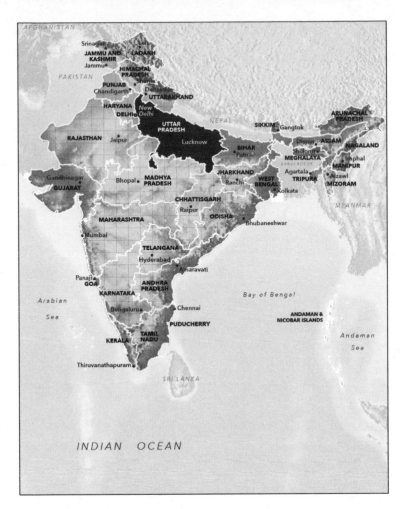

Index of Characters

THE VILLAGE OF KATRA

Padma Shakya, sixteen years old
Her father *Jeevan Lal*, a farmer, and stepmother *Sunita Devi*
Ram Sakhi, Padma's biological mother who died when she was two years old
Lalli Shakya, fourteen years old
Her father *Sohan Lal*, the Shakya family patriarch and older brother to Jeevan Lal and Ram Babu, his wife *Siya Devi* and their four other children: daughter *Phoolan* and sons *Virender*, *Parvesh* and *Avnesh*. Lalli is their youngest daughter
Ram Babu, Padma and Lalli's paternal uncle, his wife *Guddo* and their seven children
Ramdevi, Padma and Lalli's paternal grandmother who lives with Jeevan Lal and family
Manju Shakya, a cousin spending her summer holidays with Lalli's family, aged twelve
A first cousin of the Shakya brothers, *Babu 'Nazru' Ram*, aged twenty-six. He lives with his family in the midst of the Katra fields
Rajiv Kumar Yadav, a neighbour who draws Nazru's attention to the girls' behaviour in the fields

Yogendra Singh Shakya, a prosperous cousin of the Shakya brothers, who the brothers often turned to for help
Prem Singh Shakya, Yogendra's brother. He saw Lalli talking on the phone on the day she disappeared
Their father, *Neksu Lal*

THE HAMLET OF JATI

Darvesh 'Pappu' Yadav, aged nineteen, watermelon farmer
His father *Veerpal 'Veere' Yadav*, mother *Jhalla Devi* and brothers *Avdesh* and *Urvesh*, both in their twenties
Avdesh's wife, *Basanta*, and their infant daughter *Shivani*
Pappu's cousin and close friend *Raju*, in whose shack he often spent the night

THE VILLAGE OF NABIGANJ

Ram Chander, Padma's oldest maternal uncle and her late mother's oldest brother
His son, *Ram Avtar*, aged eighteen
His younger brother *Kanhaiya Lal*, who had been told a dream that predicted what happened to the girls
Ram Chander's three other brothers, who, along with their families, comprise around thirty people living together

POLICE

Sub-Inspector *Ram Vilas Yadav*, aged fifty-seven, in charge of the police outpost located in Katra village
Chattrapal Singh Gangwar, aged fifty-six, recently promoted to Head Constable
Constable *Sarvesh Yadav*, aged thirty-nine, accused of dereliction of duty towards the Shakya villagers

Constable *Raghunandan Singh Yadav*, who assisted the family

Constable *Satinder Pal Singh Yadav*, a quiet man who did as he was told

Inspector *Ganga Singh Yadav*, Station Officer of the police station in Ushait and first Inspecting Officer on the case

Mukesh Kumar Saxena, a locally powerful police officer who went on to head a Special Investigation Team on the case

Maan Singh Chauhan, Superintendent of Police, highest-ranking officer present on the day the bodies were found

POST-MORTEM TEAM

Lala Ram, the former sweeper who conducted the post-mortem

Dr *Rajiv Gupta*, general practitioner, District Hospital, Budaun, who oversaw the post-mortem

Dr *Pushpa Panth Tripathi*, gynaecologist and obstetrician, District Women's Hospital, Budaun

They were accompanied by Dr *Avdhesh Kumar*, a senior surgeon at the District Hospital and *A. K. Singh*, the hospital pharmacist

POLITICIANS

Narendra Modi, the new Prime Minister of India who was sworn in on 26 May, two days before the children were found

Akhilesh Yadav, Chief Minister of Uttar Pradesh, who was in control of the state police

Mayawati Prabhu Das, Dalit leader with cult status in Uttar Pradesh

Bhagwan Singh Shakya, a member of the Bharatiya Janata Party and a Shakya community leader

Sinod Kumar Shakya, a member of Mayawati's party and an elected member of the state legislative assembly. The Shakya family were his constituents and he was their confidant

Shareef Ahmed Ansari, Sinod Kumar's close aide. He spoke on behalf of his boss and gave the Shakya family every possible assistance

CENTRAL BUREAU OF INVESTIGATION

Vijay Kumar Shukla, Investigating Officer
Anil Girdhari Lal Kaul, Supervising Officer

MEDICAL TEAM

Dr *Adarsh Kumar*, Additional Professor, Department of Forensic Medicine and Toxicology, All India Institute of Medical Sciences, New Delhi
He was accompanied by two others, Dr *Manish Kumath* and Dr *Sunil Kumar*

Contents

Prologue

GOOD DAYS ARE COMING SOON

People called them Padma Lalli like they were one person[*].
'Padma Lalli?'
'Padma Lalli!'
'Have you seen Padma Lalli?'
At sixteen Padma was the older cousin by two years.
She was small, only five feet, but even so she was bigger
than Lalli by three inches. Padma had oval eyes, smooth
skin and collarbones that popped. She had long black hair
that she knew to pat down with water and tightly plait or
else there would be words.

Lalli's kameez hung from her frame like washing on the
line. Round-shouldered and baby-faced, she was the quiet
romantic who read poems out loud. Padma had dropped
out of school, but Lalli told her father she wanted to study
and get a job. And while it would please him to share
the memory of this conversation, they had both known it
would never happen. The school Lalli attended had a roof,
but not enough rooms – many classes were conducted

---

[*]The girls' names have been changed in accordance with Indian law which
requires that the identity of victims of certain crimes remain private.

outside, in the dirt, and there were seven teachers for 400 pupils. But even if the school had been different, a girl's destiny lay in the hands of her husband.

School broke up one blazing afternoon in May, and all the children congregated in Ramnath's orchard to shout, run and climb trees. Lalli hurried to Padma's side. As the others pelted down green mangoes, the teenagers stood aloof. They were together always, apart from everyone.

Some 3,000 people lived in Katra Sadatganj, an eye-blink of a village in the Budaun district of western Uttar Pradesh, crammed into less than one square mile of land. On harvest mornings, when it was time to cut the rabi crops, the entire village congregated in the fields. Women hitched their saris and men rolled up their trouser bottoms. By 8 a.m. the ground was tapestried with branches of tobacco, and freshly picked garlic bulbs filled the air with a biting fragrance.

Even small children pitched in. They shooed the crows that swooped through the fields like great black fishing nets, they chased away the long-limbed rhesus monkeys that prowled lunch bundles for roti sabzi.

That summer, temperatures climbed to 42 degrees Celsius. Amid whirlpools of dust, cobras slithered out of their holes, but the barefoot boys and girls paid no heed. The harvest was the one precious opportunity their families had to make money.

Economic growth had improved incomes, and elections every five years brought promises of more. The day before the harvest, on 26 May, a charismatic new Prime Minister named Narendra Modi was sworn in with an irresistible slogan, 'achhe din aane waale hain'. Good days are coming soon.

As they waited, the majority of families in Katra went without electricity, gas, running water and toilets. They bought solar panels, they lowered buckets into wells. They gathered dung for cooking fuel. They squatted in the fields, pulling their knees up to their chest as they scrolled through their phones to pass the time.

Some were carpenters and tailors; others worked as political fixers, marriage brokers, cycle puncture repairmen or tonga drivers. They sold vegetables, chickens and country liquor. They broke the law to mine sand from riverbanks. A few well-off families had tractors that they leased out. About a third of the men had a piece of land. It was just a few bighas, never quite an acre, but whatever it was, it was theirs.

Land was security, from which everything flowed – it put dal in the katori, clothes on the back. Land was power. It attracted a good quality of bride who would bring a good dowry. This would increase their security and social standing. Above all, land was identity. It made them cultivators. Without it, the men were reduced to landless labourers. They were destined to go wherever there was work, for whatever they were offered. They could be compared to the Yadav cattle herders in the neighbouring hamlet of whom it was said, they are rooted to nothing and committed to no one.

The men of Katra spent almost all day in the fields. The children studied here since the good school, which taught English, was near the orchard. In the evenings when the edges of the clouds softened and blurred and a cool breeze rippled through the crops, women came back down from the village to draw water and socialise. Boys teased the limping dogs, and the limping dogs chased rats. Girls huddled. The smell was heat, husks and buffalo droppings.

After night hooded the fields men dragged their charpoys over and hunkered down under blankets, bamboo poles at the ready, same as farmers up and down the district this time of year. They would protect their harvest with their lives if they had to, whether from the gun-slinging bandits who came for motorbikes or the herds of nilgai who sought seeds and stems.

Everything was here. Everything happened here. And so naturally it was here, in the fields, that the rumour started.

Rabi

Spring, 2014

An Accusation Is Made

Rajiv Kumar had a side job as a government teacher, but his real job was farming. While working his land he had observed Padma and Lalli. They were as alike as two grains of rice, and they spent all day in the fields. Now one girl, he couldn't tell which, had a phone to her ear. He didn't like it.

Some villages in Uttar Pradesh forbade unmarried women from using phones.[1] A phone was a key to a door that led outside the village via calls and messaging apps. The villagers were afraid of what would happen if women stepped through this door. They might get ideas such as whom to marry.

Records showed that 95 per cent of Indians still married within their caste,[2] and anyone who didn't attracted attention. In 2013 a young woman from Katra village took off with a man from a different caste. Her father was so ashamed he couldn't show his face, people said. The woman had chosen to marry against his will, to have what was known as a love marriage rather than leaving it to her father to arrange a partner for her. She had violated the honour code and would never see her parents again – for their safety, and certainly hers. A few months after that, it was the turn of a girl from the next-door hamlet of Jati.

The news of the elopements moved like a swarm of whirring insects, landing first here and then there until all the nearby villages were warned: change is coming, be vigilant, be ready to act.

In 2014, for the first time, the National Crime Records Bureau, which publishes the number of cases registered for crimes, published data on honour killings. Twenty-eight cases were reported in the country,[3] but everyone knew the true number was hundreds, if not thousands, more. Girls were killed for marrying outside their caste or outside their religion and sometimes having premarital sex was reason enough.

With the killing the family's honour was reclaimed or, at least, the other villagers were given notice that the family had taken the errant behaviour seriously and done their best to right a wrong. The Constitution had existed for only decades while Hindu religious beliefs dated back thousands of years, said one father who was accused of killing his daughter.[4]

In Katra, the rule was that boys could own phones, but girls had to get permission to use them.

Even so, Padma and Lalli knew what to do with a phone better than their mothers who could identify neither letters nor numbers. Padma often called her maternal uncles, reciprocating the effort they had put into keeping in touch after their only sister, Padma's biological mother, had died. Lalli texted her elder brother who worked for a car parts manufacturer far away. The girls used the torch feature to light their way into the pit of the night.

Rajiv Kumar didn't know this, because he didn't know them. He didn't even know their parents beyond the usual 'sab theek?' – all well? – but a girl's life was everyone's business. He was determined to do his duty. His plot was near some land owned by a close relative of the girls named Babu 'Nazru' Ram. With his bowl cut, paan-stained teeth and sloppy smile Nazru was approachable. At twenty-six, he wasn't that much older than the girls.

'They shouldn't be out in public with a mobile phone,' Rajiv Kumar said, speaking in Braj Bhasha, the language of these parts. 'Who knows who they're talking to?' Although the fields adjoined the village, the walking distance from the Shakya house to the orchard was ten minutes or more. The orchard wasn't even visible from the house, which was located in a spiderweb of lanes. Rajiv Kumar's implication was clear. The girls chose that particular time because they were alone, they chose that place because it was secluded. To remove any doubt, he used the word 'chakkar' to indicate there was something crooked about all this, something off balance. 'The girls in your family are romancing someone,' he said.

Nazru agreed that it didn't look good.

'You should let their parents know,' Rajiv Kumar said.

A few days passed, and Rajiv Kumar again saw the girls talking on the phone. He again sought out Nazru who explained that a complaint could backfire. The girls' parents might accuse him of slander. Rumours were butterflies, they might say. If word got around, who would marry Padma? Who would have Lalli?

Nazru understood that it was one thing for Rajiv Kumar to talk. It was another for a relative, a first cousin no less, to level an accusation of such grave seriousness. And there was the other matter to consider, which was that he depended on the family. Everyone in the village struggled, but he had an asthmatic father to care for and a brother people called crazy. The Shakyas sometimes hired him to work their land. If things got truly difficult, they could be counted on to come through with cash.

So Nazru said nothing – but mindful of his duty, he started to watch the girls.

His behaviour didn't go unnoticed.

'He ogles us,' Padma said to a friend with disgust.

It was while Nazru was keeping watch that he came across the spindly bobblehead boy. Katra village was small and Nazru knew everyone who lived there – but he didn't know this boy. The boy was grazing his buffaloes so he couldn't have come from far. It was natural to assume that he was a Yadav from the hamlet next door.

'What's your name?' Nazru shouted.

'Pappu.'

The young man's name, in fact, was Darvesh Yadav. He was sharp-nosed with a shock of very black hair. People called him Pappu because he was small, like a boy. Pappu wore an oversized shirt and trousers, a hoop in his ear and rubber slippers on his feet.

Although his face was imprinted with apprehension, Pappu's life was more secure than most in the hamlet of Jati. His father was a watermelon farmer who had accumulated enough savings to build one of the few brick houses in a settlement of shacks. Pappu's mother doted on him, her youngest child. Although his parents' lives revolved around the sandy riverbank home of their crop, they didn't stop their children from finding work elsewhere during the off season – picking through garbage for recyclables or hefting bricks on construction sites, even as far away as Delhi.

And because of this, Pappu had seen a world outside the one his parents were rooted to: a world in which roads were crammed with cars, and not farm animals, where there were soaring buildings and ambitious men and women doing more than just the one thing in the one way it had always been done – a modern India where the burdens and entrapments that had kept generations of his family collecting cow dung could be swept away and forgotten. And although Pappu didn't know anyone who had left the village for good, this new world was full of promise. Freedom was close.

But Pappu, although he was nearly twenty, could only write his name. And he was expected to help support his family. They had a deal, father and son – as long as Pappu contributed financially, he could do as he pleased in his free time.

Nazru wasn't having it.

'If your animals eat all my grass,' he shouted, 'what will my animals eat? Don't you come here again!'

Lalli's Father Buys a Phone

Cousin Manju was twelve and skinny, with the radiant smile and point-blank manner of all the Shakya women. She lived with her family in Noida, a heavily polluted industrial city some hours away from Katra village, in an overcrowded tenement with shared bathrooms. The walls of the building shook when trucks rumbled past.

When Lalli's father, Sohan Lal, phoned to invite her for the school holidays she was thrilled. It was mango season. And she'd get to see her first cousin, whom she fondly called 'meri wali didi' – my sister. Her uncle said he'd be away with his wife and youngest son on a pilgrimage. 'Lalli will be alone.'

It was understood that Manju, although she was younger than Lalli, would look out for the older girl.

Before leaving, Sohan Lal went to buy a new phone from Keshav Communications, which was located in the bazaar, down the road from the cycle puncture repairman and opposite a snack shop that served Coca-Cola out of an icebox. Waiting at the door, sweat beading on his face, was Yogendra Singh, Sohan Lal's cousin. He was a plain-speaking young man with a rough beard, dressed – like all the village men – in a collared shirt and sturdy trousers made from a pale fabric, which better endured the heat.

All day long customers streamed into Keshav's. They browsed his affordable range of Made in China phones, some of which had features that weren't readily available even in name-brand handsets. Then, because they didn't have Internet access, they asked Keshav to download the latest Bollywood songs by sideloading them from his desktop computer to their phones via USB. Most didn't have power either, so they also paid a few rupees to charge their phones.

As they waited, customers enjoyed the cool breeze from the whirring fan, gazing at the neatly ordered shelves stacked with boxes of cellophane-wrapped products. Keshav was a modern entrepreneur and the village boys admired him.

This afternoon there weren't very many clients vying for his attention – but even if there had been, Keshav would have served the newcomers first. Sohan Lal's cousin was Keshav's landlord's son – and according to the social hierarchies of the village, this made him the equivalent of Keshav's boss's son.

Sohan Lal wanted a handset with a long battery life. He was going on a pilgrimage, he said. It was time to get his youngest boy's hair tonsured and to pay respect to the mother goddess.

Keshav brought out a handful of phones from under the glass counter. Sohan Lal browsed them carefully, but it was his cousin who did most of the talking, asking about this feature and that. They settled on a shiny black phone with a gold and black keypad. Then Sohan Lal asked to buy a SIM card. But when told to provide proof of identity, which was the law, he said he wasn't carrying any. His cousin looked on enquiringly.

Twenty-year-old Keshav made a quick set of calculations in his head. It was only here in Katra that he could afford to run his own business. He paid 500 rupees a month in rent, a good deal. He was in debt to his uncle who had helped set him up and he owed it to his widowed mother to keep things going.

It didn't matter, Keshav assured the men. He pulled out a copy of another customer's identity card and entered the details in Sohan Lal's bill of sale. Then, because Sohan Lal couldn't write, he forged a signature on his behalf. What was more likely, he thought, the police appearing at his doorstep or his landlord's son getting angry with him for refusing to do as he was told?

Keshav knew the villagers had identity cards which they used to purchase subsidised food grains and to vote, but he also knew that these precious items were kept securely at home. He often did such favours and had never yet been caught. He had no reason to believe this time would be any different.

Sohan Lal didn't take his new phone on pilgrimage. Instead, he gave it to his niece Padma. Although it's unlikely she knew it at the time, the device had a feature that made it especially popular with nosy parents. It could record calls. The conversations were then saved on the phone.

Cousin Manju Observes
Something Strange

Some years ago, the Shakya family stopped getting along.
The men blamed the women, accusing them of submitting
to small-hearted squabbles. The house, which stretched
across a quarter acre of land, was now split into three parts
demarcated by low mud walls.

Thereafter, each of the families cooked meals in their
own kitchens, drew water from their own handpumps and
housed their black-bellied buffaloes and white-skinned
goats in separate shelters. If they had used toilets, they
would have built three. But they squatted in the fields, as
most everyone else did, because paying for something that
could be had for free was wasteful.

They were still a joint family, the Shakyas insisted. The
courtyard was for everyone to bask in, all eighteen of them,
and the dogs too. A parent of one child was the parent
of all the others. Padma called Siya Devi 'badi-ma', elder
mother, and to Siya Devi her niece Padma was 'hamari
bachchi', our girl. Sohan Lal, the oldest of the brothers
at forty-seven, was the head of the household. His two
younger brothers, who were in their thirties, deferred to
him on important decisions. Being men, they spent their
days outside the confines of the house. The women mostly
stayed in. They cooked for the men, ate after the men and

sat lower than them. If the men settled on the charpoy, the wives made do on the floor.

But a little space and some autonomy improved the quality of one's life, the Shakyas said, and so did some education. The Shakya parents were illiterate, but they sent their boys and girls to the school near the orchard. The girls were typically pulled out after the eighth class, when school was no longer free nor compulsory. Then they were married off. For their safety, the Shakyas said, for social acceptability. When she could read and write, a woman exuded sheen; she attracted a better quality of husband.

Every morning at harvest time, Jeevan Lal and his wife Sunita Devi went to their mint plot. They left Padma in the care of her grandmother with whom they shared a dark little room partitioned into two by a bed sheet hooked to some nails. The elderly woman was whispers and bones in a widow's white sari. Although she shared a close bond with her granddaughter, and was, in fact, largely responsible for her well-being, it was inevitable that Padma would drift off to see her cousin in the room next door.

Lalli had two elder siblings, Phoolan Devi and Virender, but they no longer lived at home. In the absence of her parents – Sohan Lal and Siya Devi, who had taken their youngest child Avnesh on pilgrimage with them – the teenaged girl looked out for herself, her brother Parvesh, their animals and home.

At the other end of the courtyard the third Shakya man, round-bellied Ram Babu, and his ringing-voiced wife, Guddo, shepherded several of their young towards their taro patch. They wouldn't return until it was time for the evening prayers, which they performed before a shrine indoors.

The children left behind were unsupervised. The day cracked open. In, out, in, out, they went.

When Manju's father learned of this much later, he was outraged. 'Ghar pe koi nahin tha,' he said. There was no one at home. 'They were children!'

Then there was the awkward matter, which was that the older girls didn't want little Manju around. 'We're going to cut mint,' Lalli would call out as the teenagers rushed off. 'What will you come for?'

Padma, the older one, ignored her. Later, Manju would explain, 'She never asked about me. When I tried to make conversation she would reply, "what does it matter to you?"'

When the girls returned, they were even less inclined to talk. They routinely performed hard physical labour, so it couldn't be fatigue. And while they acted like she was invisible, they kept up a steady stream of conversation between themselves. 'No big deal,' Manju grumbled.

She observed that Padma's father didn't much care for this behaviour either. When he came in from the fields and saw the teenagers sitting side by side, he acted annoyed. 'Yes, yes,' he muttered, 'keep wasting time.'

But if anything, all the girls did was work.

As the sun climbed, Padma and Lalli sat before their respective family hearths, lighting dung cakes into a flaring heap. They heated oil and kneaded dough. They returned to the fields with roti sabzi for the family members still toiling. They trudged back home to scrub the dishes with wood ash for soap. Off they went with their goats. Back they came to milk the buffaloes. They swept the courtyard. They washed the clothes. They jerked the heavy galvanised steel handle of the water pump up and down, up and down, to fill a bucket of water to wash themselves. They prepared dinner. They swept the courtyard one more time. Then they did something. Then they did something else.

Crows cawed piercingly and the sun radiated fire-like. In the sickening heat, the pyramids of garbage filled the air with a rotting smell. Grit settled on clothes, faces, tongues and feet. The Shakya girls carried on.

Cousin Manju was accustomed to chores. She wasn't yet a teenager, but it was her job to cook dinner every night. Her father had bought her a footstool so she could reach the stove. But when she was done, she would switch on the air cooler. She'd listen to music on a mobile phone. She could even leave the room as long as she went no further than the front steps. Aunties said hello. Boys grinned. Her girlfriends, out roaming with elder sisters, stopped by to gossip about impossible homework and dreaded teachers.

On weekends her father took them for ice cream. They went window shopping. They chatted and laughed and sometimes they squabbled like pigeons fighting over a handful of grain – and that was okay too.

What did her cousins do when they were done with one set of chores? There was nothing fun for a girl in the village. The day was a thousand years long.

Padma was sitting at home. Very soon she would be deposited at the threshold of a new family, as a bride to a man she had never seen. In two years, it would be Lalli's turn.

The difference in their lives, it seemed to the younger girl, was that she was made to work hard so that she would one day make a good wife. But the older girls worked like they were already wives and mothers. The burdens placed on them appeared to her extreme. She was convinced 'there was no time for them to think.'

Swatting flies in the house, Manju decided that enough was enough. One afternoon, when the older girls left for the fields, she followed. That day, and the next, she observed a pattern that struck her as odd.

It was the teenagers' job to cut the mint growing in the three family plots, which covered nearly an acre of land. But the only plot they ever visited was the one that belonged to Padma's father, immediately adjacent to the orchard.

'Every day you come here and only here,' she said. 'Kyun?' Why?

'Be quiet,' Lalli snapped.

Later, Manju saw Lalli filling a diary with poems. She saw Padma secretly dabbing on lipstick.

Every night after dinner, the children stepped out one last time to squat in the fields. Padma and Lalli waited for the younger girl to choose a spot, but then scooted elsewhere. Manju felt hurt. There were wriggling snakes. And jackals. And what if some boy flashed his phone in her face? 'Let's go!' she would whine, looking warily around as she knotted her salwar.

Padma and Lalli were never ready.

'What's the hurry?' they would say, virtually in unison, their laughter tinkling in the darkness. 'There's plenty of time.'

Nazru Sees It Too

Nazru lived in an elephant-eared taro plot near the orchard. Inside the tiny brick room, his father sat upright on a charpoy, wheezing heavily into his shrivelled chest. Some nights when the asthmatic old man injected himself with medication to clear his passageways, he was knocked senseless. Nazru's teenaged brother, who was named after an old-time Bollywood star, was 'weak in the head' according to their father's diagnosis and encouraged to keep to himself. An older brother had fled to another state where he had ended up as a moulder in the even more unforgiving world of a brick kiln, with his wife by his side and their five children running around in the beating sun. His mother tried to keep the family from coming apart, but Nazru was forever getting into scrapes.

One night he heard bandits rummaging about in a neighbour's house and instead of staying away, as others did in such circumstances, he confronted the men. They shot him in the arm. Another time he killed a neighbour's goat. There was no logic to his actions, as least not any that he articulated to people's satisfaction. Asked a simple and direct question, he laughed brayingly, hee-haw, hee-haw. The villagers made him apologise to the owner of the dead goat and pay restitution. Time and again they counselled him, 'apne kaam se kaam rakho.' Mind your own business.

How could he?

There was nothing for a young man in the village. Sometimes he gathered friends for a drink, sometimes to smoke weed. He'd once gone for a drive in a car, but he didn't remember very much because it was the time he'd been shot and was being rushed to the hospital. He was too old to hang around the teenagers who stared at their phones, and too immature to socialise with men his own age who were married and had children.

Some people thought they had him pegged. 'Dar naam ka cheez usko nahin hai.' He isn't afraid of anything. Others, who saw him rustling about on one of his evening excursions, knew he was just nosy.

By their early twenties, Katra boys were embedded in that stage of Hindu life known as grihastha, becoming a householder, maintaining a home and raising a family. Nazru was considered odd, but he was hard-working. With one brother gone, another ill and his father bedridden, the burden of feeding everyone – while tending to their only buffalo and all the tobacco – fell to him. He did what was needed. Why then was he still unmarried?

Debating the causes behind twenty-six-year-old Nazru's bachelorhood became a preoccupation among the villagers who found him annoying. Someone claimed that he was having an affair with a neighbour's wife. When the neighbour was away, it was said, Nazru slipped into his wife's bed. Someone else said that he was involved with several men's wives. A third person claimed that Nazru carried pictures of underage girls in his wallet, making him sound like a pervert.

Close relatives rubbished the rumours. He was not a pervert, the poor boy, he was a hijra, they said. They had come to this conclusion having seen him squat to urinate. The rumours grew and grew, and so the question was put to Nazru's father. 'My son,' said the withered old fellow, 'is neither a man nor a woman.'

And so Nazru was left to do as he pleased. Every night after dinner, he set off. Animals, squatting women, teenagers being teenagers – no one was safe from the flashing light of Nazru's Made in China torch.

'I saw Padma and Pappu,' he said later. The pair were in his wheat field. 'They were signalling to each other.'

Nazru saw them together again, and then a third time. 'I didn't like it,' he said. 'This sort of behaviour could destroy the reputation of our entire family.'

Unspeakable Things

Reputation was skin. And the residents of the next-door hamlet of Jati couldn't shed theirs. Their reputation grew not so much out of things they said and did, as by stereotyped impressions of their Yadav caste.

Like the Shakyas, the Yadavs came under a broad category known as 'Other Backward Classes'. The OBCs were low-caste groups that upper-caste groups had systematically kept back. Once forcibly confined to agrarian jobs, Yadavs in Uttar Pradesh were not even allowed to sit on a charpoy occupied by a high-caste Brahmin. After India became independent they were the supposed beneficiaries of affirmative action policies.

The Shakyas and the Yadavs should have found common cause, except that now the Yadavs were politically powerful. The community, which made up an estimated 9 per cent of the population in the state of Uttar Pradesh, always voted strategically, in a bloc. Their leaders formed political alliances with other low-caste groups. And the Yadav-run Samajwadi Party employed the tactics of patronage politics – they were accused of distributing freebies like clothes, cooking pots and even cash[1] to potential voters. In 2014, the party was in control of the state government, and its influence extended over the local bureaucracy and police.

Uttar Pradesh was India's largest and most powerful state, with a population of more than 200 million people. It sent eighty members to Parliament. 'The road to Delhi,' it was said, 'passes through Lucknow,' the capital city of Uttar Pradesh. In fact, eight out of India's fourteen prime ministers were from this politically significant state. Even India's new prime minister, who was from Gujarat, had contested the general elections from here in 2014.

But living conditions in Uttar Pradesh reflected none of this. As many as 60 million people in the state were poor, said a World Bank report.[2] The infant mortality rate was the same as in some war-torn countries. In times of drought, when crops perished, people ate grass to survive.[3] Against this backdrop, one chief minister had spent taxpayers' money on filling public parks with statues of herself.[4]

A state bureaucrat attempted to explain why the system was so broken: 'If you get a cow that gives you twenty litres of milk twice a day and you know you'll own the cow for only a short period, what will you do?'

The answer? Milk it dry.

Two years earlier, in 2012, Akhilesh Yadav had become chief minister. Educated in Australia, where he received a degree in environmental engineering from the University of Sydney, the forty-one-year-old had often been photographed on his mobile phone or pecking away on his laptop. The media called him 'tech-savvy'. This was shorthand for 'likely to be smart'. His father, Mulayam Singh, a former mud wrestler who had founded the Samajwadi Party, didn't think much of his son – but a senior advisor had pointed out the advantages of putting the young man forward. 'Do any of you know who Hannah Montana is?' he had said. 'Ask Akhilesh. He knows. That's why we need the young generation leading the party.'[5]

Akhilesh had some good ideas to improve the state – more power, better roads and a pension scheme. But his cabinet ministers were old-school thugs. The Association for Democratic Reforms, an organisation that campaigns for better governance, showed that about a third of the politicians who were elected nationwide to Parliament in 2014 had a criminal record.[6] In Akhilesh's cabinet, over half the members had pending criminal cases.[7] Critics were convinced that nothing was going to change.

Soon his government, like the Yadav governments that preceded him, was also slapped with the label 'goonda raj': the rule of criminals.[8] In the climate of fear and insecurity that subsequently developed, the phrase 'raat gayi baat gayi' – the night has concluded and so has the incident – circulated as often as it ever had before, meaning that victims of Yadav-led crimes might as well forget about getting justice. The reputation of this dabbang – thuggish – government tainted all Yadavs.

The Yadavs in Jati, the hamlet that adjoined Katra village, occupied the opposite end of this power spectrum. They were climate refugees who were forced out of their homes on the banks of the River Ganga when it flooded. Ganga-kateves, people called them, those whose lands the Ganga has consumed. Having lost their homes and virtually everything they owned, they lived in hovels held up with bamboo sticks. They went barefoot. Their babies were naked. On hot days they slept out in the open, by the side of the road.

But because they were Yadavs, some Katra villagers didn't feel safe around them, especially after dark. 'If they come with guns,' someone said, 'what will we do?'

One of the Jati men, Veerpal Yadav, had a fearsome reputation.

Veerpal, who was known as Veere, had moved to Jati four years earlier when his childhood home in the sandy hamlet of Badam Nagla was swept away, and with it the land on which he had grown corn, maize and taro root for five decades. He was left with a handful of watermelons salvaged from the alluvial soil of the riverbank.

Badam Nagla was not a place to be missed. It was so isolated that when a notorious bandit, who stood accused of murdering eleven policemen, needed someplace to hide this was where he took cover. There wasn't even a drainage system. When it rained heavily, the men stepped out without trousers, carrying their clothes in polythene bags that they balanced on their heads. They slipped them on again only once they were indoors. One former resident described living in Badam Nagla as 'living like an animal'.

Jati crouched at the mouth of Katra village, which had shops and two schools, with the closest town only twenty minutes away. And just as Katra was dominated by Shakyas, Jati, by some similar unspoken rule, was for Yadavs. Almost all the 187 families living in Jati were Yadav; some were related to Veere.

One of them was Veere's brother.

To start with, this brother, a single man, was around constantly. Then, suddenly, he wasn't. In next-door Katra a horrific rumour took root. Veere had shot dead his brother, people said. He had then burned the body and dug a hole in the nearby jungle to bury the remains, so he could snatch control of his brother's property – which he did, they said, by moving in his family.

Who knew where the story came from? No one claimed responsibility and no one informed the police.

No one said they had witnessed the alleged killing or even that they had spoken to someone who did. But almost everyone in Katra heard the rumour. Soon, it was a part of the frightening mythology that dogged the Yadavs next door.

They were unspeakable things, people said, who sucked the blood of even kith and kin.

The Naughty Boy

In fact, Veere's brother had died of complications from diabetes. Veere built the house he lived in from scratch, on land he had purchased years earlier. Even if he knew what the people in the neighbouring village were saying, what could he do.

Every morning Veere and his three sons, Avdesh, Urvesh and Pappu, crossed the road and walked through the rice fields towards the Ganga River. Rolling up their trouser bottoms, they waded into the cold, fast-moving water. On that side of the bank, they grew watermelons and cucumbers on public land. But they also worked the land of better-off men in exchange for a portion of the harvest. In a good year the Yadav men brought home about 2 lakh rupees from their share of the wheat, garlic and tobacco that they sold in nearby market towns. To this they added the rent from a shop they had built alongside their house.

Every rupee that wasn't spent on food or treats like tobacco was kept aside to finish construction on the house. So far it had a sturdy entrance door, three rooms and a terrace roof. The men installed a handpump in the courtyard, stretched out a piece of rope for a clothes line and painted a bright green swastika for good luck. Veere's wife Jhalla Devi would have liked a kitchen, but her husband asked what was wrong with cooking outdoors. There wasn't even paint on the walls, he scolded.

In the evenings, Veere planted himself on the charpoy just outside the house, rolling beedis and sipping chai. The thick milk cream sometimes stuck to his moustache, which he wore long and curved like a door handle.

'Jai Ram ji ki,' he called out to strolling Yadav men, taking in the evening air. All hail Sri Ram. 'Come, come, sit,' he nodded his grizzled head towards a second charpoy.

The men set down their umbrellas. They pulled out beedis. Veere handed over a box.

'And?' he said, as they plucked out a match.

Affairs in Lucknow were always discussed at length – of how so-and-so was only a puppet in the hands of that other so-and-so, then the sale price of the fruits and vegetables they grew, and then invariably someone would look up at the broad sheet of cloudless sky and complain that the monsoon was like a woman. She couldn't be relied on to keep time. When would she arrive?

Sometimes Veere remembered his sons.

'Arre!' he shouted.

He treated them like boys, even though the eldest was himself a father. He didn't let them speak. The boys had nothing to say to him either.

They trooped out of the house sullen-faced, like their feet were made of cement.

The older two were good boys, neighbours later said. They stayed close to home. One loved his wife, the other worshipped books. The youngest, on the other hand, was 'naughty', as even his father admitted to those around him. 'He liked to roam around,' one of the Yadavs said.

But what did that even mean in Jati?

Pappu had no money, no bicycle and no place to go. The next-door village didn't like his type. The Yadavs on his side had less than he did. There wasn't even a snack shop where he could sit and order a handful of hot roasted gram. The riverbank offered welcome relief for many, away from the chatter of the household, but to him it represented toil. There was the fair, but that came once a year.

Even a naughty boy like him, what could he really get up to?

The Invisible Women

The women could do even less. If Veere's wife, Jhalla Devi, stuck her head out the door, she went unacknowledged. If she lingered it was with the understanding that she'd better not open that mouth of hers.

The invisible woman preferred her own company anyway, usually in the ditch opposite the house. There she sat, patting and shaping dung cakes for fertiliser, disinfectant and fuel, in the one sari she wore day and night wrapped around her like a sack, its pallu pulled over her like a hood. Her glass bangles tinkled and her silver toe rings gleamed, but her face simmered with resentment.

The other Yadav woman didn't even make it this far. Veere's only daughter-in-law was so strictly regulated that her neighbours couldn't say for sure what she looked like. In fact, Basanta was big-eyed and fleshy-lipped; an exhausted teenager with a scrawny one-year-old. Basanta cooked and cleaned for everyone. Early on she had even offered to help her mother-in-law pat dung, but Jhalla Devi had tilted up her pinched face and glared.

Now, when Basanta was done with every possible chore in the near-empty house, she dropped to the floor. Flies nibbled at the sweat that soaked through the thin fabric of her dirty sari blouse. They clustered around her daughter's leaking bottom, settling on her rose gold earlobes. By late

afternoon, when the breezes started up, Basanta shook
herself and took her little one to the back of the house.
The family plot spilled into the Katra fields, with not even
a fence in between. Here, the bored new mother could
amuse baby Shivani without being accused by her mother-
in-law and the men of flaunting herself before strangers.

'Look, a farmer, see, grazing goats; listen, boys, look, a
kite, listen, birds, see, a well. Moo, baa, bow-wow.'

Straight ahead, at a distance covered in a few minutes
on foot, was Ramnath's orchard. That summer every one
of his thirteen trees heaved richly with fruit. One was a
fragrant-leafed fig tree; the others were mango.

Lalli Asks for a Memento

Lalli's parents returned from their pilgrimage with presents of amulets and chains. Things went quiet for a while.

Then one magical afternoon, everyone was out. Padma and Lalli asked cousin Manju to open her suitcase. They went through her clothes carefully. The blouses were brightly coloured and made of a soft fabric. They slipped like water between the girls' fingers. The jeans were very, very tight. Did Manju really wear such clothes? Could she even sit in them? Here in the village, she had been as boring as they, sticking to roomy salwar kameezes.

They decided to try on the clothes. They wriggled into the blouses and jeans and then turned to look. The same heart-shaped face, the same long hair. The solemn eyes. But the funny costumes pinched their bottoms and brought out the giggles.

'You look smart,' they said to each other when they had recovered their composure.

'Yes, yes!' shouted Siya Devi, walking through the door. 'Show off your thighs!' The jeans didn't reveal the girls' thighs; they only revealed that the girls *had* thighs. But it was more than Siya Devi allowed. She disparagingly referred to the outfits as 'tiny clothes', too provocative to wear, and ordered the children to change back into their salwar kameezes.

Later, perhaps to show her gratitude, Lalli drew her younger cousin aside. 'Yaar,' she said, 'you'll go away. We should get a photo taken together at the bazaar.' Manju brought up the subject in a phone call to her mother who was back home in Noida. Her mother wasn't keen, perhaps because money was tight. 'What's the hurry,' she complained. 'Are you dying sometime soon?'

But Manju was pleased to be acknowledged by her cousin. And it had felt nice to share her clothes. The girls weren't allowed in the bazaar, but they weren't watched all the time either. 'We went!' Manju said later. 'Chori chupke!' On the sly.

Out the door, down the lane. There it was, just ahead, a little bit further. They held hands, squeezed and then plunged forward.

The road was packed with rows of tiny, peering shops that looked like the eyes of a dragonfly. The Katra shopkeepers sat in their undershirts, surrounded by sacks of rice, animal feed and barrels of cooking oil. They chatted on their mobile phones and read the newspaper, only looking up when a customer stopped by. Some of their customers were young men who took selfies against the background of nice cars that happened to be parked there, but most reminded the girls of their fathers. There was something so familiar about the way these men retrieved the thin roll of notes from their shirt pockets, almost in slow motion, and the care with which they counted the change they got back. That look of dread was familiar too. Too much was going out, too little was coming in, everything was fragile.

There were too many men, the girls suddenly realised. They were shouting and laughing. They were roaring phat phat phat past in motorcycles. Into the shop, quickly now.

The flash went POP.

The girls blinked.

The Fair Comes to the Village

Everyone knew the fair had arrived because the music could be heard across the village and even in the fields. It was only devotional, for the annual event was organised by the local temple committee, but the Shakya girls were excited. They had never been to a mela. The highlight was a performance of the Ramlila, a theatrical enactment of the life of the Hindu god Ram, which culminated in the battle between Ram and his nemesis Ravana, the ten-headed demon king of Lanka.

That morning, 27 May, it was just the girls in the house, with the two mothers. Padma was frying slices of bottle gourd in a seasoning of salt and chilli powder. Over the wall, Siya Devi and Lalli made sure the buffaloes were fed, the courtyard was swept and an afternoon meal of curry and rotis prepared over the smoky outdoor fire. Siya Devi reminded her daughter to keep the food covered. 'These brazen monkeys will steal every last roti if they can; given half a chance they will run off with the aate ka dabba.'

When Lalli picked up her sharp-tongued sickle to lend family members a hand with the harvest, Padma insisted on tagging along. Cousin Manju had succumbed to the heat and was asleep on a charpoy.

In the fields, the perspiring men had roped turbans around their heads. The women wore rubber slippers. The high temperature had turned the ground into a thousand pieces of glass. Padma wandered off with her goats.

It had been a good year for the mint harvest, and Sohan Lal had more than thirty kilograms of fragrant green leaves bundled up and ready to go. He would sell the oil to a wholesaler in the bazaar, and that man would sell it on to factories that made toothpaste, tobacco, medicines and mouthwash. Sohan Lal's mint would travel from Katra village across towns and cities in India and perhaps even go abroad.

But first, the leaves had to be taken to the oil distillation machine sixteen kilometres away. A cousin with a tractor had agreed to help out, but there was still plenty to do. As Sohan Lal was stuffing some things into a polythene bag, he asked his daughter Lalli for assistance. Would she make a call on his behalf, he said, handing over his mobile phone. Sohan Lal had two sons still at home, but they were little. For now, Lalli, who was her mother's right hand, was also her father's.

By this time, cousin Manju had recovered sufficiently to join the older girls out in the sun. Although they had never had much use for her, they now smilingly beckoned for her to join them in the shade of a mango tree. 'Ask mummy to let us go to the fair,' Lalli beseeched. 'She'll listen to you.'

To no one's surprise, Siya Devi said absolutely not.

'Ladkiyan bahar nahin ghoomti,' she scolded. Girls don't wander about outside the house.

Manju was on the threshold of adolescence, already familiar with the art of breaking down resistant parents. 'Why, why, why?' she wheedled. Why had she come to visit, if not to go to the fair? Her father had given her 500 rupees to spend.

Siya Devi had little tolerance for such behaviour, but she was conflicted. Her husband always said girls didn't go to the bazaar, what would they do there? But Lalli was her only daughter still living at home. She was such a good girl. She did everything she was asked to, immediately and devotedly. If it weren't for her, Siya Devi would have no one to talk to.

Soon Lalli would go away, to her husband's home, and then what opportunity would Siya Devi have to spoil her little girl? Surely a quick outing after the day's chores would do no harm.

But Siya Devi's mask didn't drop, and Lalli would never know the loving thoughts that had crossed her mother's mind.

'Don't eat or drink anything,' Siya Devi said, sternly, for it wouldn't do for girls to be seen enjoying themselves in a public place. 'Whatever you want your father will buy for you later and you can have at home.'

The excited girls took the advice in one ear and let it out the other. They locked the doors into the courtyard and took turns at the water pump. They washed their face and feet. Padma brushed her hair, and put on her green salwar kameez, a favourite gift from her maternal uncles. Lalli's purple and red outfit hung inconspicuously over her frame.

Sometime between 4 and 4.30 p.m. the three girls crossed the bazaar and joined the throng of villagers picking their way through the rubbish-strewn ground where the fair was set up. In the far distance, the Ganga gleamed like diamonds. Vendors in tarpaulin shacks showed off shirts and saris, bras and panties, glass bangles and bindis. Fluffy teddy bears, plastic flip phones and pellet guns. Kerchiefs for the heat, golden nose pins for special occasions. One vendor cried, 'Watermelons! Watermelons!' Another beckoned with hot jalebis. A barefoot man in a vest stirred a pot of spicy golgappa water. Children squealed with joy from the tippy-top of a clanking Ferris wheel.

The cousins immediately saw familiar faces. There was Somwati, whose father had a vegetable stall at the fair. She'd brought along her little niece. With them was a neighbour, Rekha, who was surely a saint. Rekha was now fourteen – but she was only six when her mother died of cancer, and she was pulled out of school to cook and clean for her family of four. A disability prevented one of her brothers from walking, so the task of looking after him also fell to Rekha. If the demands placed on her seemed extreme, she never said so to her friends. The span of childhood was in the hands of fate.

Shortly afterwards, Padma took cousin Manju aside and asked her to stay right there, not to move one inch. They would be back soon, she promised. But they took so long – at least fifteen minutes, as the younger girl later remembered – that she went in search of them.

Although the fair was concentrated in a small area, it was swarming with people. Some farmers were coaxing a weighing machine up the embankment towards their taro crop, and the crowd surged forward to gape. It was possible that the men would slip, and the scales would fall and crush them. At first Manju wandered through the exclaiming people, but she quickly changed her mind. All she could make out was a sea of heads and backs.

'If they don't show up,' she told herself. 'I'll go home.'

Pappu entered the fair at around 5.45 p.m.

As was often the case, he was the only one of the Yadav brothers with any time for recreational activities. After work Avdesh went straight to his wife and baby. At this

moment he was cutting tobacco plants for a neighbour
for some extra money. In fact, there was so much to do
that he had taken Basanta along. Pappu's other brother,
Urvesh, was across the Ganga with their father. When he
was done, the quiet young man would retrieve his tenth-
class exercise books. Urvesh was twenty-one, an age at
which better-off contemporaries were graduating college,
but his days working in the watermelon patch left him
worn out. He studied when he could.

Pappu, at nineteen, had no plans to marry. Nor did he
know what it meant to study. Someone had offered to
teach him how to write his name, but 'Darvesh' proved
tricky to spell; so 'Pappu' was all he knew.

That evening, he and his companion Sannu Pandit,
younger than Pappu by two years, settled on the bare
ground, ready to watch the Ramlila.

Manju found the teenaged girls near some stalls,
examining their purchases – nail polish for Somwati and
Rekha, a tube of cream for Padma. But the mood was
weighted and sour. Her cousin Lalli looked upset, 'as
though she'd been in a fight', she later remembered.

Padma was cursing to herself.

Manju was taken aback.

'You took your time,' she said lightly.

'Keep quiet!' Padma snapped. 'Let's go.'

The moment passed for Manju, who enjoyed herself
on the Ferris wheel while the others gazed up at her. 'You
go on,' they had said, 'that thing gives us a headache.'
Disregarding her aunt's advice, she treated everyone to
packets of hot, greasy vegetable pakodas, and they made
their way to the play.

They arrived at a pivotal moment in what was, to them,
the greatest love story ever told. Lord Ram, upon lifting

the divine bow to string it – a demand that was made of all the men who had come to win the hand of the beautiful princess, Sita – ended up breaking it instead. By doing so, he had proved his extraordinary strength and worth.

> Like the thunder's pealing accent rose the loud terrific clang,
> And the firm earth shook and trembled and the hills in echoes rang,
> And the chiefs and gathered monarchs fell and fainted in their fear,
> And the men of many nations shook the dreadful sound to hear!
> Pale and white the startled monarchs slowly from their terror woke,
> And with royal grace and greetings Janak to the rishi spoke:
> 'Now my ancient eyes have witnessed wond'rous deed by Rama done,
> Deed surpassing thought or fancy wrought by Dasaratha's son,
> And the proud and peerless princess, Sita glory of my house,
> Sheds on me an added lustre as she weds a godlike spouse,
> True shall be my plighted promise, Sita dearer than my life,
> Won by worth and wond'rous valour shall be Rama's faithful wife!'[1]

The girls couldn't tear their eyes away.

Padma Lalli, Gone

The sky drained, signalling that it was time to go home, and so the girls got up. Around this time, Pappu and his friend also brushed the dust from their clothes. The two groups followed a similar route, exiting the fairground, ambling past the police chowki – outpost – and then entering the bazaar. But while the girls crossed over into Katra, the boys walked five minutes further to their hamlet.

On the way, Padma and Lalli divided up the remainder of the day's chores. Typically, they packed Manju off. 'You sweep the courtyard,' they ordered. Then they took to the fields with the seven goats the family owned.

An age passed, or so it seemed to Manju, until finally boredom prompted her to seek out the older girls. She walked down the sloping path that led into the alleyway. There they were on their way back from the fields. They had one more job to do before they came in, they said. Offering a perfectly reasonable explanation – they had to tether the goats in their shelters – they insisted, 'run along now.' They assured her they would promptly follow.

To Manju, it was obvious that the older girls were reluctant to return home. The fair had turned out to be a whole lot of nothing as far as she was concerned, no better than the hawkers at home, but she knew that for Padma and Lalli, it had been a day to remember.

All through the evening the heat had leached out of the village and now the night air was perfumed and cool. The aroma of taro and soya coming to a boil on wood fires, the creak of a front door swinging shut, a mother's call beckoning her children home – all signalled the day's end.

A crescent moon rose in the sky.

Padma and Lalli finally walked through the courtyard. The two best friends who did everything together, now unclasped. Padma joined her stepmother, Sunita Devi, in the kitchen and started to roll out rotis, toasting the circular discs carefully over the fire with a pair of tongs. As Lalli went over to Siya Devi, a set of small solar panels filled one end of the courtyard with a watery grey light.

Separated by the wall, the girls started to discuss the evening's events. What a wonderful thing a mela was!

It was too much for Sunita Devi who had thought it undignified for them to have gone at all. 'Shut up!' she roared. 'Get on with the food.'

Over the next hour, the women sweated over fires and laboured over small errands. The children brought down grass brooms, beating out the day's dust from the courtyard. There was a button to thread, a broken slipper to twist into a knot, nits to comb out, wicker fans to wipe clean. The men were out, smoking beedis and talking among themselves.

Sunita Devi was feeding the animals in her corner of the courtyard when her husband Jeevan Lal returned for dinner. Padma laid out a stack of rotis and the bottle gourd left over from lunch. Over in the next section of the house, the visitor from out of town, cousin Manju, had succumbed to the heat once more and was snoring peacefully on a charpoy.

After dinner, Padma's father rinsed his mouth and started for his animal shelter, which was perched on the edge of the fields. The shelter had high walls and a sturdy wooden door to protect his buffalo and calf. 'Where there are animals,' he always said, 'there are thieves.' There was also a charpoy in the shelter, so that he and his wife could keep an eye on things and still enjoy some privacy.

Sunita Devi was at the handpump rubbing ash into a pile of dirty dishes. She'd join him soon, she promised. Their daughter Padma walked the few feet over to the end of the courtyard to catch up with those of her cousins who had skipped the fair to milk the buffaloes.

Meanwhile in Jati, the Yadav men polished off the dal that Basanta had placed before them. Pappu's father then left for their riverside plot to guard the watermelon harvest. His sons gathered their rolls of bedding and headed to their respective charpoys. The eldest went up to the terrace to await his wife and child. The second liked to sleep outside the house, on the main road – there was barely any foot traffic once the sun had set and the leaves of tall trees delivered silky breezes.

As Jhalla Devi pottered about, her daughter-in-law finally sat down to her meal. When Pappu walked out of the house the women assumed he was going to see his cousin, who lived in a shack just down the road.

In Katra, at this time, Padma complained loudly of a stomach ache. 'I have to go to the toilet,' she said. Lalli piped up from the centre of the courtyard. 'Me too! I'll come along.'

Their mothers barely gave them a glance. It wasn't very late, and there would be others in the fields taking a final squat for the night. Anyway, Padma had a phone.

It was common knowledge that the girls would be half an hour, since they usually went to the set of family plots near the orchard. But thirty minutes passed and there was still no sign of them. 'Where have they disappeared to,' grumbled Sunita Devi.

Her mother-in-law, who was particularly attuned to Padma's welfare, hobbled to the door. 'Padma,' rasped the old woman. 'Lalli!'

At around 9.30 p.m., Pappu bounded into his cousin's shack. The two were good friends and often chatted late into the night. Pappu sometimes used Raju's phone to make calls and send text messages to girls he liked. They would fall asleep side by side.

He was coming from the orchard, Pappu explained, where he'd been 'to the latrine'. His stomach was off, he'd probably eaten too many spicy snacks at the fair.

Raju commiserated. Would Pappu like some watermelon? They had enjoyed a bumper harvest and would take a lorry to Delhi to sell the lot. But for now, they could make a dent in this pile that stood six feet high, no one would notice. Pappu agreed, and the two young men devoured the juicy red fruit.

'How was the fair?' Raju asked.

'I saw the girls,' Pappu replied, munching loudly. 'But they were with some others so we couldn't chat.'

Thieves in the Tobacco

Jeevan Lal was stretched out on a charpoy dreamily awaiting the company of his wife, when a furious knocking brought him to his feet. It was his nosy cousin, the one who was always roaming about. 'Khet mein admi hai!' Nazru shouted. There are thieves in your field.

Jeevan Lal's elder brother, Sohan Lal, had taken the family's mint that very morning. The tobacco was also gone. That left little worth robbing. Even so, Jeevan Lal grabbed hold of a bamboo stick. With Nazru by his side he turned right from the animal shelter, taking a shortcut straight into the fields. As he hurried along, he pulled out his mobile phone to call for backup. His first instinct was to phone Sohan Lal, but he still wasn't home from his long journey to press the mint; so, he tried his other brother.

It was 9.29 p.m.

Ram Babu, who was at home, hurriedly informed his wife of what had happened. Then he grabbed a torch and a lathi and took off. But where his brother had turned right, he took a left, unthinkingly traversing a longer route. He pounded down the road, diving through an opening between two brick houses. The fields frilled darkly before him. A melancholic tune wafted down from the fair. 'What if they shoot us?' Ram Babu thought.

So many people in western Uttar Pradesh had access to a gun that the area had come to be known as Tamancha Land. Although some strapped manual-loading Lee Enfield rifles proudly to their backs, most packed sanitation pipes or automobile steering rods to make long-necked tamanchas to stick down their trousers. It was mostly 'dabbang dikhane ke liye' – a display of swagger – but showing off had tragic consequences. Between 2010 and 2014, the state accounted for 40 per cent of all deaths from gun violence in India.[1] In fact, there had been armed robbers in the fields just a few days earlier, so Ram Babu's fears were warranted.

He looked around and saw a figure lying on a charpoy. 'Thieves in the tobacco field!' he shouted. 'Thieves in the tobacco!' The man jumped up to join in the search. Soon three other men were striding alongside Ram Babu. What was there to be scared for, he thought. If they saw the thieves, they'd catch them!

His brother and cousin Nazru were already in the trio of family plots, craning their necks as they peered this way and that. Just ahead was the orchard, at a distance of less than a hundred feet. The ground was mostly bare, and it should have been easy enough to see far. But in the darkness, it was like staring into a well, hoping to catch a snake in the gaping chasm.

The men felt a deep familiarity with the fields. It was everything to them, their ancestral land, the home of parents, grandparents and great-grandparents. They themselves had worked on this land when they were children. They had tagged alongside their elders just like their sons did now, learning how to tend for the earth, how to invest in it, how to protect it from pests like jungli cows and thieves like moneylenders. This was where they had spent the happiest times of their lives and where they had confronted their greatest fears. In fact, their fields were so intimately familiar to them that although they couldn't see much, they believed they would sense if something was amiss, just as one can sense a change in the texture of one's palm.

But this was not the case. They were unable to make out any telltale signs of intruder activity.

The men dispersed, and so did Nazru.

Congregated under a tree, the two brothers were dissecting the matter when some of the Shakya women emerged from the village, walking quickly towards them.

'The girls aren't back,' cried Siya Devi.

The horrified men started towards home. There they would plan how to proceed. The other women followed, but Siya Devi hung back.

The first time Lalli's mother saw Katra village was also the first time she saw the man she was to marry, whose name she then had inked on her hand as a sign that she now belonged to him. She was beautiful, with a straight nose, regal cheekbones and paper-gold skin. Sohan Lal was small and loud. He told her to shut up all the time – 'chup kar, chup kar, tu chap kar!' But although she was then only a teenager, she was no pushover. When she got angry, she turned her back to him. She shouted at others, when really, she was shouting at him. Whatever method she chose, the message was always received. Siya Devi was tough, she knew it, and you didn't want to provoke her.

The seasons rolled on, rabi, kharif, rabi, kharif, rabi, kharif over and over. She carried six babies to term. Children take their toll. Men take everything. She spent most of the day on her feet. And she was unsentimental. She refused to name her dogs because what was the point of naming something that would leave without saying goodbye?

And now here she was, still only in her forties, but her hair was falling out and some teeth also. Her golden face was crinkled with gloom. But she was still beautiful, and she was still tough, more so now that she was the mother of a young woman. 'Maine control mein rakha tha,' Siya Devi said later, bleakly. I was firm with my girl.

And so, even though she couldn't imagine what had happened, her thoughts didn't stray to dark places.

Treading slowly through the indigo night, Siya Devi came upon her husband's cousin, Nazru. The young man was urinating by the side of his house in the fields.

'Was it really thieves you saw or something else?'

Later, she didn't explain what she had meant by 'something else'. Nazru was known to muddle easily, to say one thing when he meant another.

'Something else,' he replied, zipping his trousers.

'The children aren't home yet.'

'Pappu took them,' he said. 'Pappu Yadav.'

Siya Devi ran home so fast her feet swallowed the earth.

In the subsequent turmoil that engulfed the family, no one wondered aloud why Nazru hadn't told the truth to begin with. Why did he say he saw thieves when what he actually saw was Pappu taking the girls?

Where Are They?

The phone that Padma had been carrying was now switched off.

Cousin Manju was shaken awake.

'Did something happen at the fair?'

'No,' she replied groggily. Then she remembered something odd. 'Padma didi was cursing at someone, but I don't know whom.'

Jeevan Lal turned to his mother, 'You sent the girls to the fair!'

This wasn't true, of course; it was his sister-in-law Siya Devi who had given them permission to go.

'I'm going to kill you,' he screamed.

Then, because this was a matter far bigger than the sighting of thieves in the fields, far bigger than he could even imagine, he dialled his brother Sohan Lal, still many villages away.

As it turned out, the oil extraction machine had broken down and Sohan Lal was unable to immediately process his harvest. By the time the matter was dealt with and he had twelve litres of oil in cans, darkness had embraced the unfamiliar village. A relative named Harbans, who lived nearby, urged him to spend the night instead of returning immediately to Katra. They had eaten dinner and then climbed up to the roof to sleep.

'Bhai!'

'Hello?'

'Brother, the girls have disappeared. Come home quick!'

'Hello?'

'Hello?'

Sohan Lal looked down at his phone. It was dead.

In Katra, Jeevan Lal tried dialling a few more times. Then he called Harbans. The reception this far out was so poor, the calls kept dropping, and it was past 10 p.m. when Lalli's father heard the full story.

As was often the case, practical matters took priority. Sohan Lal needed to get home right away, but to wake early one went to bed early. And almost everyone around him was already asleep. So he called a cousin in Katra, the same man who had helped him buy his new phone.

'I have to get home,' he told Yogendra Singh, whose prosperous family owned several vehicles.

'Is it an emergency?'

Yogendra Singh's white Mahindra Bolero SUV had been giving him steering trouble. He had a motorcycle, but Sohan Lal and Harbans were with two others, and a motorcycle could hardly accommodate all five of them. Then he remembered a problem with the chain of his bike, which was just as well.

'I won't come out at night,' he said.

There were no street lights in these parts. Some drivers compensated by turning on their high beams, even though it meant blinding oncoming traffic. But it was equally possible, Yogendra knew, that he might be waylaid, robbed and killed. What was an extreme scenario elsewhere was a legitimate concern here. Uttar Pradesh was the murder capital of India.[1]

Beside Yogendra lay his wife – and at her breast, suckling contentedly, was their newborn daughter swaddled in a piece of sari cloth.

'I won't come alone,' he said firmly.

Sohan Lal hung up.

Then curiosity got the better of Yogendra. Why would his cousin venture out in the dark?

Taking along his father, Neksu Lal, and two brothers, he set off to investigate. The tall sturdy men carried torches to illuminate the inky night into which they now waded. Up and down, the unpaved streets were empty. All the doors were shut. Even the stray dogs that animated the hottest days with their relentless barks heaved with sleep.

There were a number of people milling about the Shakya courtyard. Their girls had gone to the toilet, the newcomers were told. They hadn't returned.

The Shakyas didn't say that someone had taken them.

Even with this limited information it was clear that the matter was of the utmost seriousness. Girls didn't disappear into thin air. But not a single person present suggested walking over to the police chowki that was located not five minutes away. If they were aware that there was a number they could call for help, they didn't dial it.

Every Eight Minutes

To the Shakyas, the threshold of a police station could feel as insurmountable as a fortress wall. The Indian police were known for their dismissive attitude towards the poor. They were meant to serve and protect, but they were just as likely to kill.[1] The roughly shaven, khaki-clad men of the local force had the most terrifying reputation of all. 'UP police ka koi bharosa nahin,' it was said. You never know with the UP police.

There was plenty of truth to this notion. Around 2005, children from a slum in Noida started to disappear. The slum dwellers, who worked for the wealthy occupants of the city's towering apartment blocks, repeatedly went to the police and begged them to intervene. To one distraught mother an officer said, 'Why do you people have so many children if you can't look after them?'[2] Scrutinising the photograph of her missing twenty-year-old daughter, he declared, 'She looks so beautiful. She probably eloped.'[3]

Missing person cases continued to stream in, but by many accounts the police refused to take them seriously.

Then in 2006, officials found seventeen chopped-up bodies, including those of several children, in a sewer behind the home of a wealthy businessman who lived near the slum. The clothes of the missing young woman were also found there. The gruesome details made headlines, and only because of this was the case even investigated in the first place.[4] The killers – the businessman and his domestic help – had gone undetected for years, most likely because they had chosen their victims from among the city's poor.

Since police stations were evaluated on the number of cases they solved, officers had an incentive to open only those with a chance of success. Solving the mystery of a missing child required time, manpower and resources – things that the police were generally short of. Between 2012 and 2014, the police filed FIRs – First Information Reports – in less than 60 per cent of such cases.[5] This negligence contributed to an epidemic of missing and exploited children, many of them trafficked within and outside the country.[6]

In the year that Padma and Lalli went missing, 12,361 people were kidnapped and abducted in Uttar Pradesh,[7] accounting for 16 per cent of all such crimes in India. Across the country, one child went missing every eight minutes, said Kailash Satyarthi, who went on to jointly win the Nobel Peace Prize with Malala Yousafzai.[8] And these were just the reported cases.

The economist Abhijit Banerjee, who later also jointly won a Nobel Prize for his approach to alleviating global poverty, explained that 'parents may be reluctant to report children who ran away as a result of abuse, sexual and otherwise.' He added that this was likely 'rampant'.[9] In fact, some parents sold their children or deliberately allowed unwanted daughters to stray in busy marketplaces. No one reported them missing, and so, no one looked for them.

Even in a tiny village like Katra where everyone was of the same social class, the Shakya family believed that the police would still take sides. They would choose to favour the person of their caste. And told that the culprit was Yadav, they would most likely wave away the Shakyas, being Yadavs themselves. 'Raat gayi toh baat gayi,' they would say, grunting back to sleep. The night has concluded and so has the incident.

'It was easy to ask why we didn't immediately go to the chowki,' Jeevan Lal would later complain. Time was scarce and he preferred not to waste it on a thankless task.

There was, however, another reason that Padma's father held back.

Jeevan Lal's Secret

By 10.15 p.m., a dozen men were searching for Padma and Lalli in the Shakya family plots. Some in the group assumed that the girls were injured and unable to call for help. Around the search party, termites crawled, mosquitoes buzzed and moths fluttered. As the heat drained out, the field rustled with snakes slipping back into their holes. Nazru excused himself – to eat dinner, he said.

The others waded through the upturned earth of Jeevan Lal's property. They tramped into the orchard. They arrived at the dagger-leafed eucalyptus grove. They went as far as the tube well that adjoined the Yadav hamlet. They moved quickly and, at the request of Padma's father, they didn't call out the girls' names. They were as quiet as they could be.

A villager who lived some 400 feet from the Shakya plots had gone into the fields to empty his bladder several times that night, but when questioned about it later he said he didn't hear or see anything. Certainly, there was nothing to suggest that a group of men armed with torches and tall, heavy sticks were in search of missing children.

Jeevan Lal didn't need to spell out what was at stake, but he did anyway: 'Our daughters are unmarried,' he said. 'Why would we ruin their chances of finding a good match?' The other villagers would have asked why the girls had been allowed out at night with a phone, and without a chaperone. 'There's no point crying after the birds have eaten the harvest,' they would have said.

But the girls had been taken by Pappu. Nazru had said so – and Jeevan Lal knew this, even if the others didn't. 'This is the sort of place where people cause a commotion over a missing goat,' a village storekeeper later said. 'If the girls were taken by Pappu, as Nazru said, why didn't the family make any noise or call out to anyone?'

They didn't, because it wasn't just the girls' honour that was at stake, it was the family's too. And the family had to live in the village.

And so, just like that, in less than an hour since they were gone, Padma was no longer the quick-tempered one. Lalli was no longer the faithful partner in crime. Who they were, and what had happened to them, was already less important than what their disappearance meant to the status of the people left behind.

Adrenaline in the Fields, Tears at Home

It was a quarter past eleven when Lalli's father arrived in Katra. Every man that Sohan Lal had approached for help that night had turned him down, refusing to drive around in the darkness. His relative Harbans had finally persuaded a friend to bring out his motorcycle.

The villagers were regrouping around Sohan Lal when they saw a light on the path adjoining the fields. They looked at it with interest, until they realised it was just another motorcycle. There were plenty around here. Most paid it no more heed. They still didn't know that Pappu had the girls. But the two Shakya brothers, who did know the truth, grew agitated. The motorcycle was leaving Jati, where the Yadavs lived, for a road that led out of the district. If there was even the slightest chance that the girls were on it, now was the time to act. 'Let's go!' they cried.

Some of the men took off on foot, grunting through the crops. The brothers tried to get a car, but where to start? They quickly settled on a more easily available two-wheeler. But by the time they were back in the fields, fifteen minutes had passed, and the motorcycle was gone. Ram Babu who had led this effort looked helplessly around.

At 11.30 p.m., Sohan Lal had a run-in with Rajiv Kumar, the man who had seen Padma and Lalli talking on the phone and had complained about it.

'What's the matter,' Rajiv Kumar said, glancing curiously over at the gathered men. The men fell silent.

'It's nothing,' Sohan Lal replied. He didn't want any more people getting involved. Understanding that he had been dismissed, Rajiv Kumar went home.

The men continued searching, and it seemed to some like they were doing a thorough job. But while the plots were tiny, the fields were vast, deep and full of hiding places: groves of trees, ditches, piles of dung cakes. Haystacks, shacks and taro plants two feet high. A search party twice the size, with the benefit of daylight, would still have their task cut out for them. At night, only chance could reveal someone who wished to stay hidden.

Two small girls, they could be anywhere.

Later, a farmer said that the search party didn't venture into some partly constructed houses located in the fields. 'There could have been any number of men hiding inside, and we wouldn't have known,' he said. They missed several plots of land just because they were full of dunghills. They didn't even make it all the way into the orchard.

At 12.30 a.m. on 28 May, members of the search party started to make their excuses and peel away. A friend said that he really must keep watch over his harvest. Another pressed his hands against his temple and complained of a headache. The relative, Harbans, fell asleep on a charpoy outside the Shakya house.

Inside the house, the Shakya women were clustered in heaving groups. They didn't know for sure, but they knew, nonetheless. With the men gone they relied on friends to call relatives and forewarn them.

The caller who phoned Lalli's older brother to pass on the news was so distraught that she couldn't make herself understood. Virender was hours away in Noida and unable to be of immediate help. He dialled his older sister who lived with her husband in a village closer to home. 'Something has happened,' he said. 'Call and find out what.'

Phoolan Devi wasn't in a position to help either. Her husband had a motorbike but there was no question of plunging into the night. 'It would be good if they are found soon,' she thought. 'Our honour will be saved.'

In Katra, their ten-year-old brother, Parvesh, ran to a neighbour's house and begged him to try Padma's phone. The neighbour called twice but the handset was still switched off.

The girls' grandmother had convinced herself that since Padma had left the house complaining of a stomach ache, the child was simply having trouble defecating. 'Sometimes,' mumbled the old lady, 'if you delay too long it doesn't come out.'

The others knew better.

'We were weeping unstoppably,' Padma's stepmother would remember.

Nazru Changes His Story, Again

Over in the fields, the men were baffled. The persistent chirp of crickets aside, there were now no signs of life. Where were those two?

The situation felt so surreal that one member of the search party was convinced he was sleepwalking. Around this time, someone started prodding the Shakyas for details. Where exactly did the girls go? Did anyone see them? Was there anything else they remembered?

Now, finally – and perhaps only because they weren't getting anywhere – did Ram Babu tell the truth. The girls hadn't disappeared. A Yadav from next door had taken them. His cousin Nazru had said so.

The news landed like a thunderclap. The girls had been kidnapped, the family knew who was responsible, and yet here they were roaming impotently with sticks?

The Shakyas wouldn't budge. What if the Yadavs had guns? By confronting Pappu, they would jeopardise the safety of their clan, they said. Better to let the girls show up. Then the matter would be over, and no one need mention it again.

The village men looked at one another as though to say, are you listening to this. The Shakya brothers were making no sense at all. A man who took a girl did not return her in one piece.

The two groups started to argue: go, stay, go, stay. They bickered and grumbled in the darkness. Then, as suddenly as he had gone, Nazru reappeared and sidled up to his cousins. Sohan Lal threw an arm around him. The oldest Shakya brother had arrived late to the scene and wanted to know everything from the start.

'Tell me,' he said.

He'd been snacking on some corn, Nazru started, keeping watch for wild animals when he heard voices near Jeevan Lal's plot. 'I thought they were women talking among themselves,' he told the group. But, listening carefully, he realised that the women were screaming for help. He moved quickly, looking here and there and shining his torch into the darkness. In the weak light, he saw something startling. 'What's that? Four men scuffling. With Padma and Lalli!' He recognised one of the men, it was that troublemaker Pappu. He was forcing the girls to go with them! 'Padma and Lalli called out, "mujhe bacha do! Save me!"' Nazru flung himself at Pappu, throwing him to the ground. Then Pappu's friend pulled out a gun.

'If I'd known they had a tamancha,' Nazru told the villagers, 'I would have first attempted to snatch it and then rescue the girls.'

But he had to save himself, didn't he? He had to run.

Jeevan Lal and Ram Babu were taken aback. This latest story bore no resemblance to the ones Nazru had told before. At first, he claimed to see thieves. Then, to the family's horror, he had said that Pappu took the girls. Now he had modified his story yet again, adding four men and a gun. What was he up to?

But the brothers didn't make a scene. The essential fact was the same. The girls were gone. And what was more, Nazru was here now. All night the young man had slipped in and out of the search party like he had better things to do.

'If you're sure it was Pappu, we should go to his house,' said Vijay Singh, a hawk-faced farmer with a no-nonsense directness. Before the Shakyas could protest, the thirty-six-year-old picked up his iron rod and called for a friend to accompany him. They cut quickly through the dark.

The Yadav house gleamed in the moonlight.

A single bulb flickered at the front door.

'Pappu!' Singh called out. 'Pappu!'

Pappu's elder brother stirred.

'What is the matter?' Urvesh said, heaving himself up from the charpoy outside the front door. 'Why are you calling Pappu?'

'I have some urgent business.'

Urvesh yelled thickly down the road, 'Pappu! Ai, Pappu!'

Pappu emerged from his uncle's shack. He was wearing a vest and trousers. According to his cousin Raju, they had nodded off on a charpoy after eating a watermelon from the harvest supply.

'Kya yahan par koi chalta purza hai?' Vijay Singh asked. Are there any busybodies around?

By using the term busybody, he was asking the Yadav boy whether he'd seen any troublemakers in the area. It was, of course, just an excuse to confirm whether Pappu had been at home.

'There's no one here,' Pappu replied, rubbing his eyes.

His mother, Jhalla Devi, stepped out of the house – to draw water from the handpump, she would later claim.

'What's the matter?' she said from behind her sari veil. The men from Katra waved her away. 'It's nothing.'

Avdesh, the oldest Yadav son, climbed down from the terrace. After a desultory back and forth the outsiders took their leave.

'What's going on?' one of the brothers said to Pappu.

'I had kind of a fight with Nazru,' Pappu replied sheepishly.

'When will you stop playing the fool,' his brother scolded.

If anything further was said, the family later kept it to themselves.

Pappu turned back. Urvesh lay down, closed his eyes and brought his knees up to his chest in his usual position of sleep. Avdesh climbed up the stairs. Their mother scuttled in and bolted the door behind her.

The villagers went on looking.

'The orchard,' Singh later recalled, ticking off the places they searched next. 'The eucalyptus grove.' But some members of the party remembered it differently. After this encounter, they said, they limited their search to the vicinity of the Yadav house. They saw nothing. They heard nothing.

Sometime later, the men decided to take a break under an enormous quince tree. They wiped their faces and hands and shared a drink of water.

Another one of the Shakya cousins then spoke up.

A little before 6 a.m. that morning, Prem Singh said, he had driven his tractor up to Sohan Lal's plot to load the farmer's mint harvest. The thirty-two-year-old's grocery store was losing money like you wouldn't believe, and he made up the deficit by transporting people and goods for cash. As he chatted with Nazru, who also happened to be hanging around, he had seen Sohan Lal's daughter, Lalli, speaking into a mobile phone.

The search party leaned in with interest.

This titbit promised to revive their energies. Perhaps it was a clue that could be mined for leads.

But Prem Singh hadn't heard the conversation. 'I thought she was talking to a relative,' he shrugged. He'd only mentioned it in case it meant something to her father. Lalli's father remembered that he had asked his daughter to make a call for him that morning. Then he'd wandered off, leaving his phone with her.

'Check the recorded calls,' Sohan Lal ordered Yogendra, Prem Singh's brother.

The list showed three calls. Two were outgoing, one was incoming. The incoming conversation had taken place at 6.01 a.m. that morning.

'I played the recording,' Yogendra would remember. 'And everyone present heard it.'

'Where are you?' Lalli asked.

'Across the bridge,' said a reedy voice. 'Where are you?'

'In the fields. They are cutting the crops.'

'Didn't you go to the fair?'

'Did you give us money to go?'

'I'll give you money, go to the fair. And when will I get the chance to enjoy myself?'

'Meet us in the evening. You will enjoy yourself.'

'Bastards, Go Look for
Them Yourselves'

The contents of the call were so shocking that after the night had finally passed, the brothers would sometimes claim that they hadn't heard it. As though willing it out of existence, they spoke about it only in vague terms, as something that might have been but of which they themselves had no direct knowledge. In fact, someone had anticipated the conversation and then switched on the phone's recording facility. This Made in China handset, like the one Sohan Lal had given to Padma, could record calls – but it wasn't pre-activated to do so.

As the men stared down at their feet, Jeevan Lal declared that he was going home. Ram Babu offered to accompany him.

The two brothers walked off. No one blamed them. The voice on the other end of the line had belonged to a boy, a boy like Pappu.

The police chowki was located in an alleyway just opposite a government nursery school. To get there, Sohan Lal and the others in the search party had to cross the bazaar. Upon arrival, the metal gate was padlocked, and inside, an oil lamp placed on a table had long died out. Attired in night clothes, the five police officers were sprawled on charpoys, legs outstretched and potbellies heaving. It was between 2 and 2.30 a.m. The night was cold. The moonlight was thin.

The villagers rattled the gate.

'Sahib,' they called out deferentially. 'Sahib, wake up, sahib!'

One of the officers opened his eyes but showed no signs of moving. The group raised its collective voice.

A frustrated Sohan Lal tried another tactic.

Srikrishen Shakya lived down the road. As he saw the officers come and go, Srikrishen did them small favours to keep in their good graces and they in turn grew friendly with him. Knowing this, Sohan Lal hurried over to his house. By this time the group was making such a racket that while the police continued to sleep – or *pretend* to sleep – Srikrishen had jumped out of bed, wondering what on earth was going on. He was fumbling for a light when Sohan Lal arrived at his doorstep.

'My girls are gone,' Sohan Lal said. 'The police won't wake up. Time is being wasted.'

Srikrishen agreed to accompany Sohan Lal to the chowki.

'Babuji,' he cried to the sleeping officers. 'Babuji!'

It was only now, on the urging of a familiar voice, that the police roused themselves. 'Yes, yes,' muttered Sub-Inspector Ram Vilas Yadav, the top-ranking officer at the chowki.

Barrel-bellied and heavily moustached, Ram Vilas had an unfortunate speech impediment that made him sound as though he had two tongues. He stammered and slurred. Strangers reacted with open rudeness, dismissing him offhand. His colleagues were kinder, pointing out that it required just a little patience to figure out what he was saying. But even they avoided him at mealtimes.

'Watching him eat could make you vomit,' one officer said, referring to the manner in which lentils tended to dribble out of Ram Vilas's mouth, soaking his collar.

Ram Vilas also had visible scars that some people attributed to brave encounters with bandits. In fact, said his colleagues, he was a drunk who had been involved in seven motorcycle accidents in one year. This didn't influence any promotions that he was due. Even the villagers judged him less harshly for his drunkenness than his speech – every police officer they had ever known was a drunkard. And the fifty-seven-year-old man was said to be fair. The villagers respectfully called him 'darogaji', police chief.

Sohan Lal kept it brief. His girls were missing, he said. Pappu Yadav of Jati had them. Would they please come with him to Pappu's house?

'He listened to us,' Lalli's father later said. 'But no one listened to him.' He meant some of the other policemen, who acted as though the complaint was entirely made-up.

One of them was a lanky man with stiff grey hair and pitted cheeks named Chattrapal Singh Gangwar. Gangwar had recently been promoted to head constable. The good news, arriving shortly before he was to retire at the age of sixty, had given him an excuse to exceed his daily quota of alcohol. He had cut loose that day, spending several hours on duty downing cheap whisky at a roadside eatery.

As Ram Vilas prodded Gangwar – saying, 'utho yaar,' wake up – his subordinate shot back in language that shocked his colleagues. 'His behaviour was indecent,' said Raghunandan Singh, the other officer who went on to help the family.

Ram Vilas wasn't deterred.

'Get up!' he shouted.

Again, Gangwar swore.

One of the villagers claimed to smell his alcohol-laced breath all the way from the gate.

The older man shared a friendly relationship with his boss, and the two were known to engage in what was considered playful banter of the sister-mother variety – casually swapping digs that invoked sex and sexual violence. But now, Gangwar was mistakenly under the impression that his boss was pulling his leg, the way he did when they got drunk together in the chowki.

Finally, he gave in.

'Nothing but drama,' he groaned.

The fourth officer in the chowki was Constable Sarvesh Kumar Yadav, then thirty-nine years old, with a jutting mouth and a stubborn disposition. Sarvesh was used to doing as he pleased. He thrashed around a bit but remained where he was. 'Bastards,' he muttered at the villagers. 'Go look for them yourselves.'

In the back and forth, some of the officers had changed into their uniforms. They climbed onto their motorbikes and made for Pappu's house, less than half a kilometre away. The villagers trudged on foot. Sarvesh and Gangwar were taking far too long to sort themselves out and were left behind.

The village was eerily quiet, the fifth officer present that night later recalled. 'It felt desolate,' Satinder Pal Yadav said. It was as though the people had left, the animals had wandered off and all the birds had flown away.

A Finger Is Pointed

Outside the Yadav house, a figure lay curled on a charpoy. Ram Vilas demanded to see Pappu. For the second time that night, Pappu's brother Urvesh scrambled up. This time he knew better than to yell, and he walked quickly down the road.

There the boy was, tightly asleep beside his cousin.

'Wh-wh-what's your name?' Ram Vilas stammered.

'Pappu,' replied the startled young man.

'Wh-wh-what's your fa-father's name?'

'Veerpal Yadav.'

'I-I-I need some information from you.'

As Pappu pulled on a shirt, Ram Vilas pointed to Urvesh and ordered him to follow. Avdesh came down from the terrace and was also told to come along to the chowki. Ram Vilas offered no explanation and it wouldn't have occurred to the brothers to ask. There was no point antagonising the police, as it was they made life hell.

A Yadav neighbour peered out the door. 'What has Pappu done,' he protested.

Padma's father Jeevan Lal and her uncle Ram Babu, who had returned to the fields to keep an eye on the Yadav house, now emerged from the shadows and blended in with the group of villagers.

A motorcycle then came to a screeching halt. Sarvesh and his colleague dismounted. Bleary-eyed Gangwar had little to say for himself, but Sarvesh presented himself as the protector of the Yadav brothers. 'Pappu is right here, idiots! Would he be here if he'd been out kidnapping girls? You people don't keep an eye on your children and then harass us.'

He turned to his boss. 'Let Pappu go. I will answer for him. Bunch of motherfuckers. Are we really going to listen to these sister-fuckers?'

'It was clear Sarvesh felt sympathetic towards the Yadavs,' a fellow officer would dryly recall.

Sohan Lal didn't react to the abuse. It was all one could expect from the police. They treated the poor like insects to be squashed under their shoes. But the suggestion that Pappu should be exempt from questioning made him lightheaded.

'You can't do that,' he begged. If Pappu was allowed to stay back, whatever chance the family had to find the children would be lost, he said. If the boy had abducted the girls, who knows what he would do to them.

Ram Vilas agreed.

With the three Yadavs huddling it was hard to say which was which. The ragged sameness of their faces and slight limbs prompted some confusion.

'Which one was it?' squinted Constable Raghunandan. Which one took your girls, he meant.

It was his cousin Nazru who had seen them, Sohan Lal explained. But he was at home. Should they go get him?

In the chowki courtyard, Ram Vilas got down to business. He slapped Pappu across the face. 'Where are the girls?' he shouted.

As the crying teenager clutched his cheek, Ram Vilas drew out the strip of rubber he kept for one purpose only.

He started to whip Pappu, bringing the rubber down on the teenager's thighs, knees and ankles, places that filled the body with a severe and stinging, but outwardly invisible, pain.

'I'm in my vest,' Pappu squealed, trying to convey that since he was partially dressed at the time the police came for him, he was obviously asleep then and not wandering around somewhere. With this response he made it clear that he didn't have to be told what he was being accused of; he knew.

'Idiot!' snapped Constable Raghunandan. 'Does it take years to take off a shirt?'

'It was him!' Nazru said, sitting on a charpoy. The older Yadav brothers sat on the edge of a second charpoy. The villagers spread out; some stood, others squatted by the chowki gates. Tired and red-eyed from lack of sleep, every one of them was determined to see this through.

At the gates, Sohan Lal pulled up the recording on his phone. Several more people now heard it.

The beating continued with Ram Vilas shouting, 'Where are the girls? Where are the girls? Where are the girls?' Pappu responded with more squeals. The villagers watched without flinching. The fellow was only getting what he deserved. Beat him, beat him; what else was there to do?

Only one person reacted viscerally.

Nazru put his head in his hands and howled.

'Why are you crying?' said Constable Raghunandan. 'No one is saying anything to you. No one is even asking you questions.'

Ram Vilas made it clear that the beating wouldn't stop until Pappu started to talk.

Finally, he got what he wanted.

'They were with me,' Pappu admitted, tears rolling down his face. He'd met them that evening, at around 9.30 p.m., to give them money for the mela. A hundred rupees each.

'Kiya maine kuch nahin,' he sobbed. I didn't do anything.

'If you didn't do anything,' Ram Vilas shouted, 'who did? Someone has them, otherwise they would be home, wouldn't they! Idiot!'

'I had just handed over the money to them when he pounced on me.'

Everyone looked in the direction that Pappu was pointing at.

Pappu's finger pointed unwaveringly at Nazru.

'He threw me to the ground,' Pappu said. 'I picked myself up and ran away. I don't know where they are now, but when I left them, they were with *him*.'

Constable Sarvesh barrelled towards Nazru as though to slap him.

Sohan Lal couldn't believe it.

'Pappu just said he was with the girls,' he cried. 'Why are you involving one of our people? Pappu has been talking to our girls on the phone, I have proof!'

The conflicting narratives set alight a firecracker of chaos.

The village men shouted that Pappu was lying. Constable Sarvesh shouted that *they* were the liars. Everyone stood up to point fingers.

The hours immediately after a child goes missing are critical: in that time, they may be sexually assaulted, transported out of the state for trafficking purposes or even killed.

Some police officers responded to a report of a missing child with only an entry in the GD, or General Diary, a record of daily events. The previous year however, in 2013, the Supreme Court had ordered the police to also file an official FIR in all such cases. This was the document required to start an investigation.[1] The decision had been made in response to the growing epidemic of missing children.

Ram Vilas was only a chowki officer. He wasn't authorised to file the report. But he might have done something.

He might have looked for the girls.

Sohan Lal Storms Out

Nazru's tears were so relentless even the villagers were taken aback. The young man was crying as though a cobra had fallen into his lap.

Only Sohan Lal was sympathetic. His cousin was being toyed with as a distraction, he said, to give Pappu the time to come up with an alibi. And what about Pappu's brothers?

Ram Vilas heaved with annoyance. 'They have nothing to do with the matter,' he replied. After all, Nazru hadn't implicated the older Yadav boys in the night's events. He hadn't even seen them.

Pappu, meanwhile, tried to make himself inconspicuous by saying nothing further.

'I'm telling you,' Constable Sarvesh shouted, banging his chest theatrically. 'The girls are not with him.'

'I'm leaving,' declared Sohan Lal. He was fuming.

Having started the night refusing to approach the police, notify the rest of the village or even raise his voice, Lalli's father said he would go to Ushait. It was the closest town with a full-scale police station, and he could file an FIR.

Sohan Lal took Nazru by the hand and walked out. 'We won't get justice here.' They went looking for a car to take them.

Some of the villagers lingered in the chowki, attempting to piece together the chronology of the night's events. Pappu and the girls had met, but then Nazru surprised them – that much was settled. Then what? Pappu said he ran away leaving behind the girls, but Nazru claimed that *he* was the one who had run off. The last two people known to have seen Padma and Lalli were accusing each other of having taken the girls.

The roosters crowed. The sky was shot through with light. The village awoke as if to an alarm. Fires were lit and tea brewed. The smell of boiling milk infused the air with sweetness.

Then doors opened and people left their homes in ones and twos, rubbing the crusts of sleep from their eyes. Some carried round-mouthed lotas brimming with water. Others went to check on their animals.

The night had passed, and they had no idea what had happened. These were the last quiet hours.

The Shakya brothers had come to an agreement over the price of renting a neighbour's car, a nine-seater Mahindra Maxx. Some of the villagers had changed their clothes; others had sprinkled water on their hair and slipped shoes over their feet. They were ready to look dreaded authority figures in the face. They squeezed into the car.

A few young men, who by now felt personally invested in the case, insisted on following on motorbikes. They included Rajiv Kumar, the man who had set Nazru spying on the girls.

As the sleeping village came to life, the cavalcade roared out of Katra.

Finally, News

There had been no question of Jhalla Devi sleeping that night. Now, finally, her sons were back. 'Nazru is saying he got into a fight with Pappu,' one of them told her. 'He's accusing Pappu of snatching Sohan and Jeevan's daughters.'

'How's that possible?' Jhalla Devi snapped. 'When the village men came for him, he was at his uncle's. When the police came for him, he was still at his uncle's. How and when could he have taken the girls?'

'I'm going to gather fodder,' she said. Her daughter-in-law started to sweep the house, but her sons wandered off.

Jhalla Devi was filling her arms with hay when a car full of men drove past. They shouted abuse at her, she would later claim. They called the Yadav family fucking scum and threatened to burn down their house. The timing would suggest that they were part of the convoy heading to the police station.

Jhalla Devi slipped into the house and went to the backyard.

'I was feeding the buffaloes,' she later said, 'when some crying women walked past.'

What she heard startled her into dropping the hay. She ran quick as a shadow. 'We have to leave,' she told her daughter-in-law.

The Yadav women were gathering their things when Avdesh and Urvesh returned home. At exactly one minute past five in the morning, Avdesh dialled his friend in the chowki, Sarvesh, with the news.

As soon as he hung up, several family members packed whatever belongings they could carry on their head. They fled, but the others stayed awhile, leaving a little later.

Constable Sarvesh had come to know the family over the past few months, ever since his boss, Ram Vilas, started sending him to Jati to keep an eye out for the sand mining mafia. The riverbank sand was trucked out to factories and mixed with concrete and bricks. It was a hugely profitable operation, sometimes deadly and entirely illegal.

Sarvesh would take to striding up and down the road opposite the Yadav house. As he was only a few years older than Avdesh, the two got along. Many people saw them sharing tea, talking over dal and rotis.

A friendship with a police officer was a coup. The relationship with Constable Sarvesh burnished the Yadav name, elevating the family of climate refugees in their new neighbourhood.

Now, Sarvesh hung up the phone without asking further questions. He passed the information he had received on to his boss, who made preparations to leave. Ram Vilas took two officers with him, but told Sarvesh to stay back – ostensibly to keep an eye on Pappu, who was still hovering uncertainly, but really because Sarvesh was more trouble than he was worth.

A man standing outside the police chowki saw the officers leave and was overcome with dread. 'They have been found,' he thought.

Shortly afterwards, Prem Singh – the cousin who had overheard Lalli on the phone – was walking to the fields, when he heard a youngster shouting the news. Prem Singh immediately phoned his father.

'The girls are in the aam ka bagh,' he said. The mango orchard.

The older man – part of the group on their way to Ushait – immediately told the others, but their phones were now ringing too. The car resounded with chimes as one after the other villager, friend and relative called to say: the girls are dead, the girls are dead, the girls are dead.

'An Unspeakable Sight'

Lalli's mother picked up the hem of her sari and ran. The news had spread and it seemed as though everyone around her was also running. The crowd was packed with men and women. Babies were at their mothers' breasts; children hurried alongside in raggedy trousers and filthy dresses. Siya Devi's ears filled with a thundering sound.

Padma and Lalli were hanging from a mango tree.

The tree had a broad base, with a trunk that branched off at a few inches short of three feet. Padma was higher up above the ground. One knot secured her dark green dupatta to the tree. A second knot, looped tightly around her neck, kept her aloft. Lalli was nearly two feet lower, secured in near-identical fashion. Their eyes were closed. Their hands sloped inwards. Their toes pointed to the earth.

They looked like 'dangling puppets', a villager later recalled.

Siya Devi didn't cry. It was as though the forces that had extinguished her daughter's life had taken her tongue with them.

The last time she had seen the girls they were radiant. The visit to the fair had been a real treat, and she had come to accept that Padma and Lalli would chatter about it for days, driving her crazy. Yesterday was the best day of their lives, but today?

'Kisne kiya,' someone shouted. Who did it?

One man said that he was about to have a heart attack.

A teenager muttered, 'They better hang the culprits.'

A family friend turned away. 'An unspeakable sight.'

Padma and Lalli weren't just cousins, someone said. They were best friends. Wasn't Padma admired for her fine hand embroidery? She loved mangoes. She loved devotional songs.

Lalli had wanted to be a doctor; no, she wanted to be a teacher. 'I want to be *something*,' she had always said. But Lalli would never be anything at all.

Finally, Siya Devi found her voice.

'My girl is hanging. Why? What did she do? She didn't do anything. She didn't go anywhere. She only used to graze the goats. Why did they hang her? Is she worth nothing? Do our children mean nothing?'

No one expected Siya Devi to stay. She would go home, and they would carry her. In anticipation that she might faint, some men quickly moved in.

But Siya Devi placed her lathi against the mango tree and lowered herself onto the bare ground. 'Meri bacchi,' she moaned. 'My child, my child, my child, my child, my child, my child.'

Padma's mother Sunita Devi sat down too.

The children's grandmother sat with them.

Other women came forward. Without question, without permission. Their faces were covered, but their intention was beyond a doubt.

With their bodies they were guarding the bodies in the tree.

A Policeman's Suspicion

The Shakya brothers had to push their way through the teeming crowd. A neighbour ran past clicking pictures.

There they were, their children.

'Maar dali ladkiyan hamari,' Sohan Lal crumpled.

'Maar di!' Jeevan Lal echoed. 'Maar di!'

They have killed our daughters. Killed them.

Friends rushed forward to steer the brothers to the protective awning of shady trees, far from the hanging bodies. Sohan Lal didn't seek out his wife. He turned to the other men. 'My daughter is dead. My daughter is dead,' he said, as though wanting a contradiction.

The men nodded and sighed.

The Vedas had a prayer calling for people to die in the right order. Parents, always, before children. But you didn't have to subscribe to a particular theology to know that no parent should have to bury a child. And yet, time and again, the Shakyas had done just that. Sohan Lal and Siya Devi had lost their eldest child after she gave birth. Jeevan Lal and Sunita Devi had suffered many miscarriages. And Sohan Lal's mother had once had a daughter too, not just three sons. There were very few people in the village who didn't understand the loss the family was going through. But here were two girls hanging from a tree. No one knew how to respond. Most stepped back and looked fearfully on from afar.

Cousin Manju went up close. Lalli was covered in dust. Thorns poked out of her salwar kameez. 'Someone killed her,' she thought, with despair.

A breeze started to blow through the orchard, scattering dust from the ground. It picked fallen leaves and shook the branches of trees. The breeze lifted the girls' kameezes and they swayed gently from side to side as if they were jostling each other to share a secret, suno, listen, I have something to tell you.

A neighbour picked up his lathi and hurried off. The dead were supposed to be still, he thought, but it was as if these girls were alive. The horror stalked him between the walls of his house all the way in the village. 'All I could hear was moaning,' he said.

The searing heat started to smite people. 'Manju,' someone called, 'run and get water for us.'

By the time Manju was back, her father had come for her, having left the previous night. Despite his sister Siya Devi's pleas that they stay, he refused. 'What if the same thing that happened to your daughter happens to mine?'

Padma's maternal uncles, who lived in another village, arrived shortly afterwards. 'I lost my mind when I saw her,' Kanhaiya Lal later recalled. He threw his arms around the body of his niece. His ribs shone in the heat like copper wire. His eyes were pressed shut. He said something, but it was hard for the others to make out what. Then, it sounded to some like he had indeed lost his senses.

'Your cousin saw you in a dream,' he sobbed. 'You were dead, she said. She asked me to bring you to us. But I didn't. I didn't even phone you. All I said was dreams don't come true.'

'Justice!' someone called out.

As Padma's uncles found their way to the Shakya men, the gathered villagers took up the call on their behalf. 'Justice!' they said, lifting their voices. 'Justice!' they said, banging their lathis to the ground, stirring tiny dust storms.

Members of the search party started talking, circulating their version of the night's affair. Pappu was declared the culprit, the man who had killed Padma and Lalli. Constable Sarvesh, his protector.

'Come forward, you cowards!'

'Bring Pappu and Sarvesh, let's hang them from a tree the way they hanged our girls. Only then will we get justice!'

Sub-Inspector Ram Vilas phoned his subordinate.

'The crowd is growing,' he whispered. 'They may kill Pappu. Go, hurry, drop him off at the station.'

Ram Vilas had finally understood the gravity of the situation, if only through its potential impact on him. Sarvesh would manage; he was that sort of guy. But if the crowd got out of hand, they would lynch the Yadav boy. A lynching would lead to an investigation, and when Ram Vilas limped, stammered and slurred before his superior officers the game would be up for good.

To make sure the teenager didn't act funny, Head Constable Gangwar clasped Pappu firmly around the waist. The three men sped out of Katra on Sarvesh's motorcycle, on their way to Ushait, as villagers watched in disgust. The officers had placed Pappu between them to protect him, they said.

The news travelled quickly back to the orchard. A Yadav boy had killed the girls, and Yadav policemen – emboldened by the protections they received from Yadav politicians – were protecting the accused.

'Maro police ko!' someone shouted. 'Maaro salon ko.' Thrash the police. Thrash the bastards.

'Let them be,' Jeevan Lal mumbled. He didn't need a fight breaking out.

'He's old,' said his brother, gesturing at Ram Vilas.

The villagers knew Ram Vilas well but now they assessed him. Look at those watery eyes, that saggy jaw, the belly that spilled out over his wrinkly brown trousers.

Was he guarding the house of a politician or patrolling neighbourhoods where the rich lived? No, he had been offloaded on Katra, because the villagers were considered mere keede makode, vermin, that deserved no better. They were despised.

And now that they could do so openly, without fear of retribution, they expressed their true feelings for Ram Vilas. Darogaji, my foot. He was a good-for-nothing.

A tailor, ordinarily a docile man, hurled himself against Ram Vilas, almost toppling him into a plot of mint. When the policeman's colleague stepped forward to intervene, the tailor pushed him aside and made for Ram Vilas again.

Ram Vilas shrank.

'He was afraid,' the colleague later recalled. 'He must have thought, "I can't even run, what will I do?"'

It was too much for Padma's father.

'Bacha nahin paonga,' Jeevan Lal said, folding his hands pleadingly. I can't protect you.

But even as the Shakyas stood up for Ram Vilas, his feelings towards them changed. The moment he arrived in the orchard he asked himself one question – 'yeh mar kaise gaye?'

How did they die?

Then he cycled through the evening's events in his
mind, hoping to recall something that would provide a
clue to the truth. The Shakyas had behaved very oddly, he
felt. Several hours had passed since the time their girls had
gone missing and they had shown up to file a complaint.
They hadn't wanted a private matter to become public,
theek hai, but was that the smart choice in a matter of life
and death?

Ram Vilas was a father of sons, but his daughters made
him proud. They had left the village years ago and now
lived in Noida in a flat that they shared. In his village, if
a girl left home it was to marry. But Jyoti was a business
student and Babli worked for a multinational company
with Americans.

He was in awe of those two. He loved them. If anyone
dared to lay so much as a finger on them, he would peel
off their skin.

But when their girls went missing what did Sohan Lal
and Jeevan Lal do? They didn't go to the police. Then they
refused to let the police speak to the only witness to the
girls' meeting in the fields.

But it was the way the brothers had reacted to the sight
of the bodies that convinced Ram Vilas that his hunch was
accurate. It wasn't so much about what they did wrong.
Indeed, they had acted just right.

He assessed the pair with distaste. Padma's father and
Lalli's father were still sobbing.

'They killed them,' he told himself. 'They hanged them.'

The Poster Child for a New India

In the remote parts of the district, important information was still broadcast on a loudspeaker. But all the men here had a phone. Rooted to the orchard, they shared the news with everyone they could think of. They took photos of the girls, they recorded videos. The digital souvenirs were sent around via the social network WhatsApp and soon caught the attention of farmers dozens of kilometres away. It was a pivotal time in the harvest, but the opportunity to look death in the face was a 'naya tamasha', an exciting new spectacle, as one man observed.

The road to Katra was soon jammed with horse carts, motorbikes and tractors. The farmers brought their wives, their wives toted children, and some even carried guns. The visitors gazed up at the girls. 'Ladkiyan tangi!' Girls hanging!

The crowd staked their positions around the tree, just behind the Shakya family. Women sat cross-legged on the bare ground with their faces covered to ensure modesty. 'When they cannot control us, they kill us,' they agreed.

Behind them, older men sat on their haunches with their cotton dhotis pulled up to their knees, beedis clutched in their fists. The younger ones strolled about in their trousers and loose-fitting, Western-style shirts, clicking pictures. As temperatures soared, they stripped down to their vests. Some teenagers climbed to the tops of trees for a bird's-eye view.

Everyone believed Padma and Lalli had been killed. They were children who were found hanging in a public place. The hangings, people said, were meant to serve as a reminder of the powerlessness of the poor. No one was safe from the better-off castes, not even tiny girls.

Shocking events were hardly a novelty in the district. The previous year, in 2013, two members of a family in a nearby village had died by suicide, an aunt and nephew allegedly in an illicit love affair. That same year, the police beat a young man to death because his sister had married outside their caste.

And the year before that a teenaged boy from the district was among those arrested, and later convicted, in the appalling crime that haunted the nation – the Delhi bus rape.

One cold December night in 2012, a twenty-three-year-old physiotherapy intern and her male friend were returning home after watching the movie *Life of Pi* in an upscale Delhi mall. It was around 9.30 p.m., but the streets were brightly lit and crowded. The roads thundered with fast-moving traffic. After they had boarded what seemed to be a passenger bus, the men inside took hold of the young woman. Six of them gang-raped her and tortured her, shoving a metal rod up to her diaphragm. Then they threw the couple from the vehicle. They tried to run them over. When the victim was brought into the hospital, she was alive, but her intestines were spilling out of her body.

The victim, the daughter of an airport porter – whose name and identity was withheld as per the requirements of Indian law – was the first in her family to go to college. Her parents had glimpsed her potential early on. 'Boys cry when you send them to school,' her father Badri Singh said. 'But she would cry if you didn't let her go to school.'[1]

He sold most of his land to educate her, and when that wasn't enough, he took on debt and double shifts. This was more than most would do for a girl.

The victim might have been the poster child for a new India – the porter's daughter who went on to become a doctor, fulfilling the highest aspiration of every educated Indian. Instead, the ease with which she was captured, raped and then murdered – in the national capital no less – was a klaxon: listen, there is something very wrong with this place.

When the victim died in a hospital bed in Singapore, Indians responded with the largest demonstration against sexual assault the country had ever witnessed. The victim was widely known as *Nirbhaya*, meaning fearless, and her struggle and death became a symbol of women's resistance to rape around the world. The six culprits had been quickly apprehended and would stand trial in record time, but the protests reflected the fact that too many victims of sexual violence never saw justice.

The protests were so forceful that police employed tear gas and enforced curfews. Eventually, the government had to respond. They launched public awareness campaigns, helplines and women's shelters. They strengthened existing laws: the definition of the word 'rape' was expanded to include any object being inserted into any part of the body – this was in recognition of the fact that the victim's rapists had tortured her with a metal rod. And for the first time ever, acid attacks, intent to disrobe a woman, voyeurism and stalking were each made an offence.

The minimum punishment for anyone convicted of gang rape was raised to twenty years, rape that led to death was punishable with the death penalty. And the age of consent was raised from sixteen to eighteen. The changes to these laws would have a powerful impact on the rape cases that did make it to trial. In 2019, four of the six men convicted in the Delhi bus rape case were hanged.[2]

The lesson that many ordinary Indians took from the aftermath of the Delhi bus rape was that protests mattered. They forced the hand of power. The villagers of Katra had also understood this. And, as far as they were concerned, the deaths of Padma and Lalli were more disturbing even than the attack in Delhi. The way they saw it, the children hadn't died in a city far away, pushing their boundaries and asserting their independence. They hadn't died watching an English film with a boy, then taking public transport at night. They hadn't died doing something that girls like them should never have thought to do. They had died where they were born. They had died pissing in the fields.

But Delhi, where the high-profile rape had taken place, where the most powerful politicians lived, where the media conglomerates had their air-conditioned offices, was hundreds of kilometres away. The villagers couldn't go to them.

Would they come to the village?

A Reporter's Big Break

The morning birds had only just begun their chorus when Ankur Chaturvedi, a reporter with Aaj Tak – one of India's most popular Hindi-language news channels – started to receive calls from Katra.

The twenty-seven-year-old had reported from western Uttar Pradesh for several years. He circulated his mobile phone number liberally and encouraged sources to call him night or day. They phoned in news of gang rapes, acid attacks and randua pratha, when family members killed single men for their ancestral property. They called when nilgai stampeded, laying crops to waste, or when a child slipped and fell headlong into a well.

Chaturvedi didn't always follow through. In Uttar Pradesh, where bad news was commonplace, he was under pressure to find stories that would bring light relief.

Aaj Tak's more than 100 million viewers liked to watch news that boosted their self-esteem. The middle class, particularly, wanted to hear of the India that had survived the worldwide economic recession virtually unscathed, the India whose economy was now the third-largest in Asia. They enjoyed news about cricket and Bollywood. And they relished global lists featuring Indian names, because these reiterated the country's growing place in the world.

On 28 May, the day the girls were found, *Forbes* magazine published its list of the world's most powerful women. It included five Indian and Indian-origin women – among them, the chief technology and strategy officer of Cisco and the newly appointed chairperson of the State Bank of India.[1] A few months later, *Fortune* published its list of the most powerful women in the Asia Pacific, in which eight Indians made the cut.[2]

To many Indians these lists were evidence that the country was on track to become an economic superpower. The promise was implicit in Prime Minister Modi's speeches – 'good days are coming soon,' he had said, over and over.

India had been poor for so long; but now, rather than being dismissed as a lumbering elephant, it was a tiger, and its economy measured favourably alongside China's. As people's vanities were stoked, their appetite for news stories about girls like Padma and Lalli shrank. While monitoring six major national newspapers over a two-month period later that year, Delhi's Centre for Media Studies found that coverage of rural India made up only 0.23 per cent of the news.[3] The world was watching India, but no one was more bewitched by the transformation than Indians themselves.

The largely ignored parts of the rural countryside, where 70 per cent of the population lived, were also witnessing change. Here, people were eating fewer nutrients than were required to stay healthy, as compared to forty years ago.[4] The number of farmers who had died by suicide over farm-related debt had crossed 290,000. And as more people lost their land, a vast new underclass emerged – one that was forced to leave their ancestral village and to migrate to towns and cities where they had no choice but to serve better-off Indians as nannies, gardeners, dog walkers, cooks and cleaners.

The richest 1 per cent owned 53 per cent of the country's wealth, according to Credit Suisse. The top 10 per cent owned 76.3 per cent. That left, on the opposite end of the spectrum, the poor – with a mere 4.1 per cent of national wealth.[5]

Chaturvedi knew that his boss could not care less about Padma and Lalli. The thing about India, he would say, was that there were *a lot* of people. And this was an ordinary killing, just two girls in some village.

He forgot about the calls and went on with his day. He slipped on his spectacles and perched his laptop on his belly to post a lament on Facebook about wanting someone to love. He drank some tea. The post had accumulated fifteen likes by the time a police officer called.

Did Chaturvedi know that the girls' parents were refusing to allow the bodies to come down?

No, he did not.

They had created quite the scene. The crowd was a seething mob.

A fatal crime was more of the usual. But the same report with the victims still in the frame was so unusual, even in these parts, it would definitely be telecast. The clip might make its way to Facebook.

Chaturvedi followed up with other sources. 'It had all the elements,' he said later. 'The accused were Yadavs, the state government was Yadav, and the police were Yadavs.' It was a crime of caste, he said, and it confirmed popular, negative stereotypes about Yadavs. He could just see his audience tut-tutting as they chewed on their breakfast sabzi parantha.

Grabbing his dinged-up laptop, Chaturvedi phoned a cameraman colleague and arranged to meet him. With one hand on the steering wheel of his zippy little car, he plugged in his Bluetooth headphones and called his boss to relay the news.

'Send me the clip immediately,' his boss ordered.

As Chaturvedi sped forward, he saw a man a few feet ahead lying in the middle of the road, his open eyes looking up at the sky. He was very likely drunk but perhaps he was dead, and Chaturvedi swerved to avoid hitting him.

'I can get a great shot,' he promised his boss.

'The Matter Will End'

The object glinting in Padma's clothing was clearly a mobile phone, and Ram Vilas was eager to have it. It would offer clues to the case, which would redeem him in the eyes of his superiors. On the other hand, if the crowd caught him rifling through the teenager's bra, they would kill him.

It was foolish for a police officer to even contemplate collecting evidence with his bare hands, but the idea at least showed initiative. So far, Ram Vilas had behaved more like a spectator, except that actual spectators had been far more useful at documenting the event by capturing images and videos. He would later be unable even to recall what time he had arrived at the orchard.

It was true that the police weren't adequately trained or equipped to do their job. An acceptable method of securing a crime scene, for example, was by chasing away onlookers like they were pigeons. There was no question of protecting the area from encroachment or procuring evidence, even though the scene of a crime is one of three resources investigators rely on to interpret events. Another is the body of the deceased, which is why criminal investigations develop around post-mortems. A third vital resource is the body of the culprit. Pappu Yadav was on his way to the police station, but his family,

who had rather mysteriously called in with news of the
bodies, had been all but forgotten.

'Bheed kafi hai,' Ram Vilas muttered, digging into his
pocket for his phone. There's quite a crowd.

Better to let someone else take over.

In the nearby town of Ushait, Ram Vilas's immediate
superior was in a deep sleep. It was 5.37 a.m. He listened
with groggy irritation as the caller stammered his way
through a greeting. 'Is someone else around?' Inspector
Ganga Singh demanded in his hoarse voice. He couldn't
follow a word.

Ram Vilas handed the phone to a colleague who swiftly
summarised the events of the past few hours. He was in
Katra village, explained Constable Raghunandan. Two
girls, having attended a play the previous evening, had
failed to return home. This morning they were found
hanged from a tree.

Raghunandan had got the first part wrong. The girls had,
of course, returned home; they disappeared much later.

Ganga Singh wasn't sure he had heard right. 'If a man is
woken up and told that two girls were found hanged,' he
later remembered, 'wouldn't he be taken aback?'

Raghunandan piped up again. A father of three – his
youngest, a boy in the fifth class – the officer had reacted
to the sight before him with predictable shock. But he
was first and foremost a policeman; it was all he knew to
do since he had joined the force some twenty years ago.
There was an aspect of the scene that he found so striking
he had to mention it right away.

Two pairs of footwear stood at the base of the tree
almost immediately beneath Padma's gently dangling feet.
The sky-blue slippers were hers. Lalli had owned the black
ones with the distinctive red straps. The slippers might

have been expected to slide off the girls' feet after they'd been hanged, but in that case, they would surely have been strewn on the ground.

Instead, here they were, side by side against the tree, as upright as stems of wheat. The precise and delicate placement baffled Raghunandan.

He then told Ganga Singh that a crowd had gathered. 'Like cattle let out of the pen,' he whispered.

The grim pallor of the early morning sky appeared to reflect the mood of the crowd. The officer was eager to be off. 'Come quickly,' he begged.

'Theek hai,' replied Ganga Singh. 'I'm coming.'

'I didn't do Colgate,' he would recall. In the interest of saving time, he splashed cold water on his face but skipped brushing his teeth. He pulled on his uniform, calling on four of his men to wait by his car.

The officer had spent the previous day, 27 May, overseeing security arrangements for a nearby fair commemorating the life of Dr Bhimrao Ramji Ambedkar, the iconic Dalit leader who had drafted India's Constitution. It wasn't really part of his job – but like most police officers, he spent more time patrolling religious, social and political processions than he did investigating crimes. By the time he returned to the station it was 5.30 p.m. He attended to some paperwork and then set off again on his daily patrol through the nearby villages. He was back only at midnight, at which time he hurriedly swallowed his dinner.

Ganga Singh was a career policeman, accustomed to the long hours and lousy food that went with his line of work. Some days, though, the collision between age and sleep deprivation was a body slam. This morning he felt as though weights had been strapped to his ankles.

When he arrived in Katra, shortly after 6 a.m., the
road was blocked by a tractor trolley. The villagers had
placed it there, possibly to prevent visitors from driving
their vehicles into the orchard. A public bus attempting
to get past had also been forced to adjourn. The curious
passengers pressed their faces against the grime-smeared
windows but stayed in their seats.

The orchard was about 150 metres away, and Ganga
Singh was striding towards it when some village men
charged forward to intercept his advance.

'You won't go there,' they warned, waggling their
fingers at him.

'Why not?' he asked.

'The bodies will not come down.'

'Why not, don't we need to investigate the case? What
about the post-mortem?'

The men started shouting at him.

Not once in his three-decade-long career had Ganga
Singh faced such a situation. The decision – whether it
came from the family or evolved out of public anger,
he didn't know then – startled him. Then the chaos of
voices started to make sense. Let the district magistrate
come! Call the chief minister! Where's the prime minister?
The crowd insisted that the most powerful people in the
country see them.

The Shakya women had put the lessons that everyone
had learned in the aftermath of the Delhi bus rape to the
test. By refusing to let the police touch their children, they
had expressed their protest. Their family and friends built
on this strategy. The police, they said, acted like they were
the kings of Katra. And until yesterday that's how they
had been treated. But they were actually useless. They
couldn't be trusted to solve the disappearance of a goat.

'If we bring down the bodies,' a family member said, 'the matter will end in the village.' They would wait for the politicians to arrive.

And with this, the Shakya family demonstrated their keen understanding of how India functions. The wheels of justice move only under pressure from the powerful.

Ganga Singh sighed and called for reinforcements.

The First Politician Arrives

The first politician to reach the village on 28 May, between 8.30 and 8.45 a.m., was a man who had no real reason to be there.

Bhagwan Singh didn't represent Katra. He probably had to feed the address into his GPS. But he was a Shakya, which was why he'd been asked to come by friends of the family. The stout man with the tepee-shaped moustache didn't warrant the villagers' trust. The one time he had made the news was for harbouring a fugitive wanted for kidnap and murder. 'He ran into my house,' he had told the police, expecting them to believe him.[1]

He was also an infamous 'party-hopper' – someone who changed political parties often, and for whom principles were secondary to opportunity. The sometimes this, sometimes that man was now roosting with the Bharatiya Janata Party.

Ganga Singh's reinforcements had arrived and Katra village was brimming with testosterone and khaki. Like the farmers, the constables in flak jackets and bowl-shaped helmets carried heavy bamboo sticks in their hands. Unlike the farmers, they weren't permitted anywhere near the girls. The crowd jeered and heckled. Stripped of what little power they had, the police remained apprehensive and unsure of their authority.

The first person to approach the political arrival was Mukesh Kumar Saxena, a sixty-year-old circle officer in charge of several police stations. Like some of the men who would show up that day, Saxena had a reputation. He was said to be a 'darpok type', a timid man who craved neither attention nor much more responsibility, but kept his thoughts firmly on the time when he would collect his pension. He had been so intimidated by the crowd in the orchard that he had parked his car at a petrol pump several kilometres from the village. Then he had phoned a subordinate officer to demand an escort in.

Saxena walked the politician to a chair placed for him under a leafy tree. Bhagwan Singh pulled out a handkerchief to wipe the beads of sweat rolling from his face. Then he waited for his supplicants.

The Shakyas had other plans.

After the initial shock, the family had split along the usual lines, defined by social decorum. Lalli's father, Sohan Lal, didn't seek out his wife. Whatever their relationship was in private, in public they followed the rules – and he didn't give her a second glance now. From this point on, the family would act as one, and Sohan Lal would tell them what to do.

He wasn't really much of a talker, but he may have been held back by his lisp. His tongue sometimes protruded when he spoke, and when this happened, he smiled shyly, folding his hands together to show just how sorry he was. But as the patriarch of the family he was used to telling people what to do. And he was stubborn. Everyone in the village knew this about him, although they didn't think that he would stand up to the police. They were wrong.

Maan Singh Chauhan was the highest-ranking officer present that day. The superintendent of police

was well educated, with a master's degree in history. He
spoke several languages and came across impressively in
interviews to news channels. A sinewy man in his fifties,
with rimless glasses and a khaki cap pulled down his
receding hairline, he had observed the Shakya men from
afar. Now he approached Lalli's father.

Rather than focusing on the potential criminal aspect of
the deaths, as most were doing, Chauhan talked about the
girls. He called Padma and Lalli 'bachiyon', little children,
and offered his condolences. It was a terrible thing, he
said, with a regretful expression.

A muscular firmness then entered his voice.

'It is time to take down the bodies.'

'No, it isn't,' Sohan Lal said. 'Sorry, so sorry.' He folded
his hands in an apologetic namaskar.

The officer was taken aback. He wasn't some incompetent
chowki policeman, or even poor Ganga Singh of whom
it was said, 'where Ganga goes scandal follows'. He was a
top-ranking officer. He expected people to do as he said,
and he had even asked politely.

'Look,' Sohan Lal told him, 'even if I give the go-ahead,
the crowd is worked up. They will stop you.'

Chauhan then instructed his deputy to make it clear
that they were nothing like the chowki policemen. 'We're
not here to shield anyone,' his deputy boomed into a
megaphone.

The crowd murmured with discontent.

Chauhan's face compressed into a grimace. 'Where was
the honour in keeping the girls hanging?' he would later
say. 'It was a disgraceful thing.' He called for a chair and
sat next to Bhagwan Singh at the edge of the orchard like
a guest waiting to be invited in.

The politician interpreted the Shakya family's position differently. They were simpletons. It was one thing to blame the police; it was another to antagonise them openly. It was his duty, he believed, to teach the brothers how to behave, to show them how to survive. 'Hum tumhare saat hai,' he said. I'm with you. 'I'll ensure justice.' He urged them to allow the police to remove the bodies and even promised to supervise the process.

At first it appeared as though he was getting through. When he grunted up from the chair and moved towards the laden mango tree, the police cautiously followed. Then Sohan Lal changed his mind.

'Stop!' he called frantically. 'Stop!'

The police switched tactics, using the relatable matter of honour to coerce him. '*You* asked Bhagwan Singh for help,' they said. '*You* made him come all the way to the village. Now you won't listen to him. Aren't you offending his honour?'

'In this way,' Ganga Singh later said, 'we tried to apply pressure on him. It didn't make any difference.' He laughed with admiration.

With even this latest lot of officers stripped of authority, the orchard became a virtual free-for-all; contaminated by more than a hundred people in just the first few hours of the day.[2] The spectators tramped in and out. They ate, smoked, spat tobacco, and later at night, some squatted.

The Matter Should Be Settled

At lunchtime, some of the crowd started to eat their dal and roti, their appetite not spoiled by the sight of the dangling corpses. Constables yawned. A group of men sitting at the feet of the politician gossiped about the upcoming local elections. Then Lalli's elder brother Virender arrived from Noida, took one look at the bodies and fainted.

Chauhan, the superintendent of police, was still working out how to remove the bodies. It was the right course of action.

Speaking to the family hadn't worked; appealing to the crowd made no difference. He wasn't above delivering a few cracking slaps. Later, he would be caught on camera striking rule-breaking motorcyclists across their faces.[1] But in a situation where onlookers outnumbered his men, he wasn't about to start a riot.

He leaned back.

Five years earlier, when he was posted to the city of Aligarh, his men discovered about a hundred skulls and other human remains languishing at the bottom of a pond. The officer tracked this discovery to a state-run mortuary whose doctors couldn't be bothered to dispose of unclaimed bodies responsibly.[2]

The year after that, in 2010, a professor of literature at the renowned Aligarh Muslim University was secretly filmed having sex with a rickshaw puller. The crew from the local television station who did the filming kept recording even once they were discovered. They went so far as to ask the professor, 'Aap sharminda hain?' Are you ashamed? Over and over again, the man pleaded, 'Haan, main sharminda hoon. Ab mujhe jaane dijiye.' Yes, I am ashamed. Now, please leave me alone.[3]

The video was widely circulated on the conservative college campus and the publicly humiliated professor was outed. Then he was suspended on grounds of misconduct. The suspension was revoked but less than two months later, the professor was found dead in his flat. After the death was ruled suicide by poison, Chauhan considered the matter settled. He let go the people who had illegally filmed the professor and triggered the sequence of events that had led to his death.

What the policeman now wanted was for this case to follow something along those lines. The girls were dead. The matter should be settled.

The politician Bhagwan Singh was also stirring with annoyance. It wasn't the scene in the orchard that was on his mind, although he was put off by Virender taking pictures of his dead sister with his mobile phone. It had been hours since he'd arrived, and the Shakyas were still ignoring him. He didn't understand what he had done to cause offence but he didn't want to look a fool.

By 12.30 p.m. the politician was overheated, out of patience, and covered in a thin film of dust. Grunting his goodbyes, he heaved back out through the fields and drove off. Already, his mind was on other matters.

Someone to Solve Their Problems

It wasn't the politician; it was the party. Bhagwan Singh was a low-caste Shakya, but he belonged to a party that favoured upper-caste people. The Shakya family had no illusions of where they stood on the Bharatiya Janata Party's list of priorities.

The new prime minister, Narendra Modi, was the first national leader to use social networks rather than mainstream media to express his views. On Twitter, his followers numbered upwards of 45 million. He tweeted incessantly. As part of his agenda to position himself as a global leader, in keeping with the destiny he promised India, he also tweeted at heads of state. He expressed condolences when disasters took lives in other countries. And he wished celebrities – in Bollywood and beyond – a happy birthday.

The Katra hangings were the most high-profile crime to take place in India since Modi had come to power just days earlier. It was natural to assume that he would reach out to the Shakyas on his favourite social media platform.

On 28 May, however, when the hangings made the news, Modi tweeted about Vinayak Savarkar, the early twentieth-century Hindu supremacist who had been in thrall to Hitler. An associate of his, named Nathuram Vinayak Godse, who was inspired by Savarkar's view that

Gandhi was responsible for the Partition of India because he had a soft spot for minorities, had shot the Mahatma at point-blank range. Savarkar was also arrested, but subsequently acquitted, for his role in the plot to kill Gandhi.

Hindu nationalists like Modi admired Savarkar. Like their hero, they too viewed secularism as inimical to their idea of India.[1] They wanted to transform secular India, by whatever means necessary, into a Hindu state. In his tweets, Modi rehabilitated Savarkar as 'a prolific writer, thinker, poet & a social reformer'.[2]

The Shakyas hadn't voted for Modi's party. It wasn't that they didn't believe his promise of 'achhe din', good days. They just didn't think it extended to people like them. The upper castes had mistreated them for so long that even Modi, the son of a tea vendor, who belonged to a low caste, was seen as lacking moral authority because of the people he worked with. Under the Bharatiya Janata Party marginalised groups were subject to increased discrimination and violence. 'Some senior BJP leaders publicly supported perpetrators of such crimes, made inflammatory speeches against minority communities, and promoted Hindu supremacy and ultra-nationalism, which encouraged further violence,' said Human Rights Watch.[3]

Across India, but particularly in caste-ridden Uttar Pradesh, it was said, people didn't 'cast their vote, they voted their caste'. The Shakya family voted with religious enthusiasm – in elections for the farmers' union, the village council, the legislative assembly and Lok Sabha, the House of the People – and they always followed the same principle. Their clan was large, with around 300 people, of which 70 adults were eligible to vote. This number made them a voting bloc, and they voted as such.

Shakya politicians courted them and sometimes the
family even put forward their own candidates. In the
last election for village head an uncle had lost, and the
winner – who had secured the appointment by a mere
forty votes – punished the family by uprooting some
electricity wires in the vicinity of their home. (The wires
weren't for their use; the new village head was simply
making a point.)

Overall, the Shakya family's allegiance was with the
Bahujan Samaj Party (BSP) and their national president,
Mayawati Prabhu Das, the only politician in whom they
saw themselves. Mayawati, who used one name, wasn't a
Shakya; she was Dalit. Her father was a clerk in the postal
system and her mother couldn't read.

Even now, violence against Dalits – once classified as
so polluting they were treated as outcasts and declared
'untouchable' – was widespread. This violence was in
fact a systematic attempt by some upper-caste groups to
maintain status and power.

In the same year as the hangings, a Dalit boy was
lynched for talking to an upper-caste girl,[4] while another
was set on fire for letting his goats stray into land owned
by an upper-caste family.[5] A Dalit woman was accused of
being a witch and force-fed faeces.[6] And these were not
isolated incidents.

And yet, Mayawati was such a singular individual that
she had become chief minister of the state four times.

Opposition leaders alleged that she spent a
disproportionate amount of this time settling scores.[7]
And she had actively pursued financial gain, even raffling
election tickets to the highest bidder. The going rate,
according to a US diplomatic cable released by WikiLeaks,
was 'roughly $250,000'.[8] The cables claimed that as chief

minister Mayawati had nine cooks, two food tasters and once sent her private jet to Mumbai to buy her preferred brand of sandals. She denied the claims.[9] The state, meanwhile, slid deeper into a development black hole.

So what if she was corrupt, her loyalists said, she was a politician. As a Dalit and a woman, she was simply scrutinised more than all her male, upper-caste colleagues put together.

The Shakyas' love for Mayawati actually went beyond a feeling of identification. As chief minister she passed an informal order that her voters would never forget. She insisted that police stations register complaints by lower-caste people as soon as they were received. This was obviously a basic right, and she wasn't doing anyone a favour. But like the idea of a Dalit wielding power, the idea of fairness was such a foreign thing in these parts, it was startling to behold and impossible to forget. Investigations, when they took place, were hardly less shoddy, and incidents of crime remained high, but the memory of this tiny correction burned like a fire in the hearts of the people who benefited from it.

In 2007, when Mayawati's partyman Sinod Kumar, then only thirty years old, stood for election in Budaun's Dataganj assembly constituency, where Katra was located, it was inevitable that he would win. He had her blessings after all.

There was low literacy in Budaun especially among women, only 40 per cent of whom were literate.[10] Around the same percentage of women were also married before the age of eighteen. The new mothers were often anaemic, a condition linked to poverty and poor sanitation, and so were their children, only slightly over half of whom were fully immunised. While Dataganj was electrified in

1960[11] – on paper, certainly – in 2014 Katra still had areas of darkness. The majority of households in the village practised open defecation.

These were staggering problems, but there is no indication to suggest that Sinod Kumar even attempted to make a dent in them. The villagers' one link to the state machinery didn't speak up on their behalf in the legislative assembly. He didn't alert the media to the problems that overwhelmed them.

Furthermore, while his constituents remained poor, his fortunes soared. In 2007, he declared total assets worth 9 lakh rupees.[12] By 2012, his assets had grown considerably. He was now worth 3 crore rupees.[13] And yet, when he stood for re-election that year, he won handily.

Sinod Kumar's success came down to the practice of small corrections, a trick he'd picked up from his boss.

India's often fabulously rich politicians were far removed from the poor people they represented – but the government was linked to this same group, certainly in rural areas, via the enormous tentacles of an endless number of state programmes that provided education, employment and food. Despite their promise, these institutions weren't always able or even willing to serve everyone fairly. It helped to have someone with pull to nudge them along.

As Akhilesh Yadav's food and supplies minister had famously said: 'What do poor people really need? What the people need is someone to intercede for them when they get into trouble with the police; someone to speak on their behalf to government babus and get their work done. Someone to solve their problems.'[14]

This someone was a politician like Sinod Kumar – who pressed his calling card with his personal mobile phone number into voters' hands, insisting they call him at the first sign of trouble. They should use his nickname, Deepu bhaiya, he said.

When his voters took him up on his offer and called to ask if he would put in a word with so-and-so, he did so promptly – or, his aides did. They conjured jobs, school admissions, hospital appointments, even police investigations. The concept of instant justice worked so well in states like Uttar Pradesh because politicians made it clear – and the people they served accepted – that nothing would really change. The people could either wait for the education system to be overhauled, for example, or they could just get their own child into a good school.

Kumar's Yadav constituents, it goes without saying, didn't have the same access to his influence – and they were fine with this. When one of their people won, the position would be reversed. A popular saying in the district was, 'Aaj police tumhari sunti hai, kal meri sunegi.' Today the police are with you; tomorrow they will be with me.

The Shakya voters were happy to let their leaders live well, just as long as they didn't forget who they owed. And Sinod Kumar hadn't. Although his party wasn't in power – the Yadav-run Samajwadi party was – he responded promptly to complaints. On one occasion, he had even helped the Shakya family take a neighbour to court over a land dispute.

What they were now hoping for was far bigger. Their children had died. He must protect them and support them for as long as it took to deliver justice.

The Politician's Aide

Sinod Kumar was hours away in Lucknow, still in bed. His trusted aide asked his driver to wake him.

'Do the needful,' Kumar replied. He didn't know what needed doing. Whatever it was, his aide would do it, dispatching the matter out of the orbit of Kumar's responsibilities. The aide did the work, the politician took the credit; such was the axis on which the relationship between politics and the public moved.

With a broad smile and stoic eyes, Shareef Ahmed Ansari had an easy manner with high and low, making him the perfect ambassador for such a job. He usually passed mornings in the courtyard of Kumar's majestic, white-walled, high-ceilinged home in Dataganj, sipping strong tea in tiny white cups as he heard out a procession of complainants who had arrived on the backs of motorcycles, lugging folders full of documents to support their claims.

Later in the day, he would drive around in one of his boss's five SUVs, visiting village leaders to gauge the mood.

This western part of Uttar Pradesh was more prone to trouble than the rest of the state. But Budaun district, in which Kumar's constituency was located, wasn't particularly volatile. The last major riot had taken place twenty-five years ago, in 1989, when the area's Hindus protested a proposal to introduce Urdu as the state's second official language after Hindi. They had fired from rooftops and mobbed a train, killing nearly thirty people,[1] but the bill had been passed.

Religious riots were most likely to break out in areas where there was, among other things, population parity between Hindus and Muslims. This heightened competition for opportunities, at least in the eyes of the perpetrators. But in Budaun 78 per cent of the population of just over 3.6 million people was Hindu.[2] It wasn't religion that sparked troubles, but inter-caste rivalries.

Ansari went to Katra with his boss's brother. While the brother chit-chatted with the police, the aide threaded his way to the family. The culprit, according to most people he spoke to, was definitely Pappu. He had kidnapped the girls, people said, but after news of the disappearances had spread, filling the fields, Pappu panicked. He killed the girls so they couldn't identify him. Then he made it appear as though they had hanged themselves.

Others told Ansari that Pappu had the help of the police, particularly Constable Sarvesh.

The real culprits, argued someone else, were a gang of men who were right this minute sitting on the banks of the Ganga River, laughing and smoking beedis.

Ansari wasn't convinced by the most popular theory – the one that involved Pappu and Pappu alone. The idea that one man could kidnap and then hang two girls stretched the imagination. But he listened carefully. His

boss would demand a report, which meant knowing
what people believed, rather than just accepting what the
police said.

And the police clearly weren't doing their jobs because
the bodies were still hanging from the tree. 'What's going
on?' he asked a constable.

The Shakyas were being very unreasonable, the
constable complained. Would he like to give it a try?

Ansari did his best, assuring Sohan Lal and Jeevan Lal
that their leader was on the way. The brothers accepted
this explanation and said they would wait.

In fact, Ansari wasn't at all sure that his boss would
show up. And if he did, it wouldn't be for many hours.
The thought of the bodies' condition by then made him
shudder. When he reported the Shakyas' response to
Chauhan, the superintendent of police briefly shut his
eyes. 'What do they want?' he said.

Ansari promised to take the question back to the family,
but he didn't really, because he knew the answer already.
Instead he told the Shakya men, 'Look, there's a lot of
pressure.' He urged them to change their minds. 'By the
time the girls are down, their bodies wrapped and sealed,
boss will arrive.'

The brothers refused, forcing Ansari to shuffle
embarrassedly before the police officer who sent him back
to the Shakyas. Back and forth Ansari went, carrying
proposals and rejections like a marriage broker.

The family's stubbornness might have offended another
man, but not Ansari. His background was modest. He
had trained as a mechanical fitter but was unable to find
steady work. He then started a tailoring service, but it
didn't take off. Then he opened a car rental service, which

was also plagued with ill luck – until, with a wife and children to support, he turned to salaried jobs. His quest ended at Sinod Kumar's doorstep.

Although he didn't earn very much, Ansari's proximity to power made him appear powerful to some. And he hadn't forgotten how it felt to be dismissed. A person's worth was judged by factors out of their control. Ansari was a Muslim, so in his case, religion was that factor; in the case of the Hindu Shakyas, it was caste.

And the Shakyas, clearly, had been judged lacking by all the powerful people who had so far entered the orchard. But here they were, just look at them, won't you, Ansari thought. In the ashes of their lives they had found the courage of mighty warriors.

None of this made Ansari's job easier. He called his boss to ask him to intervene. From Lucknow, Kumar phoned Lalli's father. 'I told him to allow the police to remove the bodies,' he later claimed. 'But he was determined to wait for me.' Sohan Lal, he said, was convinced that without the politician present, the police would find a way to damage the bodies, by either removing or planting evidence and thereby protecting Pappu Yadav.

The family had every reason to be wary of the police. But it was in Sinod Kumar's best interest to let the brothers obstruct procedure. The police answered to the state government. By making them appear incompetent, unable even to deliver bodies for a post-mortem, the Shakyas made the party in power – the Samajwadi Party of Akhilesh Yadav – look foolish.

Later, when he was asked why the state government should be blamed for something that had happened in his constituency, Kumar was at a loss. 'From the time the FIR was written to the post-mortem to the final rites, it was I alone among the politicians present who did anything,' he said.

But politicians didn't think it was their job to make life better. It was enough to just show up.

'Liars, Thieves and Fucking Scum'

The police station in the town of Ushait was a tidy building in a breezy, tree-filled compound. With many officers now in Katra village, there was no one senior enough to attend to Pappu.

Constable Sarvesh and Head Constable Gangwar wandered about with their suspect dragging his feet miserably behind them. The older man decided to borrow a motorcycle and return to the village to help control the situation there. Sarvesh, who had gauged the mood, refused.

Gangwar was taken aback by the thronging crowd on the road leading into the village. As he nosed his motorcycle past, some people recognised him. They blocked his way, demanding to know where his colleague was. 'I'm here aren't I?' Gangwar replied. 'Tell me the problem.'

Then Ganga Singh, the inspector from Ushait, walked over. 'They're very angry,' he warned. 'You should leave.' He ordered Gangwar to return to the police station. Gangwar nodded dutifully but went straight to the flat that he shared with his wife and five children. He had been wrong to poke his nose in this business, now he would lie low.

After a lifetime of repeated transfers – a standard tactic to keep police officers honest in a notoriously corrupt state – Gangwar had landed in obscure Katra only two years ago. When he first arrived, he was taken aback by the state of the chowki. It looked like a cowshed. The courtyard was choking with weeds. At the water tap, an elderly cook sat on his haunches, rotating a metal scrubber on dirty utensils.

When he had looked for the staff quarters so that he might refresh himself, Gangwar realised there were none. His new colleagues were sitting around yawning. They told him he would have to make his own arrangements. One officer spent the nights in the government nursery school opposite the chowki. Another made do in the health centre. Gangwar would take to the open courtyard. In the hottest weather, the others joined him, bringing over their charpoys to partake of the breeze.

The lack of resources was felt in more important ways. Although it wasn't a 'reporting' chowki – that is, the police weren't empowered to file the First Information Reports required to start investigations – they still had to respond to disturbances. These often involved stolen cattle. In instances of grave complaints such as assault, however, the officers didn't have any equipment to move things along. They didn't have phones. They didn't have computers. Their travel allowance extended to the use of a bicycle. If they had to contact the police station, they used WhatsApp on their personal devices.

In this way the team of first four, then five, men policed Katra and as many as forty-six other villages.

'Government kuch nahin karti!' The government does nothing for us, they moaned, flinging open their shirts, sticking their legs out on chairs and drinking on duty. The outpost came to be known as an adda of alcoholics.

One day, the fed-up cook ran away, and no one could be convinced to take his place.

Gangwar liked the chowki. It was as close as he had ever been to his family, who were now only an hour away. And the work was straightforward. Taking along his Lee-Enfield, he got on his motorcycle whenever the mood struck and toured the nearby constellation of villages. 'Baatcheet se samjhata tha,' he said. I would counsel in chit-chat. 'Fighting is futile. File a case and you'll only end up making the rounds of the court.' Actually, since filing a complaint forced the police to open an investigation, by advising villagers to avoid such procedures what Gangwar was really doing was saving his colleagues hours of work.

As half-heartedly as he did his job, he came to be known as a 'good man'. The villagers called him 'daddu', grandfather.

Around this time, another officer had moved into the chowki. Sarvesh Yadav was a college boy with a bachelor's degree. He came from a farming village in Etah, a district that was roughly three hours' drive away. He gave the impression that he was well connected and, therefore, above the rules. One of his brothers was in the army. Another held a factory job. This information came out in dribs and drabs, for Sarvesh liked to keep to himself.

The other officers didn't probe. 'If you don't want to talk,' one said, 'why should I?'

Sarvesh had been transferred from a chowki in a village named Bhoora Bhadraul. The relatively well-off farmers there had donated some temple land for the policeman's quarters. They warned Sarvesh against consuming alcohol and meat. If he wanted those things, which pious Hindus considered sinful, he was to leave the chowki and attend to his needs unobtrusively.

Often the only fights in the village involved the pint-sized, brown-backed monkeys, who descended on the apples and bananas that temple-goers deposited as offerings at the shrine. When the shrieking animals made off with a handbag, Sarvesh chased them down.

With this experience, he arrived in Katra where he was tasked with keeping an eye on the sand mafia.

While differing vastly in age and temperament, the two newcomers, Gangwar and Sarvesh, exhibited extreme behaviour. The men were all drinkers, but Gangwar was a sodden drunk. They all lolled about, but to get lazy Sarvesh out of bed you had to slam the chowki gate a few times. And his behaviour towards the villagers was something else. He made it clear that it was beneath his dignity to talk to them. He described the men who dared to walk into the chowki as 'liars', 'thieves' and 'fucking scum'.

Another colleague, Constable Raghunandan, didn't think that Sarvesh was influenced by caste. 'We are Yadavs!' he exclaimed. By this he meant that as low-caste people they weren't in a position to look down on anyone else. Sarvesh's problem, he believed, was that he trusted no one. People had to prove themselves to win his confidence. 'I would often tell him to change his ways. To get to know someone before judging them.'

But the villagers weren't obliged to prove their integrity to Sarvesh. Rather, he was obliged to serve them.

The day the girls went missing, 27 May, hadn't started off in quite the usual fashion at the chowki. The men usually woke up when they wanted, then groaned and wilted through the day's high temperatures. That morning, however, they had received a tip-off about a cache of illegal liquor in a nearby village. After they were done recovering the goods there, Sarvesh and Gangwar were instructed to keep an eye on the movement of some buses. This was a matter of routine to ensure the security of passengers in areas that were usually targeted by bandits.

As they waited for the buses, the men decided to drink. They toasted Gangwar's promotion to head constable. The alcohol unstoppered Sarvesh who grumbled about a leave application being rejected. When would he see his brothers, he said. They had a meal and more whisky. Gangwar revealed that his promotion didn't come with a pay rise. He wouldn't bother treating the others to mithai. This made the men cackle and they drank some more. The buses were all but forgotten.

When they stumbled through the chowki gate it was still early, around 5 p.m. They were on duty, but it was too hot to work. They drank some more and chatted. The other policemen joined in. When they ran out of things to say to one another they drunk-dialled friends.

At about 11 p.m., the five chowki policemen pulled out their charpoys, muttered their good nights, and collapsed into sleep.

Cable Wars in the Katra Fields

When the reporter Ankur Chaturvedi arrived in Katra village, the sun was high, the sky enormous and the fields glittered with heat. Some female constables were now present. They had been summoned from the women's police stations in Budaun, Bareilly and elsewhere to keep an eye on the mothers sitting at the foot of the mango tree – but they were outnumbered by the visitors streaming in. As it was, there were only around 7,000 policewomen in Uttar Pradesh, making up less than 5 per cent of the state force.[1]

The women in khaki looked here and there, and then looked away – there wasn't much else for them to do.

Chaturvedi was in time to hear the latest rumour. The girls, people were now saying, had been gang-raped and then hanged. There was no way anyone could have known this with the bodies still unexamined but the rumour spread fast.

A local journalist posted a photograph on Facebook.[2] It was through this highly emotive image that urban India learned what had happened.

In the image that they saw, the girls appear to be asleep. Their heads droop, their chins tucking into the cove of their necks. Their shoulders slope downwards and their arms hang loose. Their hands look as though they are grasping for something. Their bare feet are grey with dust, but their clothes are as bright as blossoms.

The image appears to have been captured from amid the group of mourners, for only women fill the bottom half of the frame. They are mostly seated on the ground, with their chins resting on their knees and their faces covered. There is a tiffin box, some bamboo sticks and a dog with pointy black ears.

Some of the women would later become familiar to television viewers. The one in the widow's white sari with the curly hair and overhanging buck teeth was the children's grandmother. The one in red, with the broad nose and deep black wells under her eyes, was Padma's stepmother. The fact that they weren't crying, that they didn't seem to be saying anything, made for a strikingly unusual portrait of grief. It was as though the women weren't reacting in expected ways because they weren't convinced that what they were seeing was real.

In the photograph, you could see at the edge of the field, just walking out of the frame, a man with a piece of cloth roped around his head, trudging to work. Even when confronted with death, life must go on.

The image migrated to Twitter where the outrage was viral. If social media conversations that morning were taken at face value, it seemed everyone was in favour of ending caste, patriarchy and gender violence, of bringing education, professional opportunities and toilets to rural women. If they had all these things, the comments implied, then none of this might have happened. The hashtag #BudaunRape, referring to the district in which Katra village was located, started to trend.

The growing interest caught the attention of more cable news channels. They sent over local reporters at first. Then from Delhi, which was a six-hour drive, they dispatched recognisable faces. Soon, so many production vans had lined the road to Katra, disgorging so many teams of journalists, that village women seeking privacy were left stranded. They had to dig holes in the floors of their courtyards to urinate.

'Move out of the way,' shouted a reporter.

'The first to reach here,' crowed another.

Some struggled to pronounce the name of this district that they had never been to before. They settled on 'ba-dawn'. (It was actually 'ba-da-yoo'.)

A 'media mela!' Chaturvedi exclaimed, updating his Facebook feed in the midst of the chaos. He had got the shots he wanted and was pleased with himself.

The media was ravenous for information and, at first, the family was eager to talk. A colleague of Chaturvedi's at Aaj Tak pounced on Sohan Lal. Lalli's father wore a white shirt, white trousers and a piece of checked cloth tied around his neck like a scarf. His clothes were worn out by repeated washings and his ribs were visible through the thin material.

Other than Pappu who else is responsible, the reporter asked off camera.[3]

'Veere,' Sohan Lal replied. '[Pappu's] father.'

Someone in the crowd of men pressing around him offered a prompt: 'Avdesh.'

Sohan Lal nodded. 'Avdesh, that's one of the brother's names.'

Another prompt: 'Urvesh.'

'Urvesh.' This was the other brother.

Sohan Lal looked around expectantly. When no more names were forthcoming, he left it at that.

'Three brothers,' he said. 'And the father.'

Then someone mentioned Sarvesh, the constable.

This set Sohan Lal off.

'Sarvesh sipahi! Murder usne karwaya.' Constable Sarvesh! He masterminded the murder.

'And the staff,' he added, referring to the chowki policemen.

Now Sohan Lal's brother, Jeevan Lal, was pulled in front of the cameras. He wore the same sort of clothes, but his scarf was hanging around his neck like a bath towel. His voice was low, his manner tentative. He always hung back, allowing his older brother to talk for him and in this terrible moment, too, he didn't stray from his accustomed ways. When he was asked to name names, he hesitated. Sohan Lal, off-camera, impatiently cut in, shouting responses.

Some hours passed, and even Sohan Lal's face took on a hunted look. The police might have come in handy now, but they were still being kept at a distance. Every time Sohan Lal wanted to take a break he was reminded that this was what he had hoped for, that the media attention would make all the difference.

Two months earlier, in March, four Dalit women in the neighbouring state of Haryana were abducted by upper-caste men. They were drugged, raped, then dumped at a railway station.[4] The police arrested the men, but upper-caste groups ganged up on the victims and their village. Fearing for their lives, eighty Dalit families picked up their belongings and fled.

But right here, in Katra, Sohan Lal was inundated with people who were anxious to hear his side of the story. They wanted to draw attention to the children's deaths, so that he wouldn't have to cry himself hoarse. They wanted to right a wrong – and for this he was grateful.

Anyway, as he later said, left to themselves, who knows what they would have come up with.

In that, he wasn't wrong.

Some journalists erroneously claimed that Head Constable Gangwar was a Yadav, even though his surname clearly stated his caste. Then they made an even greater blunder by claiming that the Shakyas were Dalits. Both errors, likely the result of the pressure to produce instant news that fed the appetites of viewers, had an impact on how these people were perceived by those on the outside. To declare the family Dalit was to sharpen their experience of victimisation. To call Gangwar a Yadav was to cement his status as a loutish thug.

In a Delhi TV studio, a cable news anchor wiped away imaginary tears. Another shouted 'gang rape, murder!' 'gang rape, murder!' over and over. A third channel reconstructed the alleged crime, showing a woman being strangled. Two male actors set upon her, pulling apart her legs.

Histrionics had been the main ingredient of several cable TV news channels for a while now, but this was the first time they had been applied to a story concerning the death of children. An editor at Times Now, the nation's top-rated news channel, which had styled itself on America's incendiary Fox News, later told a reporter, 'We brought in a lot of what was happening in TV soap operas into the way we were treating our stories. We brought in alarmist music and a soundtrack to our reportage.'[5]

The former bureau chief of another news channel said they had been greatly encouraged after making a half-hour show around a YouTube clip that they promoted with the words, 'Eyes of Satan, watch the eyes of Satan'. 'People couldn't stop watching,' he said.[6]

Complaints Are Written, Then Torn

It was now the afternoon of 28 May. Sweat was pouring down people's faces. They started to follow the shade. Old people and small children napped where they were. The Shakya brothers were still refusing to let the police remove the bodies; but they had lost support from some of the crowd. 'It's disrespectful to the girls,' said one man. 'The bodies are spoiling.'

The Shakyas' own neighbours openly speculated about the brothers' involvement in the deaths. 'They were fed up with the girls' behaviour,' one declared. 'They killed them to protect the family from further dishonour.'

'Well, it wouldn't have happened if the girls hadn't had sex with Pappu,' said another.

The superintendent of police decided to address the problem in a roundabout way. If the family filed a First Information Report, he would be empowered to start an investigation, Chauhan told the Shakya brothers. Wasn't that what they wanted, to learn what had happened? What he didn't say was that criminal death investigations were informed by post-mortems. Once the FIR was filed, the bodies would have to come down, by whatever means.

Filing a First Information Report was the job of the police officers who had received the complaint, but without the chowki men to furnish details, the superintendent had to ask the Shakyas what had happened.

This latest request presented a new problem for the family. The brothers couldn't read or write. They could tell the police what had happened, but they didn't trust them enough. 'Police tod mor ke likhegi.' They will twist our words and write what they want.

Some friends were literate, but on being approached for help they made excuses. The Shakyas had made it clear that they intended to implicate the chowki officers. The villagers had no wish to be involved in such squabbles.

A farmers' union leader from a neighbouring village stepped forward. He settled down on the ground and took careful notes. Then he wrote up a complaint and read it out loud for the brothers' approval. They responded with sighs of frustration. 'It doesn't sound right,' one said, 'tear it up.' They dictated a second complaint. That didn't sound right to them either. They walked off.

A journalist was then handed a blank sheet of paper by a family friend and begged to intervene. But the man had watched the back and forth. 'They are going to waste my time,' he thought, excusing himself on the pretext that he was thirsty.

As the eyewitness, Nazru should have been the one dictating the complaint. But the Shakya brothers weren't bothered with him. If they had paid attention, they would have seen their cousin was acting stranger even than normal. He was coming apart like overripe fruit.

It was still early afternoon when Ansari, the politician's aide, started to sag with defeat. He had been dispatched to protect the family from the police, but who would protect the girls from their family? The blazing sun was frying his skin. What was it doing to the children? The bodies should have been examined hours ago, or refrigerated, at the very least.

He was deeply sympathetic – of course he was. Their girls were dead and they were heartbroken, but they had to stop arguing over who was to blame. The family had changed three versions of their complaint and were just getting started on another when Ansari forced himself to intervene. 'Tell me what to write,' he begged.

The Shakyas told Ansari that Pappu, his brothers, his father and the police had 'raped the girls, killed them and hanged them'.

Ansari hesitated. He had, many times by now, looked at the bodies up close. He had seen nothing to suggest that acts of such violence had taken place. 'Only a doctor can prove whether they were raped,' he said. 'Let the post-mortem report come out. The matter will be clear.'

Some villagers also stepped up. Veere wasn't home last night, they pointed out gently. Pappu's father had been across the river guarding his watermelons. Everyone knew this. If the Shakya brothers insisted on claiming otherwise they would embarrass themselves and the village.

The brothers refused to listen.

Eventually, Sohan Lal and Jeevan Lal finalised their complaint. The three Yadav brothers, they said, had pounced on their daughters Padma and Lalli while they were in the fields. Their cousin Nazru and their brother Ram Babu happened to hear the girls' cries for help and immediately intervened, but they were threatened with a gun. Then, when the family approached the police for help, Constable Sarvesh assaulted them. Later, along with his colleague, Head Constable Gangwar, he told them to go to the mango orchard, which is where they found the girls. (This last line was meant to suggest that the police officers already knew where the bodies were because they themselves had put them there.)

Several villagers present were aware that this complaint was mostly made up, but it was not their place to say so, they told themselves. Time would pass, the truth might come out, but they would continue living in the village alongside the Shakya family. Good relations must be maintained.

At 3.50 p.m. Sohan Lal handed over the complaint to the police. As soon as it was in his possession, Chauhan grew deaf to the brothers' insistence that the bodies remain where they were. His men converged around the mango tree.

For a while now, the orchard had echoed with the question, 'Kab utrengi?' When will they come down?

Now, it seemed, there was an answer.

The Bodies Come Down

A local man volunteering with the police as a home guard was tasked with climbing the tree. He bounded up in his sports shoes.

Leaning across a branch, he was able to easily unfasten the dark green dupatta. It had been attached by a simple single knot. He let go, and the child's body floated into the outstretched arms of some female constables. They untied the second knot, around the neck.

The home guard then attempted to free the other body, but it wasn't so easy. This one was secured with a double knot. He tugged and tugged some more, but then he slipped, almost ripping his blue denim jeans. The branch wouldn't take his weight for much longer.

'Halka admi chadha dijiye,' he called down. Get someone skinny to climb up here.

The crowd groaned – was there no end to police incompetence?

'Please help,' said the home guard, catching Lalli's older brother's eye. Although he was small for his age, Virender was strong from years of helping his father in the fields. He was a good climber. The teenager stretched himself flat on the branch that held the second body. The knot really was tight, and he couldn't undo it either. He sunk his teeth in, tearing into the skin of the cotton fabric until it loosened enough for him to use his hands. The body parachuted down. The moment passed in a blur.

Later, Virender couldn't remember which of the girls he had helped with. 'It could have been the older girl,' he said. 'It was so crowded, there were so many people.'

He was mistaken. The reddish-purple dupatta had belonged to Lalli.

Virender's confusion may have arisen from the fact that it was his second attempt at freeing his sister. Earlier in the day, he had briefly lost his head and darted up the tree. He had untied Lalli, but before he could do more, his mother had intervened, shouting at him from down below. The bodies mustn't come down yet, Siya Devi said. 'Leave your sister alone.'

To be on the safe side, Virender then made a double knot.

This wasn't the only time the children's bodies were manhandled. Padma's mobile phone was no longer in her bra. Her gold chain was not at her neck – it would never be recovered. And both sets of slippers were now gone from the base of the tree.

The police didn't make any attempts to investigate further. 'They wanted to send the bodies to the city,' said Chaturvedi, the journalist. 'It didn't look like they were interested in evidence.'

The inspector from Ushait, Ganga Singh, blamed the crowd. 'We needed time to observe the bodies and gather details,' he said. 'But it was chaos.'

He did get started on an inquest panchnama – a written description of the scene in which a person believed to have died in suspicious circumstances was found. The panchnama was written by the investigating officer, now Ganga Singh, but it was based on witness testimony.

Ganga Singh picked five men randomly from the crowd and asked them to look at the bodies up close. Observe the injuries, if any, he said. What was the apparent cause of death?

To the men it appeared as though the girls had been killed. Why else would they be in a tree?

'I agreed,' Ganga Singh later said. The witnesses, who were not literate, inked their fingerprints on the panchnama.

The bodies were then carried through the fields and into the main road where a van had been mobilised to take them to the post-mortem house. Ganga Singh wrapped the bodies in stiff white cloth. He dipped the police seal into a melted bar of red wax and stamped the cloth.

The van was winding its way through the crowd when the promise of another upheaval presented itself. Ansari, the politician's aide, received a call from his boss Sinod Kumar – who said that he was about to arrive. 'I will reach in five minutes.'

When Ansari passed on this information, the Shakya brothers couldn't contain themselves. 'Stop the car!' one of them shouted. 'Stop the car!'

Someone reached into the moving van and plucked out the key. With the driver trapped in his seat, the crowd put all its weight onto the vehicle and started to push it back towards the orchard. The path was so uneven that during one particularly steep dip, a body rolled out of the back of the van and fell to the ground with a loud thud. The impact was so severe that the seal popped open, revealing the child.

The second body was then removed from the van and, as the Shakya brothers looked on, its seal was opened too. The girls were now back where they had been all day.

They were placed side by side at the foot of the tree.

The Shakyas had waited for their leader, anticipation building hour after hour. They wanted comfort certainly and also direction. But when Kumar arrived, the scene in the orchard took him aback. He stood there in his politician's white kurta pyjama, his boyish face crinkled in confusion, his double chin dipping into the folds of his neck. Although he was up to date on the day's drama, he was at a loss for words when he saw the girls staring up at him. 'Calm down,' he told their family members, wiping a hand across his moustache. 'Let the law take its course. Arguments won't get you anywhere.'

A long-anticipated moment passed within minutes.

Kumar led the entourage out of the village in his Toyota SUV. The van with the bodies and the brothers rattled behind. As many as twenty-five cars, including several police jeeps and news trucks followed. Village men jumped into whatever vehicle they could find. No one thought to ask Padma and Lalli's mothers if they wanted to come along. They were women, what would they do there.

When the convoy had left the crowd far enough behind it came to a halt. The children were lying exposed on the floor of the van. Their bodies hadn't been resealed to avoid giving people yet another opportunity to delay matters.

Once again Padma and Lalli were covered, the pieces of cloth sealed and stamped. The cars set off over the bridge that led out of the district. Beneath them the Ganga River gently flowed, shimmering and rustling. The riverbank was covered with burial mounds, and stray dogs panted at the water's edge.

The convoy was soon caught in a traffic jam, lodged between trucks piled with timber and carts drawn by horses. The police activated their sirens but it was just for show, there wasn't an inch of space. They would wait, same as the frustrated drivers slamming their horns, same as the farmers bringing down their whips, same as the daily wage labourers grimacing as they pushed forward on their cycles.

The politician's air-conditioned car was ice-cold, but the Shakya brothers crammed into the van with the bodies of their children were barely able to breathe.

Windows down, windows down, one of them begged.

From the side of the road vendors came running up to the car offering fizzy drinks, whole roasted corn and boiled eggs. The Shakyas looked over their heads at the hospitals, the banquet halls and the car showrooms that lined the road in a boast of prosperity.

By the time the men reached the city of Budaun, two hours had passed and the day was leaching out. But even here, in this relatively well-off urban area, there were no lights along the road. The houses too were dark. Everything was as filthy as though a storm had blown in all the garbage of the world. In the sky, birds were screeching.

A Sweeper and a 'Weaker' Doctor

The post-mortem house was located in a buffalo field. On one side flowed a river, on the other a track whistled with passenger trains.

News of the hangings had reached the man in charge, Lala Ram, early that afternoon when he had happened to switch on the TV in his office, around twenty minutes' walking distance from the house. At fifty-one, Lala Ram had lost most of his hair but he had retained his calm disposition. Sitting with the hospital pharmacist, A. K. Singh, sipping milky tea during a rare break from the chaos of government hospital life, he didn't find anything unusual to comment on. He didn't know where Katra was, but he knew such things happened.

About an hour later, Lala Ram received a call from the physician who was on post-mortem supervision duty that day. Dr Rajiv Gupta told him to get hold of surgical gloves, glass slides and a pack of cotton buds for swabs. Even such small essentials were often out of stock at the hospital, and had to be ordered in advance. They were to examine the bodies from Katra, he said.

Dr Gupta then made a second phone call, this time to the chief medical officer of the hospital. He told his boss that he had heard the girls were raped. He had very little experience of rape cases, he said. They should summon a female doctor.

The administration couldn't get any of the female doctors in the hospital to volunteer for the job. 'The case was too high-profile,' Ansari, the politician's aide, later learned. No one wanted to touch it. 'Only the weaker doctors had no choice but to do as told.'

Pushpa Pant Tripathi – who was fifty-one, and from the nearby Women's Hospital – was that doctor. She was 'weaker' because she didn't assert her authority. She said yes when others said no. Dr Tripathi was a general practitioner and had never performed a post-mortem.

The hospital performed on average two or three post-mortems a day, primarily on victims of violent or suspicious deaths. A man pulled under his own tractor, a female baby discarded in a garbage heap. One rule of thumb with regard to how many post-mortems a person should conduct in a year was 250; at the most, 325.[1] This was to prevent errors. Lala Ram said there was 'no limit' as to how many post-mortems he was expected to do. Padma and Lalli were the eighth and ninth such examinations he was to perform that day.

Lala Ram had been doing this job for almost two decades, but he wasn't at all qualified to do it. For years he had worked alongside his father, Bulaki, skipping school to tend to animals and crops. When he read an advertisement for a job at the hospital, he thought, why not? He would get to move to the city. He would be a salaried man.

In 1992, he was sweeping, washing and disinfecting the hospital wards. Three years later, when the person whose job it was to examine dead bodies quit, Lala Ram was asked to step in. He obviously didn't have a

medical degree, but neither did his predecessor. There
were famously few pathologists in the country and most
government hospitals entrusted the job to people like Lala
Ram. Hospital records continued to list him as a 'grade
four' employee, a category reserved for unskilled labourers
of low rank, such as sweepers.

The first time Lala Ram found himself alone in the
post-mortem house he looked around for a set of medical
instruments. He found none, because the hospital couldn't
afford them. So, just like the man before him, he set off
to the bazaar and purchased knives, a hammer, a wooden
mallet, some needles, a spool of thread and a set of scales
from a vegetable vendor. He bought an apron and a bag
of latex gloves. He liked to work in slippers because blood
washed easily from rubber.

Lala Ram was hardly fastidious, but the post-mortem
house was too filthy even for him. The great metal bed
was inches deep in dirt, bloodstains and the red welts
of the wax sticks that were used to seal medical reports.
With loose wires hanging dangerously all over the place,
he took to examining bodies outdoors. It was easy to do,
in terms of visibility at least, because post-mortems were
usually carried out in the day.

The outdoor table, however, was a British colonial-
era relic. At the first incision, flies descended, clustering
thickly. Even after he'd wrapped the body in cloth,
running a needle to secure it in place, the insects persisted,
clinging to the blood that soaked through the fabric. As
birds circled overhead, Lala Ram joked about not wanting
to feed them between meals.

But out here, at least, he could catch the breeze – and on
hot days, of which there were plenty, this lifted his spirits.

In the early 2000s, the hospital's chief medical officer had agreed that the situation was untenable, and approved the construction of a new post-mortem house adjoining the current one. With a price tag of several million rupees, the new addition promised to have cutting-edge facilities.

In 2014, the building was finally ready, and hospital doctors flocked to admire the well-equipped rooms. The tiled floors glistened and sunshine flooded in through the large windows. There was to be power and running water twenty-four hours a day. It was one of the few 'good' buildings in Budaun, the doctors agreed – a euphemism for fully functional. They looked forward to working there.

But it was inevitable that things wouldn't go according to plan. The location of the building, in an isolated buffalo field, began to attract the same sort of supernatural rumours that shrouded the original post-mortem house next door. Hospital personnel claimed they couldn't find anyone to guard it at night. The police shared responsibility for the place; but constables always found an excuse to slip off by sundown.

Thieves pounced. They drilled out the metal window grilles. They took medical equipment, light fittings, washbasins and even plug points. Before the first post-mortem was scheduled, the place was picked clean. The empty rooms attracted a new menace. Now drug users came to shoot up. By the end of the year there had been at least three break-ins. One lot of desperate thieves took a rake and spade the gardener had tucked away in a crook of the now-deserted building.

It was only a matter of time, the beleaguered Lala Ram said, before they marched off with the front door.

The Post-Mortem

When the convoy of vehicles from Katra drew up at the gates of the post-mortem house, it was only around 6.30 p.m. but the place was soaked in darkness. The district magistrate had to be petitioned for a power generator. Then paperwork had to be filed. And then, the police had to find digital cassettes to record the examination. Finally, someone offered the police his wedding video to tape over. It had now been more than twelve hours since the girls' bodies were found.

At 7.05 p.m. the camera lens was focused on the post-mortem bed around which were five people: three doctors, one videographer, out of shot, and Lala Ram, who had stripped down to his vest to avoid soiling his shirt. A. K. Singh, the hospital pharmacist, was also present, but he was waiting in the adjoining room.

The police had asked Dr Rajiv Gupta, who was leading the post-mortem, to record the cause of death, the time of death and to say whether or not the girls were raped.

The process was immediately beset with problems. Dr Gupta's job wasn't to perform the post-mortem; he wasn't a pathologist and made it a point to never touch a dead body. Lala Ram, of course, wasn't a pathologist either, but as per their usual routine the doctor gestured instructions at Lala Ram. This evening, as the generator juddered with noise, Lala Ram struggled to focus. 'I couldn't hear a thing,' he later said.

So he did what he knew. He took scissors to the girls' clothes. Then he picked up a knife.

On one of the hottest days on record, the team was working in a small, airless room with camera lights that radiated heat. There was no air-conditioning and no fan. Lala Ram's hands skated with sweat. Someone threw open a window, but this made things worse. The team had been cocooned from the convoy from Katra. Now they were exposed to it. Dr Tripathi, who was wearing a salwar kameez with a dupatta flung around her neck, excused herself to get some air. She would later say that the sight of the crowd gathered outside 'scared' her.

Padma's tongue was protruding. Her eyes were congested and there was stool present around her anus. Lalli was in a similar state. There was post-mortem staining on the bodies, which were in rigor mortis.

A cable news channel had reported that the children had 'injury marks all over them'. Lalli's father, Sohan Lal, claimed to have seen blood. Cousin Manju remembered thorns. But apart from dust, 'an abnormal amount', the doctors saw no visible injuries. There was no blood and no scratches. The girls' hair was neat. Their glass bangles were intact.

Then Lala Ram noted that the 'little girl', meaning Lalli, had bled from her vagina.

The tape ran out and the videographer slipped in a new one. This second tape had been used to record a music and dance performance.

'Hurry up Lala Ram,' Dr Gupta chided. 'It's very hot.'

Lalli's post-mortem took fifty minutes, which was a brief span of time given the circumstances. Padma's examination was shorter by ten minutes. By 9.15 p.m. the doctors gathered in the adjoining room to collate their notes in the presence of the hospital pharmacist. They concluded that Padma and Lalli were sixteen years old and fourteen years old respectively. The cause of death was hanging. They put the time of death at 2.30 a.m., or around the time the search party was banging on the gates of the chowki, attempting to wake the police.

Dr Tripathi, who had been called in specifically to determine whether a sexual assault had taken place, felt that the clotted blood 'in and around [Lalli's] vaginal orifice' – which Lala Ram had pointed out to her – as well as the presence of 'abrasions' in the area, indicated exactly such a possibility. She didn't mention the number or the size of the abrasions in the post-mortem report.

There was no blood on Padma, but the doctor noted what appeared as abnormalities: a bluish and swollen hymen, a vaginal tear and some discharge. She instructed Lala Ram to take vaginal swabs.

Two months earlier the Ministry of Health & Family Welfare had published a set of guidelines for doctors examining survivors and victims of sexual violence.[1] Like the changes to the rape laws, they were framed in response to the 2012 Delhi bus rape.[2]

Among other things, the guidelines stated that the purpose of a forensic medical examination was to ascertain whether a sexual act had been 'attempted or completed', whether such an act was recently committed and whether harm was caused to the survivor's body. These guidelines also contained a reminder that the decision on whether a rape had occurred was to be left to the court. 'A medical opinion cannot be given on whether "rape" occurred because "rape" is a legal term.'

Dr Tripathi – who was unaware of the guidelines – told Dr Gupta, who was writing the report, to record that the 'findings' on both girls were 'suggestive of rape'. Dr Gupta, as her supervisor on the post-mortem, should have corrected the error, except that he didn't know the guidelines either. 'To be honest,' he said later, 'I only learned that "rape" was a legal term afterwards.' He had come upon it while browsing the Internet.

In fact, Dr Tripathi didn't know if the girls had been raped or not. 'As soon as she saw signs of blood on the vagina,' said a doctor brought in to assess the post-mortem, and in whom she confided, 'she made up her mind that the crowd outside were right, that the girl had been raped. She did not wait to look further.'

Her conclusions leaked immediately to the anxious crowd. The tragedy they had named had come true.

Left behind with the bodies, Lala Ram cleared up as usual. Then he picked up the girls' clothes to bag them for the police. That's when he found the money. There was no question of giving it to the police, they would only pocket it. Instead, when he stepped outside to wash the medical instruments under the tap in the garden, he asked to talk to some family members and quietly slipped it to them.

The amount he gave them – two notes of a hundred rupees each – was the exact amount that Pappu said he gave the girls when they met the previous night.

Farewell Padma Lalli

It was shortly after midnight when the police brought the bodies back to Katra. They were followed by Sinod Kumar, the politician, the Shakya brothers in the van and the villagers who had accompanied them. The sky was an enormous jaw that threatened to swallow them whole. The sound was of whispers; the smell was woodsmoke and tobacco leaves.

Siya Devi surged forward. She was carrying clothes for the children. But the bodies had been resealed in cloth, and although the girls' faces were partially visible, it was less than Lalli's mother had expected. She thought that once the post-mortem was done she would have her child back, to hold one last time.

She sobbed in fury.

In normal circumstances the family would have invited priests. They would have washed the bodies and shrouded them in white sheets. But they didn't know how to deal with what was before their eyes.

Hindus were usually cremated; their corpses covered in clarified butter, laid across wood, then lit on fire. But the rules were different for babies and for children under three – they were buried or submerged in a holy river, their bodies tied with bricks so they would sink. A child's soul was never in the body long enough to develop an attachment, it was said; whereas adults, weighed down with the baggage of their sins, must be cremated to help the soul separate from the body. In some communities, this rule extended to those who were unmarried, and now the gathered villagers started to argue over whether Padma and Lalli should be buried or cremated by the Ganga.

The argument ended quickly – it was decided that they would be buried. Those who might have objected were now too tired to make a case against it. 'We have to go home,' someone said. 'We've been hungry and thirsty since morning.'

Inspector Ganga Singh said that anyone who wanted to come along to attend the funeral proceedings had better hurry up and follow his car. As doors started to slam, Siya Devi stepped back. Hinduism didn't strictly forbid women from participating in death rituals, but they weren't encouraged. The village erred on the side of conservatism, and Siya Devi knew better than to ask permission from her husband who still hadn't come up to her.

She watched the convoy, now comprising nearly thirty cars, pull away. Even the news trucks went, but she had to stay behind. The River Ganga was walking distance, but as far as she was concerned, it could have been the end of the world.

At a length of 2,500 km, there is no one Ganga. Starting in the Himalayas and emptying out in the Bay of Bengal, the river takes on different forms in different places. Its colour reflected the sewage, pesticide and industrial waste that was regularly poured into it. It was known to be 'highly contaminated' with 'carcinogenic and poisonous heavy metals, including lead, cadmium, chromium, mercury and arsenic'. According to one scientist, 200

tonnes of half-burnt human flesh were discharged into
the river every year.[1] In this part of Uttar Pradesh the holy
river was fish-grey and bubbled like stew.

Parking the vehicles near the bridge, the men descended
the stairs down to the water using their phones to light
their way. The Shakya brothers shouldered the children's
bodies.

Over the years, thousands of corpses had been burned
at the water's edge, their ashes scattered to transport the
souls to heaven. The last member of the Shakya family
cremated here was Sohan Lal's father, Zorawar. The girls
were the first in the family to be buried here.

The rituals that followed were laden with anxiety. The
police were afraid that the brothers would change their
minds. The brothers were worried about breaking religious
rules which warned against conducting last rites after
sundown. To avoid yet another delay, the police worked
quickly, bringing in priests from a temple that was tucked
under the bridge. At the same time, they wanted to be
sure that the bodies wouldn't be tampered with.

'Villagers normally bury bodies close to the surface –
in the process, attracting wild animals from the nearby
jungle,' Chauhan, the superintendent of police, later said.
'In this case, we took precautions and dug deeper graves.'
It wasn't just wild animals that Chauhan was worried
about, of course.

The Shakya brothers chose a spot near a small, blue-
skinned statue of Shiva, the Lord of Destruction, who
was said to meditate among the ashes of corpses. They
pitched in with spades, digging out a cocoon of sand that
was three feet wide and six feet deep. They lowered their
girls and covered them with the clothes their mothers had
chosen. Everyone bowed their heads in prayer.

With this, the hydra of vehicles split. The politician Sinod Kumar went back to his palatial home. The journalists went to hotels. Tomorrow, they would be back in the village.

Inspector Ganga Singh went to Jati, somehow expecting to find Pappu's family waiting for him.

And the Shakya brothers returned home to Katra.

When they arrived, they found the courtyard teeming with so many relatives who had come from faraway places to express their condolences that some had to be sent up to the roof to pass the night. The men locked the courtyard doors behind them – and people may indeed have slept. But when the sun rose, Sohan Lal and Jeevan Lal were awake.

Siya Devi was on the ground, her legs stretched out before her. She hadn't changed her sari. She hadn't eaten. And for the first time in her life she wasn't attuned to the needs of men. She didn't look once in their direction.

She looked up, instead, at the light breaking through the darkness, bringing with it a new day and, for her, a new way of living.

Kharif

Summer, 2014

The Worst Place in the World

Within the week everyone had heard of Katra, where children were said to be raped and killed. The village continued to attract curiosity-seekers from faraway places. Hundreds of police officers were deployed to monitor the situation. Their schedule was so relentless they set up charpoys in vacant animal shelters. They bathed at handpumps. Some families took pity on them and sent over fresh milk from their cows. The village children hung around, hoping to catch a glimpse of a real gun, something that wasn't made from spare parts.

The international media quickly picked up the story, which they projected as the most high-profile rape and murder in India since the 2012 Delhi bus rape. The *New York Times* led with 'Rapes in India Fuel Charges of Conspiracy by a Caste'.[1] The *Huffington Post* showed the girls' hanging bodies with a trigger warning.[2] Even the UN Secretary-General took note. Speaking of 'despicable acts across the world', Ban Ki-moon said, 'I was especially appalled by the brutal rape and gruesome murder of two teenaged women in India who had ventured out because they did not have access to a toilet.'[3]

But if the Delhi bus rape was met with horror, the hangings in Budaun were reflected on with despair.

The story of the girls' lives and deaths, as it was understood at the time, was the story of India's most persistent troubles. The country was so unsafe, immoral even, children were raped. While economic development had transformed many lives, caste rules were still followed. The police were poorly trained and thoroughly compromised. There were no toilets even just a few hours outside the national capital.

India, which in recent years was viewed through the prism of economic success, was now diagnosed in terms of a systemic social failure – the inability to protect women and children. The laws implemented in the wake of the Delhi bus rape had clearly not proved enough of a deterrent. The country had already been declared the worst place among the Group of 20 to be a woman, worse even than Saudi Arabia where women lived under strict male guardianship laws.[4] The deaths of Padma and Lalli confirmed the appropriateness of this low ranking. 'India is incredibly poor, Saudi Arabia is very rich. But there is a commonality and that is that unless you have some special access to privilege, you have a very different future, depending on whether you have an extra X chromosome, or a Y chromosome,' said an analyst.[5]

The media attention drew more politicians than even the Shakyas had hoped for. Although the prime minister stayed away, more than half a dozen of the country's most powerful people visited the family. Together they represented all the major parties – including the party in power at the centre and the party in control of the state.

With the politicians came handlers, bureaucrats and elite protection units. And with them also came the drama.

The Shakyas' favourite politician Mayawati was scheduled to visit on 1 June. Everyone was eager to see the remarkable Dalit leader in person.

Ahead of her visit, hundreds of volunteers from her political party descended on the village to get preparations under way. They brought an electricity generator, an air-conditioner and cartons of bottled water. They stacked these items, which most of the villagers had never used, in an enormous tent that they had pitched for Mayawati to relax in. Would she walk over to the Shakya house, people wondered. Probably not. They would have to come to her.

Then the volunteers appropriated a farmer's plot for a helipad and, not wanting to get their clothes dirty, they rounded up some children to dig the earth and smooth it with their bare hands. The police stood nearby and watched.[6]

Cable news channels were aghast. 'The same politicians who make laws against child labour also make small, small children work for them,'[7] said a studio anchor.

Mayawati wasn't the first high-profile politician to arrive here, and there were already barricades in place to protect the leaders from the surging crowds – many of whom had voted for them. White Ambassador cars topped with cherry-red beacons zoomed in and out of the fields with advance teams. The villagers, now separated from their land, and work, had to watch from a far distance as if they were the outsiders.

When the politician's Bell 429 appeared in the sky, the enormous crowd of waiting villagers tipped their faces up in awe. Hovering above their mint, their tobacco, the tornado of blue and white metal whipped up the dust and rocked the trees, sending monkeys jumping helter-skelter.

It was an extraordinary sight. But then these were extraordinary times.

As soon as Mayawati landed, the crowd pitched forward past the barricades like she was a rock star they had to get a glimpse of. Her enormous team of machine-gun-toting security officers kept the villagers at bay, but it was impossible to hear a word of what she was saying, so Mayawati would have to walk after all. The tiny, crop-haired politician in her stiff, cream-coloured salwar kameez, socks and sandals, proceeded to the Shakya house where she settled herself on a chair. The bereaved family members crouched on their haunches with their hands folded pleadingly before her. 'Criminal-type people won't be spared,' she told them, without going into details.

Then she walked over to the orchard, the scene of the alleged crime, to hold a press conference. The police, she said, had attempted to pin the blame on the parents. 'They tried to defame the girls and to protect the culprits.'[8]

There isn't law and order in Uttar Pradesh, there isn't governance, there is only 'jungle raj', she said,[9] invoking another commonly used phrase to describe the leadership of the Yadav government. She told the gathered press that when her Bahujan Samaj Party came back to power, she would deliver justice to the Shakyas.

Questioned about the preparations earlier in the day, a party representative said, 'The children were just playing in the mud.'

Mayawati left, never to be seen in the village again. But anticipation of the next high-profile arrival kept the television cameras and crews rooted to the fields.

Sensing an opportunity, desperate petitioners now started to appear in the village. The state had failed them, the police did nothing, perhaps the people from Delhi would be interested to know.

One mother told a reporter that it had been a month since her daughter had disappeared. 'Yadav boys took her,' she said tearfully. 'They took my darling.'[10] Another parent also blamed the Yadavs for the disappearance of his child. He even knew who the culprits were, he said, but when he had approached the police, the station head told him, 'the Yadavs will bring her back. Why don't you just go home.' 'I don't know whether she's dead or alive,' the father said.

Soon, so many complaints of missing girls started to circulate in the Katra fields that it was difficult to make sense of what was happening.

One place to look was the police. The Indian force was among the most understaffed in the world. The average police officer-to-citizen ratio was 144 to 100,000 against the United Nations' recommendation of 222 to 100,000.[11] In Uttar Pradesh, there were fewer than 100 police for 100,000 people. Here, the police functioned at 48.1 per cent of its capacity.[12]

The obvious answer was to expand the force, but the process was so cumbersome that even interested candidates drifted away. A recruitment drive was announced in 2013, but the subsequent selection would take two years and eight months to complete.[13]

Then, according to the activist group Common Cause, the state spent on average just a little over 1 per cent of its total police expenditure on training new recruits.[14] For comparison's sake, New Delhi, the national capital, spent 2.49 per cent – the most in India, but still a very small amount. The police stations in Uttar Pradesh also lacked basic communications infrastructure such as phones, wireless devices and two-wheelers.

Even if the state police came up to its required strength, it couldn't keep up with the rapidly expanding population. And, as long as politicians with criminal records continued to occupy major posts in the government, nothing would change. They were hardly likely to vote for more efficient policing.

Rather than fixing these problems, successive governments had quietly declared the situation beyond help. Since they couldn't control crime, they controlled the number of reported crimes. Police officers spoke of a 'blanket ban' and 'monthly maximum quotas' to keep crime statistics low, allowing the party in power to boast that they were at least doing better than their predecessors.

And yet, thousands of girls were reported kidnapped or abducted in Uttar Pradesh in 2014. Some were taken for ransom, others were murdered. There were 7,338 cases of kidnapping and abduction just for 'marriage' according to the National Crime Records Bureau.[15] Across the country this figure stood at more than 30,000. In fact, 'marriage' accounted for about 40 per cent of all cases of kidnappings and abductions in India in 2014.[16] In comparison, eighty-three men were reported to have been abducted for marriage that year.

At the same time, anecdotal data showed that some reported crimes weren't crimes at all. The taboo around marrying against a parent's will was still so prevalent that parents of young women who had eloped chose to allege that they had been abducted for marriage. Similar reactions followed when parents learned that their daughters were having premarital sex. They filed charges of rape to protect the family's honour. Indeed, the taboo against premarital sex was greater than the stigma of rape.

Although the police appeared to find it difficult to distinguish between real kidnappings and attempts to protect honour, there was no doubt that crimes against women were ubiquitous. And that a failure to investigate such crimes emboldened others to commit similar ones, allowing the cycle to continue. The more such crimes occurred the less likely they were to interest the media, which meant that politicians and the police had less incentive to do their job.

In fact, around the time of Padma and Lalli's deaths, there were stories of several other disturbing incidents. The morning after the girls were buried, a teenager in Azamgarh, another part of the state, was gang-raped in a field.[17] Two weeks later, a forty-five-year-old woman was found dangling in a tree by a corner of her own sari.[18] The day after, the body of yet another teenaged girl was found in yet another tree.[19]

In each case, grieving family members posited one theory, the police another; a post-mortem carried out in the standard fashion was inconclusive, and the matter was closed as though it had never happened in the first place.

The Women Who Changed India

What the political response to Katra made clear was that only public protests forced politicians to react. Moreover, a great deal depended on the extent to which the media amplified the incident. And the interest of the media was naturally influenced by whether the crime would interest their audience.

In 2012, the year of the Delhi bus rape, there were nearly 25,000 rapes reported in India.[1] Fear of social stigma and of the police, as well as a lack of trust in the justice system due to long trials and low conviction rates – around 27 per cent according to latest figures[2] – meant that sexual assault was severely under-reported. The National Family Health Survey 2015-2016, a detailed, multi-round exercise conducted by the Ministry of Health and Family Welfare, estimated that 79 per cent of women who experienced sexual violence, including rape, didn't tell anyone about the fact.[3] The financial newspaper *Mint* used this data, as well as data from crimes recorded by the police and compiled by the National Crime Records Bureau to estimate that, in fact, 99.1 per cent cases of sexual violence were not reported.[4]

The Delhi bus rape, according to a study conducted at the Harvard Kennedy School of Government, drew the media for several reasons: 'the victim was a student, she had been to an upmarket shopping mall before she was attacked, and she had also just watched an English-language movie. These factors marked her out as a middle- or upper-class Indian woman, which in turn made her story more compelling for the wealthy, urban readership of India's English-language press.'[5]

Of course, the victim was a porter's daughter from a village in Uttar Pradesh. By the time the facts emerged, however, 'the case was unstoppable.'[6]

Nearly two years later, the hanging bodies in Katra forced people to engage with the vulnerability of all children. In 2014, there were around 90,000 reported cases of crimes against children. These included infanticide, rape, murder, voyeurism, stalking, kidnapping and abduction, exposure and abandonment.[7] This marked an increase of a shocking 53.6 per cent over the previous year. Despite this, only the Katra case stayed in the news and is still remembered. Even now, all these years later, it is enough to mention Budaun in living rooms in Delhi and faraway Mumbai, and people know. In Uttar Pradesh, the death of the girls was referred to as a kand – a word that means scandal, but which implies something so terrible that it is practically unforgettable.

The Shakyas were also a poor farming family. They lived not too far from the village in which one of the Delhi bus rape victim's convicted rapists had been born and where he spent his formative years. And while the victim's father had made great efforts to educate his child and give her a future that was on a par with the dreams of modern, middle-class India, the Shakya family had taken Padma out of school after the eighth class. The family's circumstances and behaviour suggested that they were unlikely to interest the media. Indeed, the initial reaction of the reporter Ankur Chaturvedi had shown as much.

What made the difference, then, was the highly emotive image of the girls hanging in the tree. Urban Indians first saw it on social media, the place where they went to read the news and debate it. They wanted something to latch on to, to vent their personal frustrations over India's inability to change quickly enough, and the picture was it. Padma and Lalli could have been anyone's children. They were, obviously, blameless. And the manner of death was especially violent.

'It's not that people are not compassionate. But that compassion has to be aroused,' Paul Slovic, President of Decision Research, a non-profit organisation that studies human judgement, decision-making and risk perception, told NPR. 'Emotion is a critical factor in helping us understand an event, and it is a motivator that impels action as opposed to just abstract thoughts.'[8]

The Delhi bus rape was among a handful of crimes against women that had, over the years, created social awareness and led to policy changes. When these changes happened one could, perhaps, find comfort in the fact that at least something positive had come out of something heinous.

In 1972, a teenager in the western state of Maharashtra had walked into a police station to settle a domestic dispute and was only allowed to leave after the police officers present had sexually assaulted her. Her name was Mathura and she was an orphan who belonged to an indigenous community.

The assault elicited shock, a researcher on gender, poverty and health said, 'because it was new for (people) to imagine a security personnel as a perpetrator, as a rapist'.[9] The case went all the way to the Supreme Court, which acquitted the accused largely on the grounds that Mathura wasn't visibly injured and didn't call for help. The transcript read:

> [...] no marks of injury were found on the person of the girl after the incident and their absence goes a long way to indicate that the alleged intercourse was a peaceful affair, and that the story of a stiff resistance having been put up by the girl is all false. It is further clear that the averments on the part of the girl that she had been shouting loudly for help are also a tissue of lies.[10]

The decision outraged a group of four law professors who wrote a letter of protest to the Chief Justice of India.[11] Eventually, this led to the burden of proof being shifted away from the victim. A legal amendment now states, 'where sexual intercourse by the accused is proved and the question is whether it was without the consent of the woman alleged to have been raped and she states in her evidence before the Court that she did not consent, the Court shall presume that she did not consent.'[12] This meant that a woman would be taken at her word. The punishment for custodial rape was increased, and the identity of the rape victim was to be protected.

This last prohibition drew attention in 2012 after the media resorted to using a variety of lionising pseudonyms for the Delhi bus rape victim. The Hindi adjectives translated into 'fearless', 'lightning' and 'treasure'. The trend only changed after her mother publicly called for her daughter's real name to be used.

'Why should we hide our daughter's name?' Asha Devi said. 'My daughter was not at fault. And, by hiding crimes, we only allow more crimes to take place … We are proud of our daughter. She got immortalised as "Nirbhaya" but we also want the society to know the girl we raised, before she was violated by a few devilish men. Memories are painful but her name will serve as a reminder to the society to never let such things recur … I say this in front of you all that her name was Jyoti Singh. You all must also from now onwards call her Jyoti Singh.'¹³

Two decades after the attack on Mathura, in September 1992, a grassroots women's activist named Bhanwari Devi was raped by a group of Gujjars, the dominant caste in her village, for campaigning against child marriage in Rajasthan, a state that shares a border with Uttar Pradesh. Bhanwari Devi had herself been married off when she was five or six, to a boy of eight or nine. Now, she had tried to prevent the village men from marrying off a baby.

After her gang rape, instead of staying quiet as women were told to at the time, Bhanwari Devi risked social ostracism by going public with her accusations. She mobilised support from women's rights activists in cities like Delhi, and they helped her take the case forward. Over the course of the trial, reported the BBC, 'judges were inexplicably changed five times.'¹⁴ Three years later, in November 1995, the accused were acquitted of rape on grounds such as 'a member of the higher caste cannot rape a lower-caste woman because of reasons of purity.' The judgment caused outrage and led to protests across the state, but although it was challenged in the Rajasthan High Court only one hearing has ever been held.

As the rape was a direct outcome of her work, the activists who supported Bhanwari Devi then filed a Public Interest Litigation in the Supreme Court arguing that freedom from sexual harassment in the workplace was a fundamental right. The outcome of their campaign was a set of rules known as the Vishakha Guidelines. In 2013, these rules became the foundation of a law to prevent sexual harassment of women at the workplace. Bhanwari Devi continues to live in the same village as her attackers. They had married off the baby the day after she intervened.

Like the attack on Mathura, Bhanwari Devi and the victim of the Delhi bus rape, the case of Padma and Lalli became widely known. It had set off protests that had attracted powerful politicians. The question on many people's lips, in Katra and beyond, was this – would it inspire change?

The Zero Tolerance Policy

All protests ultimately faded away. Everyone agreed the system was rotten, but no one knew how to fix it – not even the people elected to do just that. Instead, politicians attempted to compensate victims for their loss with cash. Raking through government schemes, party funds and even personal accounts, they handed out cash to women who were raped and to others injured in stampedes and riots, floods and fires. Money clotted immediate concerns. Money drew a line under troublesome things.

The day she met the Shakya family, Mayawati – who was one of India's richest politicians, with assets worth more than 111 crore[1] – gave Lalli's father Sohan Lal and Padma's father Jeevan Lal 5 lakh rupees each, in cash. Another party gave them 5.5 lakh rupees each, also in cash. On 1 June, Sohan Lal's bank balance was zero rupees. By 5 June, it was 10.5 lakh rupees. The family accepted several other sums of money, large and small, from leaders of diverse ideological backgrounds. The politicians conducted the transactions openly; in fact, some waited for the TV cameras to start rolling before they handed over the stacks of notes. Although these vast amounts caused some anguish for people in Katra, most agreed that it was the least the family could expect.

There was, however, one person the Shakyas refused: Chief Minister of the state, Akhilesh Yadav.

'I will not sell my girls' honour,' Siya Devi told television cameras, after refusing 5 lakh rupees that was sent by Akhilesh Yadav through his aides. She sat on the ground of her family home, with her head tipped down to avoid looking directly at the camera, but her face was resolute. 'We do not want money. We want justice.'[2]

By accepting money from others, but refusing Akhilesh, the Shakya family made it clear that they held him responsible for what had happened. He had empowered Yadavs to behave like thugs, they suggested, and the Yadavs had done so.

The snub wasn't lost on the chief minister. Helicopters carrying politicians from Delhi now descended regularly into the Katra fields, but Akhilesh, who lived only a few hours away in the same state, didn't make the drive up.[3] He didn't even mention the bereaved family by name in public statements. All he said was that justice would take its course. In 'Horror Pradesh', as an English-language news channel had dubbed the state that Akhilesh governed, these were meaningless words.

The previous month at a public rally, Akhilesh's father had protested against capital punishment for rape, saying, 'Boys will be boys ... they make mistakes.'[4]

Since Mulayam Singh was the founder of the party, it was natural to assume that his stated position was the party position. 'You're safe, right?' the son said to the most persistent reporters who challenged him on this,[5] seeming to suggest that since they hadn't been raped or killed as yet, the problem couldn't be all that bad.

Although the Shakya family had expected as much, for many, the response from Delhi was more disheartening still. The new prime minister tweeted constantly in the days after the hangings. He tweeted about football, Bhutan, organic farming, Vladimir Putin, blood donation and World Environment Day, but he didn't mention Katra. He finally brought it up in brief, a fortnight later, during a long speech in Parliament about a host of things. 'These incidents must provoke us to look inwards and seek answers,'[6] he said.

Narendra Modi had made women's safety a prominent part of his platform for more than one election campaign. He had brought up the Delhi bus rape at the time of the assembly elections in the national capital just a few months earlier. '[Delhi] has earned a bad name as a "rape capital",' he said. 'When you vote, do not forget this. Remember [the Delhi bus rape] for a while.'[7]

A Gallup poll conducted in the midst of the general elections that took place shortly afterwards showed that only about 4 in 10 women in North India felt safe walking home at night. A majority had no confidence in the police.[8]

Modi's party, the poll noted, had increased its references to women in the 2014 campaign as compared to 2009. Close attention from international media – and the fact that some foreign governments, such as the United Kingdom, had advised women to use caution when travelling in India – had contributed to this shift.

Within days of becoming prime minister, in May 2014, Modi's government announced a 'zero tolerance' policy towards violence against women. The criminal justice system was to be strengthened for 'effective implementation'.[9]

Soon after that, in his first Independence Day speech as prime minister, Modi again raised people's hopes for change. 'In every home, parents ask daughters lots of questions as to where she is going, when will she return, and ask her to inform them when she reaches her destination,' he said. 'But have you ever asked your son where he is going, why is he going and who are his friends? After all, the person committing the rape is also someone's son. It's the responsibility of the parents to stop their sons before they take the wrong path.'[10]

Given all this, many people had expected Modi to build on the significant reforms – the new rape laws, the new medical guidelines – that were enacted by his predecessor. But Modi was no reformer. When he did talk about sexual assault, he did so in terms of 'shame for the country'. He referred to women in patriarchal language, calling them daughters.[11] And when the time came for him to demonstrate his 'zero tolerance', he sat back.

Like so many politicians before him, Modi had engaged with the subject of women's safety to win votes. And like those politicians, as soon as he came to power, it was business as usual.

A Broken System Exposed

In fact, despite the allegations of bias, the state police were doing the best they could. They had by now arrested all the Yadav brothers. Pappu was held by the police on the night of the disappearance itself; his older brothers Avdesh and Urvesh who were staying with family were brought in within the week. Constable Sarvesh and Head Constable Gangwar had been arrested and charged under a section that punishes police officers for penetrative sex with children. They lost their jobs. All five men were accused of gang rape, murder and criminal conspiracy, as well as sexual offences against minors.[1]

Sub-Inspector Ram Vilas, who was in charge of the Katra chowki, kept his job, but he was suspended for six months for, as he understood it, having 'lost control' of the situation. His subordinates were transferred. The chowki was cleared out and locked. A mulchy carpet of leaves soon filled the courtyard with a decaying smell.

Many more people were punished for their failure to staunch the tide of negative attention now directed at the state government. A superintendent of police, even a district magistrate, was suspended on direct orders from the chief minister. As many as forty-two police officers from various districts and of various ranks were transferred, presumably as proof that a broken system was being fixed.[2]

These obvious efforts to change the narrative didn't stop some powerful people from continuing to say whatever crossed their mind. Inevitably, these were foolish things.

Padma was 'the lone child of her parents', a top police officer told the media, and 'her father is one of three brothers with limited resources and if she was not alive, it could benefit others. It could be one of the motives. I am not saying that this is the motive.'[3]

The officer was implying that Padma had been killed by her own family – that the reason for the murder wasn't honour, as some believed, but to stop her inheritance from being transferred out of the family to the family of her future husband, whoever that may be.

In 2005, when Padma was seven years old, the Hindu Succession Act was amended to give women the right, among other things, to inherit agricultural property from their parents and husband.[4] But the law was one thing, and people's lived experiences were another – the officer should have known this. As far as the villagers of Katra were concerned, land stayed in the bloodline. And to them the bloodline wasn't represented by daughters, but by sons. Every woman in the village worked on the land but not a single one owned a piece of it. Across India, the situation was similarly lopsided in favour of sons.

A 2013 report published by UN Women and the land rights advocacy group Landesa showed that despite the legal amendment, only 13 per cent of women surveyed in three large states inherited or hoped to inherit their parents' land.[5] Women were likely to inherit more land as widows, the report concluded, than as daughters.

Jeevan Lal still hoped to have a boy. And if he didn't, he would reach an understanding with his brothers. They had sons. No matter what, it was highly unlikely that Padma would have inherited his property.

The investigation continued, and now the police brought in a forensic team. Several days had passed since the bodies had first been discovered, and it's unclear what they hoped to find in an area that was being treated as a tourist attraction by people from far and wide. The police also put in a request for call-detail records of numerous villagers and the officers involved in the night's events.

When the Shakya family disclosed fears of facing retaliation from the Yadavs in Jati hamlet, the police sent over armed guards to protect them. One gun-toting officer was always by Nazru's side, even when the young man resumed his night-time wanderings.

Then the state government promised to run the case through a 'fast-track' court. Fast-track courts have existed in India since the early 2000s to expedite cases – more than 1,000 fast-track courts have disposed of more than 3 million cases in this way.[6] In 2011 the courts were dissolved due to funding shortages, and then hastily revived in the aftermath of the 2012 Delhi rape;[7] six courts sprang up in the capital to deal with sexual assaults and nothing else. When rape cases went the usual route, the result could be devastating. In one instance, a teenager gang-raped in a car made more than three dozen court appearances, enduring not one, not two, but six trials.[8] It took the court eleven years to deliver a verdict.

More courts meant more judges, but here too lay a problem.

The 120th report of the Law Commission in 1987 had recommended a judge-population ratio of at least 50 per million, which was the standard in developed countries.[9] In 2010, there were still only 10.5 judges per million and 31.28 million cases pending across the country's courts.[10] A High Court judge guessed that it would take 320 years to clear the backlog.[11]

Then, on 6 June, the state government announced a Special Investigation Team (SIT) to work the case. These highly trained officers could only be appointed by the Supreme Court, or by the state and central government. They were assigned investigations that were considered too complicated or sensitive for the local police – deadly riots, for example. They also investigated the role of influential people or public servants in crimes. Bypassing the usual protocols, they handed their findings directly to the court.

With this latest gesture, the state government sent the message that they really did want justice served. But by then, they had already lost the trust of the villagers.

Mukesh Kumar Saxena, the fearful circle officer who had asked to be escorted into the mango orchard on the day the girls were found, was appointed the head of the SIT. There had been allegations in recent years that SITs were open to political influence.[12] To the villagers, Saxena's nervy behaviour was confirmation of this.

An officer who was a part of the SIT recalled that the first time he met the Shakya family, they declined to speak to him. They even refused to share their phone numbers. When he met them a second time, they told him to come back again. He faced similar resistance from the other villagers, virtually all of whom refused to answer his questions. It was utterly humiliating.

By the end of day two, just one person – a neighbour of the family – gave a statement. On day three, another man spoke up. But when the officer asked Nazru to speak to a sketch artist, the Shakyas' cousin refused. He was the one who had implicated Pappu in the girls' disappearance, but now he insisted, 'I didn't see [the suspects'] faces; I can't tell you what they looked like.' This was such a blatant lie that the officer didn't ask the question again.

By rebuffing virtually all overtures of help, the family made it clear that they believed the system was flawed because of the Yadavs. A newspaper investigation had just revealed that in major districts of the state, 'particularly those under the influence of the ruling family', Yadav officers headed nearly 60 per cent of police stations.[13] In the state capital of Lucknow, where Akhilesh lived, over 50 per cent of all station officers were Yadavs. And in Budaun, the district where Katra was located, this was true of sixteen out of twenty-two police stations. This included the station in Ushait, where Pappu Yadav was taken on the morning the girls were found.

The Shakya family took such stories as further proof of the state's complicity in covering up crimes. They refused to engage with the police investigation, and by extension, with the government. If they had something to say they said it to the TV cameras that continued to buzz around them as if they were on a reality show.

The chief minister still hadn't spoken to the family, not even over the phone. He spoke *of* them, obliquely, like he could have been talking about anyone at all. The bizarre stand-off, in which one of the most powerful men in India seemed to be fighting a family that represented some of the poorest people in India, came to be seen as a David-and-Goliath situation.

Almost everyone, of course, wanted David – the Shakyas – to win.

But perhaps the real reason the family now despised the chief minister was because of his failure to address the tragedy in human terms. This was true of most politicians, but Akhilesh Yadav had refused to even look them in the face. He acted as though the hangings were a problem for *him*. By throwing more police, experts and committees at the case he had hoped to make the problem go away.

But the death of a child wasn't a problem. It was a catastrophe. It could not be fixed, it could not be undone and it should not be forgotten. This is what the Shakyas believed.

What the Shakyas wanted was for the chief minister to address their loss. They had lost children! Why wouldn't he just come out and say so? Was it because he believed that, as Shakyas, they felt things differently? Was it, as Siya Devi had said as she wept upon seeing the hanging body of her daughter, that the children of the poor mean nothing to the rich, to the powerful?

But as Siya Devi could have told the chief minister, her daughter had meant something. To her mother, she was everything. Lalli was her mother's whole heart.

And although the police were working hard, they still weren't getting it right. One of the suspects, former Constable Sarvesh, managed to run away, taking with him two others. They were brought back in a few hours from a bus stop, from where they had been hoping to flee the state. The fact that the police had let three suspects in a major case escape on their watch showed just how little could be expected of them – even at their best.

It was in this environment that talk of bringing in the country's top investigators gained traction.

Separate Milk From Water

The Shakya brothers were later unable to recall with whom the idea originated. Like many people in Katra village, they didn't watch TV or read the papers and they weren't privy to the news that the Central Bureau of Investigation (CBI) was making for its handling of notorious cases.

Sohan Lal's eldest son would recall hearing of the agency in the context of the Aarushi Talwar mystery. Virender was living in Noida at the time when the teenaged girl was murdered in her bed one night, while on the cusp of turning fourteen, the same age as his sister when she died. The twists and turns in the investigation and the trial transfixed the nation.

In any case, the Shakyas went from knowing very little about the CBI to being convinced that the agency alone could be trusted to deliver justice. 'I *want* the CBI,' Sohan Lal told cameras.[1] He had heard that investigators could separate milk from water.

The request was heartily endorsed by opposition politicians who were eager to continue to undermine the state government, but as it turned out the chief minister was just as keen. The state police had been publicly humiliated, the Special Investigation Team embarrassingly stonewalled. Akhilesh Yadav was himself marinating in a stew of bad press.

And so, following his request to the central government, the agency stepped in on 12 June, entirely dislodging the state police from the investigation.

It was now over a week since the girls had died, and the time lag was only the first challenge the incoming team had to surmount. Neither the police nor the SIT had thought to cordon off the orchard. It was still wide open. Many witnesses were still to record their statements. Pappu and his brothers were in jail, but their mother Jhalla Devi – who claimed to have overheard where the bodies were – was yet to be questioned.

If these circumstances were unique to Katra, attributable to the location of the village, it would perhaps be understandable. But according to a former Special Director, who spoke on the condition of anonymity, 'every second case' that the CBI was called in to investigate was thus affected. A lack of training, resources and oversight at state police level meant that forensic and medical evidence was routinely contaminated, key witnesses disappeared and more time was spent fixing mistakes rather than making progress.

In the Aarushi mystery, for example, first responders didn't find the second victim, the domestic help, until a day after the teenager was discovered. All that time his bludgeoned body was lying on the terrace of the flat, slowly cooking in the sun.

The CBI had grown out of a colonial-era unit named the Special Police Establishment – which was formed by executive order in 1941 to probe bribery and corruption during World War II.[2] It was considered necessary even after the war ended, and the Delhi Special Police Establishment Act, 1946 was put into force to give it legal power to investigate and prosecute cases.[3] This Act was the genesis of the CBI, which was given its current name in 1963. In time it developed three investigative divisions: the Anti-Corruption Division pursued cases against public servants; the Economic Offences Division investigated financial crimes; and the Special Crimes Division, which threw the widest net, took on terrorism, bomb blasts, espionage, dowry deaths, sensational homicides and more. The agency also served as the official INTERPOL unit for India.

Since 2011, the agency had worked out of an eleven-storey state-of-the-art building that was modelled on the headquarters of INTERPOL in Lyon, France.[4] Built at an estimated cost of $39 million, it featured a lobby that was three floors high, a giant atrium, a gymnasium and marble floors. The price tag was a testimony to how highly the CBI's service was valued, but also how desperately it was needed.

In India it often seemed as though there was no transparency and no accountability. And that those who wanted to get rich quick could always find a way. This was certainly true in the 2000s when the economy was booming. Even as the majority stayed poor, a few took advantage of this golden opportunity to appropriate public funds into private hands. In 2014, 71.5 per cent of cases under examination by the agency were registered with the Anti-Corruption Division.[5] It was India's 'season of scams'.

The CBI was quickly outpaced. It could probe 700 cases a year,[6] but the actual caseload was almost twice that. As trust in the police eroded, it didn't take much for the public to demand that the agency get involved. The suicide of a Bollywood starlet, the assassination of a journalist, even the usual construction scam; 'almost everyone wants every case to go to the CBI,' moaned one former director.[7] It was easier, after all, to throw everything at the agency than to engage with systemic issues. In May 2014, the agency was juggling 1,122 cases, or 60 per cent more work than it was equipped to handle.[8] Of these they had been working on 11 cases for more than three years.

The untenable workload struck at the heart of its reputation for efficiency. The CBI's conviction rate started to dip. In 2014 it was at 69 per cent,[9] a figure that would continue to steadily drop.

Then vacancies started to mount. There were 1,000 posts left unfilled that year, against a sanctioned strength of 6,676.[10] The vacancies started at the top, at the post of Special and Additional Director and included jobs for inspectors and technical officers – the people whose work involved building a case and leading it to a successful conclusion. Deposing before a parliamentary committee in 2016, the CBI director would say that unless problems were swiftly addressed, the agency would 'collapse and fail'.[11]

Although the CBI's investigative skills had a mythic reputation in some quarters, its dependence on the government virtually guaranteed accusations of impropriety. The party in power at the centre provided the agency with personnel, resources and a budget. It could post officers to the CBI or transfer them out. And if the agency wanted to prosecute a government official – the reason why it had been created to begin with – it needed the authorisation of the ministry in which that very official worked.[12]

When accusations against politicians from the ruling party failed to materialise in investigations, or opposition leaders were suddenly accused of having 'disproportionate assets', which was a euphemism for corruption, and their houses raided, it appeared as though the CBI was acting on outside orders.

In 2013, the Supreme Court said the government had meddled in a CBI investigation into a scam that involved coal-field leases that had cost the country about $30 billion in lost revenue.[13] 'The heart of the report was changed on suggestions of government officials,' the court said.[14] The presiding judge lamented that India's foremost investigative agency had been reduced to a 'caged parrot speaking in its master's voice'.[15] In 2017, the CBI would be forced to file corruption charges against the man who had presided over the investigation into the coal scam – their own former director.[16]

At least two former heads told Reuters that the force was subject to political influence 'irrespective of which party happened to be in power at the time'.[17] 'The political class will never give independence to the CBI,' said a former director, who alleged that he was forced out after refusing to back off from an investigation in the 1990s. According to an internal report, the agency's conviction rate in corruption cases that often involved politicians and their cronies was 3.96 per cent.[18]

Another former head argued that even if the agency was independent, politicians benefited from making it appear otherwise. 'Every political party wants to accuse the political rival in power of misusing the CBI,' he grumbled. 'And, the cycle continues.'[19]

Whatever the actual extent of influence, the agency seemed to do better when it worked on cases that didn't implicate political leaders. Or when it wasn't in the interest of politicians in power to fix a case. And there were many such cases, the majority of which didn't make the headlines. Indeed, the ordinary public admired the agency's investigators and thought of them as honest and professional.

In contrast to the police, they were everything.

So when a CBI team of about a dozen men, led by a well-regarded investigator, was dispatched to Uttar Pradesh, it was for many people – the Shakyas, the public and some politicians – a winning moment. Now surely, justice would prevail.

A Red Flag

The investigating officer was a man who didn't leave an impression. It wasn't because of how he looked: tall, with broad shoulders, a walrus moustache and the domed forehead of a thinker. He had straight, even teeth. But he had mastered the habit of making himself small, smaller than the person he was talking to. He kept his voice low. His face gave nothing away.

After he was gone, the Shakya brothers would struggle to describe him. He was much taller than them, heavier too, and well dressed in nice suits, gleaming shoes, an Apple watch. He had come and gone for months. But he had been so unobtrusive, unlike some others on his team, that the Shakyas' memory of him was clouded.

Already twenty years into the police force, Vijay Kumar Shukla, the 49-year-old deputy superintendent of police in the Special Crimes Division in Delhi, had taken the lead on more than fifty cases, several of which had made headlines. In one instance he had helped secure a conviction against a forger who became a millionaire in the 1990s by selling counterfeit stamp papers. He tracked down the Dubai-based terrorists behind the 2002 attack on an American cultural centre in Kolkata. And in 2005, he arrested the mastermind of a poaching ring that trafficked in big cat skins for clients in China. Investigators were judged by their convictions, and Shukla had many.

A highly regarded former Special Director of the CBI, who was often asked to examine cold cases by the Supreme Court, had invited Shukla to investigate a triple murder outside of office hours. He found the officer impressive. 'He is a man of integrity,' he said, when asked for an assessment. This meant that Shukla wasn't corrupt. He couldn't be bought, and nor could he be influenced by superior officers with somewhat less integrity. 'He's hard-working,' the director added, which was to say that he dug deep. And he had a 'scientific temper' which should have been a given but wasn't, in fact, something that the police were known for.

Shukla would have to be all of these things, for Katra was a 'hot case', one of the most famous of recent times and still featuring in the headlines days after the fact.

Having set up a field office at a guest house in Budaun, Shukla and his men swarmed Katra village in their distinctive sleeveless blue jackets, which were emblazoned with the agency's initials. It was 13 June, a day after the state police had handed over the case.

'You just have to tell the truth,' Shukla said to the Shakya brothers – Sohan Lal, Jeevan Lal and Ram Babu. 'We'll take care of everything else.'

In their complaint to the police the Shakya family had named two eyewitnesses to the alleged kidnapping of Padma and Lalli. These were Nazru, their cousin, and Ram Babu.

As members of the agency's Central Forensic Science Laboratory started filming, Nazru walked the team through the fields, retracing his movements from that night.

At around 9 or 9.30 p.m. on 27 May, he said, he had been heading towards his plot when he saw two girls. With them were four men. It was very dark, but he was carrying a torch, which he aimed at the group. He recognised Pappu immediately and they launched into a fight, but then Pappu pulled out a gun. As he waved it threateningly in Nazru's face, the other men took off with the girls. Nazru had raced back to the village. 'There are badmash in the fields,' he shouted to Ram Babu. Bad men in the fields. 'They have a gun!'

The two men rushed to inform the rest of the Shakyas, who in turn told them that their girls were missing. 'I slapped my forehead and said there were two girls with the men. It had never occurred to me that they might be Padma and Lalli.'

At their field office, the investigators went through the reports of the two key witnesses. Nazru claimed that he'd bumped into Ram Babu *after* the girls were taken. But Ram Babu's statement, which was recorded right afterwards, told a different story.

On the night of 27 May, Ram Babu said, looking straight into the camera, he was with Nazru. It was around 8 or 8.30 p.m. They were in the fields when they came across Pappu with some girls. It was too dark to tell who they were. Ram Babu flashed his torch, Pappu remonstrated at the interruption, but the girls cried out, so Nazru threw himself on the Yadav boy. But as the boy was armed, the Shakya men quickly retreated. Pappu then took off with the girls.

Shukla went through the recordings a few times. Although he was baffled, he wasn't mistaken. The eyewitnesses were telling two different stories. The 'major contradictions', he would later say, were a 'red flag'.

The Villagers Talk

Three days later, six men in lab coats congregated in the mango orchard to prepare the crime scene report. The forensic scientists relied on a CBI manual listing physical and biological materials to look for. These included fingerprints, footprints, blood, semen, saliva, urine, vomit, faecal matter, hair, fibre, tissues, teeth and bite marks, skeletal remains, nails, trace evidence such as soil, as well as medicines or firearms or food. The list ran on for three pages.

The girls had gone missing on 27 May.

Today was 16 June.

That morning the team found a strand of hair on the branch from which Lalli was hanging, as well as some leaves that were stained with tobacco juice or blood, they couldn't say. Over the next few days, the officers would enlist forensic scientists in three different states – Uttar Pradesh, Telengana and Gujarat – to review this and other material.

Investigators had drawn up address lists, and they started to call in dozens of people for interviews: Shakyas, Yadavs, members of the search parties, police officers and many others. In all, they would talk to more than 200 people, from Katra and beyond. Two people were interrogated more than ten times. One was Pappu Yadav, the key accused, who was in jail. The other was the eyewitness Nazru.

The villagers of Katra had stonewalled the police and the state-appointed Special Investigation Team in solidarity with the Shakya family, but they were eager to talk to the investigators. These were serious men, they agreed. They didn't hang around with alcohol on their breath. They weren't here for handouts. More than anything, the villagers wanted to clear Katra of the smear by which it was now defined, as some place where girls were killed. As long as the rumour circulated no one would marry their boys. It was time to sow the kharif crops, but hard to focus when their character was in question.

The consequences for women and girls were naturally more severe. As some said, 'boys will be boys, but girls can't be wayward.' They had gone to the fields in ones and twos before; now they had to galvanise a group. A basic human need suddenly required advance planning and mobilisation.

In many homes the movement of phones, previously regarded as common property, was now closely tracked. There was no question, any more, of a girl of Padma's age picking up a phone and going off with it, not even to a different corner of the house. The small outings she had once enjoyed – grazing the goats, climbing trees, plucking mangoes – were no longer permitted. The door to the outside had been open by a crack, now it was pulled firmly shut. The women were to stay in at all times, they weren't to be seen. Outside, the village men lay awake, night after night, gazing up at the sky.

The villagers meant the Shakyas no harm, but by speaking honestly, they revealed things the family had hoped to keep hidden.

The brothers had known that Pappu was with the girls but didn't share this vital piece of information right away. They had kept it to themselves for several hours when it should have been clear that the children were in danger. They had chaotically attempted to find them, chasing down random motorcycles, but failing to search the fields or the orchard fully. At the police chowki, they refused to allow Nazru – who was the only one with real information at hand – to be questioned.

But it was a friend of Nazru's, Umesh Shakya, who gave the most damning evidence. The two young men often passed the evenings drinking and smoking weed in each other's company. On the morning the bodies were discovered, Umesh had made straight for the orchard, same as everyone else. There he saw Nazru sweating profusely. Umesh took his friend by the arm and walked him somewhere quiet, a mint field about forty feet away from the orchard.

'What's going on?' he asked.

He was returning home from checking in on his buffalo, Nazru told him, when he heard some khusar phusar, whispers. 'I shined my torch in the direction of the sounds and saw Pappu with Sohan and Jeevan's daughters. I was furious to see our girls with him.' When the girls saw Nazru, their faces turned ashen, he said. 'I thrashed Pappu. He lashed out at me as well, which made me even angrier, but before I could retaliate, he broke out of my grasp.'

The girls started crying and running away. Nazru assumed they were going home.

Umesh leaned in, wanting to know more. Just then, as he told investigators, some villagers took hold of Nazru.

'Listen,' Umesh overhead them say, 'it was Pappu, his brothers and the police who raped and killed the girls.'

Some hours later, when the Shakyas were arguing over the contents of the police complaint, Umesh again took Nazru to one side. 'Now what?' he said.

'Brother, don't ask me!' Nazru cried, clutching his head. 'Sohan and Jeevan tell me to say one thing, then they say another. First they told me to say that the Yadav brothers kidnapped the girls, then they said it was their father and Sarvesh sipahi who did it. They're just saying and doing anything, and I don't know who to listen to any more. I'm going mad!'

A second villager confirmed to investigators that Sohan Lal had knowingly falsified his written complaint to the police. 'Nazru saw three or four men,' Sohan Lal had told this villager. 'He couldn't identify them, so why not just say they were the Yadav brothers? They probably were.'

Like the crowd in the orchard that had called for Sarvesh to be hanged, Lalli's father had no evidence of wrongdoing. Nazru had seen Pappu with the girls, but he hadn't witnessed a crime. And he hadn't mentioned the Yadav brothers in his account, which was, in any case, sketchy and one of several that he had told on the night the girls went missing.

But the Shakyas didn't have faith in the system. Sarvesh might not have killed the girls, and Pappu's brothers might be innocent of involvement in the hangings, but they were guilty of *something*.

The constable had abused his power. The Yadav family had fed and nurtured a venomous snake, Pappu, who had seduced their children. At the very least they were Yadavs. And everyone, they said, knew that Yadavs hurt people.

The False Eyewitness

When investigators went looking to clarify matters with Nazru, they didn't find him at home. Her son was now living with the Shakya family, his mother said.

Sohan Lal warmly welcomed the men in the suits and dark glasses, with their polished shoes and the little white towels they waved around in the heat. Standing in his courtyard in bare feet, his undershirt ripped, and trousers held together with safety pins, he told them that he had invited his cousin to move in for a few days as a gesture of goodwill. The media attention was extreme, he said, and he wanted to shield the boy.

Investigators were not convinced. It was the Shakya house that was overrun with reporters. There were several even just then.

On 18 June, an amount of 75,000 rupees appeared in Nazru's bank account, which had earlier held only 502 rupees. Investigators would learn that the amount was a part of a larger payment of 1 lakh rupees. This was more money than Nazru had earned in many years. A few days earlier the same amount had appeared in Ram Babu's account. The only people who now had that kind of money in the village, and were also close to Nazru and Ram Babu, were the Shakya brothers.

Sohan Lal admitted that he had been behind the payments, but again, he said that he was just being thoughtful. The media attention had made it impossible for the men to work. The money was a form of recompense.

Shukla, the investigating officer, wasn't having it. The two men were the eyewitnesses to the alleged kidnapping of Sohan Lal's daughter and niece – why was he giving them money?

Sensing his scepticism, Sohan Lal then claimed that his brother had asked for money. His cousin had then made the same request. The Shakyas' political ally, the person they trusted most outside the family, agreed that this was indeed the case. Sinod Kumar told investigators that Nazru was upset that visiting politicians hadn't thought to give him anything. All the money went to Padma and Lalli's parents. The family was now in a position to expand their house and even buy a motorcycle. Nazru was where he had always been, in the middle of the fields with his buffalo. As far as he knew, said the politician, the Shakyas gave their cousin money to console him.

This didn't explain the money in Ram Babu's account.

Nazru repeated his story to the CBI. That on the night that Padma and Lalli disappeared, he came across two girls with four men, or 'boys' as he called them, in the fields. Sensing that the girls were in trouble, he ran towards Pappu, who was the only member of the group that he recognised. They were fighting when the Yadav boy whipped out a gun. In the meanwhile, the other boys took off with the girls.

Nazru didn't say that Pappu's brothers were involved, or the police, for that matter. He didn't even say that he recognised the girls. He had the outline of a story, but the details, as before, were fuzzy. And, he made no mention of the fact that there was someone with him – a second eyewitness.

Investigators, who were by now getting rather tired of the back and forth, called Ram Babu in for questioning again. And perhaps he was tired of the whole thing too, because this time he told the truth. He had children of his own – seven boys and girls. And they too had reputations to protect.

Ram Babu admitted that he had lied about having seen Pappu in the fields. He didn't see him, he said – he was at home at the time, relaxing after dinner. It was his older brother, Sohan Lal, who came up with the idea of manufacturing a second eyewitness. 'Look at Nazru,' he said. And they had. 'Who will believe him?'

At first the task was delegated to a family friend. He readily agreed on the condition that he could implicate someone he strongly disliked in the kidnapping. 'That will teach him a lesson.'

'We did not agree to this,' Ram Babu told investigators.

Then someone suggested that Lalli's elder brother could play the role. Virender was amenable, but he remembered just in time that he wasn't in the village the night the girls went missing. He had arrived the morning after.

Finally, they settled on Ram Babu. He was friendly, with a likeable face. He was intelligent. And he stayed calm.

'I was afraid of saying no,' Ram Babu told investigators. If he refused, he said, he would damage his relationship with his brothers. And the grieving family could not withstand further turmoil.

Investigating Officer Shukla knew people well. He knew, for example, that some fathers wrapped infant girls in soaking wet cloths or fed them salt or abandoned them in the middle of beating hot fields. If the girls survived, they were ignored, left to grow up or not. They were not treated like people, they were herded like animals. They were not loved. But Padma and Lalli, it was clear to him, were loved.

The investigator did not believe, as some did, that their parents had killed them. The fact that they had counted on Nazru – of all people – to stick to his story, only confirmed to the investigator that the family was too naive to commit a real crime. But with their constantly changing stories, the Shakyas were wasting his time.

It wasn't long before Nazru also accepted that he had lied. His cousins, he told Shukla, had paid him to say that he witnessed the kidnapping of Padma and Lalli by a group of people – among them, Pappu Yadav and his brothers. He was also told to say that Ram Babu was with him at the time.

'It wasn't true,' Nazru said. 'I only saw one person that night with the girls. And that person was Pappu.'

Purity and Pollution

The relationship between the Shakya brothers and the CBI deteriorated quickly. The brothers told the media that investigators hounded them for interviews, but that when the brothers arrived at the field office in Budaun, they were kept waiting for hours. They were even kept hungry. 'All they ever gave us to eat were a handful of samosas.' They were handed scores of letters when it should have been perfectly obvious that they couldn't read.

After the initial courtesies, they alleged, the investigator Shukla no longer bothered to give them updates on the case.

Shukla had a different take on events. He was now aware that the Shakyas' complaint to the police was fabricated. By implicating Pappu Yadav's brothers, and producing a fake eyewitness, the family had undermined their own credibility. They claimed to want to know what had happened to their daughters, but everything they did suggested that they were planting blame. 'Their conduct,' Shukla said, 'was not the natural conduct of parents.'

Sohan Lal was a particular source of aggravation. Time and again he begged off answering questions on the excuse that he didn't speak Hindi. Sohan Lal's first language was Braj Bhasha, but he understood and spoke Hindi, of that they were sure. They had seen him give numerous interviews on camera.

'We're speaking simple Hindi!' Shukla said.

The repeated refusals to answer questions became enough of an issue that the matter was kicked to a higher-up. This officer told Shukla to download a video of one of Sohan Lal's television interviews. 'Isn't this you?' Shukla asked, showing Lalli's father such a clip. 'You can speak to the media in Hindi, but you can't answer our questions?' Sohan Lal bowed his head, brought his palms together in a gesture of apology, and called Shukla sahib to show his deference – but neither man now liked the other.

Shortly after, when Shukla decided to take a closer look at the post-mortem, he didn't immediately inform the family. There was a clearly established chain of information protocol – victim's family first, always. By breaking protocol, the investigator made it clear that the family had lost his trust.

When the Shakyas learned of his plans, through friendly media tipped off by someone in the CBI, they were taken aback. The post-mortem report, which they now had in their possession, had declared the cause of death as hanging. They had been told it meant murder. What new things did Shukla expect to learn?

The pressure on the police, while they had been in charge, had been intense – and they had wanted to make it clear that they really were trying to put all their energy and resources towards working the case. Just to be sure, they had sent the post-mortem video to the state capital, Lucknow, and had asked the Forensic Science Laboratory, FSL, for a second opinion.

On 4 June, two days before the CBI investigators took over the case, a consultant medico-legal physician at the FSL called Dr Ghyasuddin Khan shared his findings. He concluded that the girls were smothered to death, and then hanged. He wrote that 'the video of PMR [showed] scientific techniques [had] been avoided.' The post-mortem team had barely even taken samples, he complained.

The CBI also had some other concerns. There was the phrase 'suggestive of rape'. And then, there was a startling piece of evidence that established not merely a lack of familiarity with protocol, but with the administration of post-mortems themselves.

On top of all this, there was the fact that Lala Ram – a sweeper, with no medical qualification to his name – had examined the bodies. This should have been reason enough for the CBI to rubbish the results. It wasn't, because the agency knew that people like Lala Ram routinely examined the dead.

There were so few pathologists in India, medical doctors were asked to do the job. Knowing they were not equipped to do so, many refused. Hospitals then claimed that they had no choice but to turn to one of the Lala Ram-type figures who roamed the corridors with a broom in one hand and a dustpan in the other.

The obvious outcome, as a campaigning professor of forensic medicine told *The Times of India*, was that post-mortem houses were really 'production-line abattoirs'[1] in which bodies were carved up. Families were left distraught and the police were denied the expert medical statement that was the backbone of a criminal death investigation.

One reason for the shortfall was a deeply embedded Hindu prejudice against dead bodies. Cadavers were seen as dirty things, whose touch was polluting. Those who touched them were also considered polluted.

The first post-mortem by an Indian in India was conducted on 28 October 1836 in Calcutta, at a modern hospital built to train Indians to help doctors of the British Army. Hindu pandits, having come to know of this plan in advance, took up vigil at the hospital entrance to ensure that no dead bodies came in.[2]

It was a full year before secret plans to smuggle in a cadaver were put in motion, and even then, the body had to be dissected in an outhouse. The lead doctor, Madhusudan Gupta, was an upper-caste Hindu, a former ayurvedic pandit and assistant to a professor of anatomy. Several medical students reportedly assisted him, but the college principal refused to reveal their identities to protect them from ostracism. The British celebrated the occasion with a fifty-round salute, but many Hindus were revolted.

The task thereafter usually fell to Dalits, people who were relegated to the outcaste group. They were already made to do work that was designated dirty, such as skinning animals and cleaning toilets. And they were already forced to live in ostracised communities. By insisting that they alone handle the dead, caste Hindus further stigmatised the process in the eyes of the wider community.

In the years since, the caste system had prevailed, and Hindu notions of purity and pollution continued to be observed at home and work. As a result, so did attitudes towards the dead, even when they came in conflict with science.

The CBI knew that they would have a fight on their hands if they dismissed the post-mortem on the grounds that it was performed by a sweeper. Who else would do the job, the villagers would say?

Instead, they said a difference of opinion had made it necessary to take a deeper look at the examinations.

A Post-mortem Undone

The agency now summoned the post-mortem doctors and asked them again how the girls had died. Did they die by hanging, were they smothered first and then hanged or did they die in a different way?

There was no sign of struggle, Dr Rajiv Gupta, who had led the post-mortem, told investigators. The girls were 'not so young', he said. And they were 'quite developed'. He used the word 'stout'. If an attempt had been made to smother them, they would have fought back. The struggle would have left an imprint in the form of scratches, splintered nails and broken bangles. And even if not, the signs of smothering were unmissable – bruising around the nose and mouth, for example – and he hadn't missed them.

The suggestion that the girls were smothered was laughable, he said, and Dr Gupta did in fact laugh out loud when recounting the interview later on.

'First the rape has been done, then the smothering has been done. Then they've been hanged to death?' He snorted. 'No. Simplicity is always truth.'

Although he didn't say as much in the report, he now told investigators that the girls were alive at the time they climbed the tree. And they had climbed it themselves. The girls' bodies, he reminded them, were virtually pristine.

'How can you hang a live person on a tree without any struggle? It's not possible.'

To show the investigators that he knew what he was talking about, he then went through the post-mortem videos with them. But unfortunately for him, he came out looking somewhat the worse for it.

In Lalli's post-mortem report, Dr Gupta had described the skull as 'congested'. But it was clear, from watching the videos, that he hadn't opened the teenager's skull.

At first he insisted that he'd ordered Lala Ram to do so. He claimed that if the man forgot it was because they were under tremendous pressure from the waiting crowd. Later, when the question was put to Lala Ram, the former sweeper was adamant that the doctor had made no such request.

'Everything was done very quickly,' he said.

Finally, Dr Gupta confessed to his mistake. 'We have not opened the skull,' he said sheepishly. 'The observation about the brain has been wrongly recorded.'

Dr Tripathi, the general practitioner from the District Women's Hospital, was then called in to explain her statement regarding the rapes — or, as she had put it, that the injuries she saw on the girls' bodies had seemed 'suggestive of rape'. She had noted 'clotted blood in and around [the] vaginal orifice' and an 'abrasion' in her report on fourteen-year-old Lalli. These findings had led her to believe that the girl was sexually assaulted.

Investigators now asked her to lean in so she could take a closer look at a photograph they had for her. This was the piece of evidence that had confirmed to them that the post-mortem results were in fact faulty.

What did she see?

A blood-soaked piece of cloth stuck to the inside of a pair of panties.

What did it look like?

'This piece of cloth looks like a sanitary pad used by females of villages during menstrual periods.'

Another group of forensic scientists, this time in southern India's Telengana state, who had been sent the children's clothes for examination, had discovered the item in Lalli's underwear.

Had Dr Tripathi seen the item on the girl?

No, she replied, 'I did not examine the undergarments.' Lala Ram had removed the clothes and she hadn't asked to see them.

'Can you comment on the source of the blood?'

'I am quite certain that this was menstrual blood.'

'You had mentioned "haematoma present over hymen." Did you examine hymen in this case? And if yes, what was the condition?'

'I examined hymen in this case which was found intact although I had not mentioned it.'

'Since hymen was found intact and she was in menstrual phase, is it possible that you had misinterpreted the finding?'

'Yes …'

The 'abrasion around hymen' she went on to explain, was a scratch. 'Since it was very small, I did not measure it … It is quite possible that it could be caused by self-scratching owing to itching especially during menstrual period.'

'Would you like to modify your opinion?'

'I submit that it was a misinterpretation on my part to label it as rape during post-mortem examination. Therefore, I am of the opinion that there were no signs of recent vaginal penetration/sexual assault in this case of deceased Lalli.'

Lalli, she now said, hadn't been raped.

The investigators then pulled up Padma's post-mortem report. Dr Tripathi had noted a tear in the sixteen-year-old's genital area, had she not? Was it new or old?

There were no signs of inflammation or bleeding, she replied. 'It can be concluded that this tear was old and healed.'

'You had mentioned that hymen was bluish and oedematous. Do you know that this discolouration and turgidity can be found in a female consequent to prolonged suspension of body?'

'No, I don't have much knowledge of forensic medicine.'

'Did you rule out that this bluish discolouration of hymen was post-mortem staining since body remained suspended for a period of more than twelve hours. If yes, then how?'

'… due to lack of knowledge. Moreover, the lighting was insufficient … since PME was conducted during night hours which might have led to wrong perception.'

'Would you like to modify your opinion?'

'I am fully convinced that it was misinterpretation on my part to label it as rape during post-mortem examination. Therefore, I am of the opinion that there were no signs of recent vaginal penetration/sexual assault in this case of deceased Padma.'

'Habitual of Sexual Intercourse'

Dr Tripathi had been unclear on the question of whether the girls were raped, but one of her her male colleagues on the post-mortem team had lied. They had one job and they failed to do it. And yet, it was she alone, the only woman on the team, who felt humiliated enough to withdraw from the public eye. Her colleague, Dr Rajiv Gupta, sometimes spoke on her behalf, mostly to explain where she had gone wrong.

She had examined many rape victims, he said, but she had never conducted a post-mortem. Without a live victim to clarify matters – the age of a scratch, for example – she had misinterpreted the physiological changes that come in after a prolonged hanging. 'The people standing outside were shouting "rape hua! rape hua!"' said Dr Gupta. 'And the police asked if the girls were raped. She had to say something.'

To draw a full criminological picture, post-mortem findings are correlated with forensic reports. For this, there have to be samples to examine – from the scalp, vagina, pubic area, anus, rectum and mouth, samples of blood and saliva and of any foreign substance that is found on the body. The rule was to take as many samples as possible. Dr Tripathi had only sent in one set of samples, from the vagina.

A trifecta of missteps, which had started with a delayed investigation and then a contaminated crime scene, was now complete.

The agency was still faced with contradictory causes of death. Dr Gupta had described the asphyxiation as suicidal. But the report from the lab in Lucknow said that the girls were smothered – suggesting that they were killed. On another case the investigators would have accepted the prognosis of the doctors who had conducted the post-mortem over someone who had watched two tapes. But Dr Gupta and his team were no longer credible. The agency decided to exhume the bodies of Padma and Lalli.

Second post-mortems weren't all that unusual in high-profile cases, especially when it was clear that the initial team had botched the job. There might even be a third one, as had been the case with Scarlet Keeling, the fifteen-year-old British tourist who had been killed after a Valentine's Day beach party in the palm-fringed western state of Goa in 2008.[1]

A first post-mortem led by the state police claimed that the teenager had drowned after drinking. On the insistence of Keeling's mother, a second post-mortem was then carried out. This time the team found more than fifty cuts and bruises and evidence of sexual assault. The police walked back their earlier conclusion, saying that the teenager had been drugged, raped and murdered. The body was repatriated to Britain, where an attempt to perform a third post-mortem showed that some internal organs – Keeling's uterus and parts of her liver and kidney[2] – hadn't been put back.

The case went to trial in Goa and, given the half-hearted manner of investigation, it came as no surprise when the accused were acquitted. In 2019, the High Court overturned the ruling and sentenced one of the accused to ten years 'rigorous imprisonment' – jail plus hard labour.[3]

In late June 2014, the CBI called in professors of forensic medicine at a top government hospital and medical college in New Delhi. This latest team of doctors, from the All India Institute of Medical Sciences, was asked to adjudicate on the matter of whether the girls were raped and how they had died. Then, in direct contravention of government guidelines introduced in the aftermath of the 2012 Delhi bus rape, if the girls had been sexually active. The exact question put to them was 'whether any of the victims were habitual of sexual intercourse'.

This ugly phrase was a familiar presence in post-mortem reports as well as courtroom trials. It was used to dispute the account of rape victims who were sexually active at the time of their assault, by attempting to show that they were trying to pass off consensual sex as rape to protect their honour. Sometimes the argument was introduced to create a character profile of a 'loose' woman. A woman who may as well have asked to be raped.

It even showed up in legal judgments. In 2002, a court in the eastern state of Orissa set aside the conviction of a man charged with rape on the argument that 'the medical evidence supported by [the alleged victim's] physical features revealed that she was habituated to sex … Though there is no apparent motive for Ms X to falsely implicate the appellant,' stated the court, 'it may be that Ms X must have changed her mind when she came to know that others must come to know of her conduct.'[4]

To determine whether a rape victim was sexually active, some doctors carried out a virginity test known as the 'two finger test'. It was exactly as invasive and humiliating as it sounded. They checked the condition of the hymen and the vagina with their fingers, even though they should have known that neither offered conclusive proof of virginity. In 2013, the Supreme Court was forced to intervene, describing the test as a violation of 'privacy, physical and mental integrity and dignity'. An affirmative report, it said, which claimed to know that the victim was sexually active, was not proof of consent.[5]

Although in the case of the Shakya girls, the doctors from the All India Institute of Medical Sciences would not be administering the two finger test to determine virginity, the enquiry as to their sexual proclivity was worth paying attention to. It showed that Shukla believed, and imagined that the doctors believed, the long-held myth about the hymen – that it breaks after a woman's first vaginal penetration. In fact, as medical experts have long held, the virginity test is a sham procedure. 'You can tell if someone has had a vaginal delivery but to tell if someone has had vaginal intercourse is not possible,'[6] a doctor told the New York Times.

Shukla's desire for a hymen test showed that while he may have had a scientific temperament it was only relative to those around him. He wanted to confirm if the girls were sexually active at the time of death, because then the call between Lalli and Pappu, in which she invited him to the fields that last night, and the fact of their meeting itself, would make a whole lot of sense.

Of course, there was no way of knowing this, and by asking the doctors to find out, the investigating officer was only sending them on a wild goose chase – no different from the one Lalli's father had earlier sent him on.

A Mother Goes 'Mad'

The woman in the courtyard refused to speak. She sat with her back to the wall with her face covered. At first it was the reporters she shooed away, like they were settling flies. Then she stopped speaking to her children. If they tried to console her she grew frustrated by their lack of understanding. Lalli's mother then refused all food. The roti stuck to the roof of her mouth, she told her only living daughter, Phoolan Devi. The young woman had arrived with her children within hours of the bodies being found on 28 May, and here she still was, weeks later, ministering to her mother's needs. Phoolan Devi should just leave her and mind her own family, her mother said.

At unexpected times, Siya Devi opened her mouth as though to say something. Then she shouted.

The men kept their distance.

Padma's stepmother went about her business as usual. She still had to feed her husband. And Ram Babu's wife had her seven children to care for. Even though they came by as often as they could there wasn't much they could do. When Siya Devi started on one of her rants, the women turned their faces in despair.

Phoolan Devi had seen her mother cry over the death of a child before. Phoolan Devi's elder sister, Sunita, had died while she was pregnant with her second child. The

child, too, had died. It was Siya Devi who had then asked
Phoolan to marry her widowed brother-in-law. There was
a toddler to look after, a girl named Khushboo, perfume.
A child needs a mother, Siya Devi had said.

Phoolan was only eighteen then, and she did as she
was told, she married her sister's husband to look after
their child. Her new home was a village where people
were poorer than any she had ever seen. The children
attached string to the filthy plastic bags they had foraged
from the dump and called them kites. Although she grew
accustomed to her new family and soon had a child of
her own, Phoolan Devi's state of mind was clear when she
said things like, 'Dil ke arman dil mein reh jaate hain.'
The desires of the heart stay in the heart.

Phoolan Devi understood something of what her
mother was going through and delivered what comfort
she could. She would later remember those days as the
time her mother 'went mad'.

Around the two women, the courtyard bristled with
activity. Reporters with camera crews and photographers,
production fixers and translators; people who introduced
themselves as leaders, lawyers and activists came and went
as they pleased. They wanted an accounting of every toilet
in the village, a list of all the politicians who had come
by. They asked for tours of the mango orchard. Sohan
Lal lost count of the number of times he was made to
pose for photographs under the tree where his daughter
was found.

One day the family counted twenty broadcasting vans.
Another day they ran out of tea to give to reporters.

The reporters asked for pictures of the girls, but how
many times could the Shakyas explain that people like
them didn't take photographs? The only photo they had

of the girls together was of them hanging in the tree. Someone had given them a copy and Sohan Lal had stuck it on the back of his door.

Then Sohan Lal remembered that Padma and Lalli had been photographed for some school forms. He asked the teacher for them back and had them copied in the bazaar.

In her photo, Padma's gleaming hair is neatly parted and smoothed away from her face. A red dupatta is draped modestly over her shoulders. She isn't smiling, but neither does she appear unhappy. It is as though when the photographer told her to stay still she responded by calming all the turmoil within. Lalli wears earrings and a necklace. Her hair is a fuzzy halo. Her eyes are big and stunned.

Sohan Lal handed out the postage-stamp-sized pictures to anyone who asked. Almost every day one tiny Padma and one tiny Lalli left the house in the palms of a stranger.

In the hamlet next door, the Yadav house was secured with a padlock. The relatives down the road were looking after their two buffaloes. Veere told reporters that if his boys were guilty of the crimes they were accused of then they *should* be punished.[1] 'But,' he said, choking up, 'if they are innocent they should be set free.' He alleged that his family had been forced out of Jati. '[The Katra villagers] didn't let us stay,' he said. 'They came with lathis.' He and his wife now lived with a friend some villages away. Their daughter-in-law and her baby lived separately. All their children were in jail.

The family's lives had been dismantled once, by the River Ganga. Now, it seemed to them, they were again without a place to call home.

Visitors to the Jail

The Budaun District Jail had been built in 1840, when the area was notorious for violent acts, particularly infanticide: the deliberate killing of newborns, almost always girls, with the consent of their parents. Even after the rate of reported deaths started to decrease, more than three decades later the district gazetteer noted, 'less care is habitually taken of girls than of boys.'[1]

In 1857, in the throes of India's First War of Independence, a treasury guard broke open the gates and released 300 convicts.[2] The jail was destroyed along with numerous other public buildings, possibly burned to the ground, which led the British to use a mausoleum to house some of the revolutionaries. After the redcoats crushed the war, they constructed a red-brick fortress where the original jail once stood.

The new jail was still very small and could only accommodate a few hundred people, a tiny number relative to the convictions being handed out to the revolutionaries, cattle thieves and grain rioters. It became necessary to erect sheds to contain the overflow. In the 2000s, the jail could still only accommodate 529 people, but somehow squeezed in three times the number.[3] Inmates were made to live barracks-style, side by side, on mattresses that were laid out in great halls. The jail regularly made the papers for stories of violent inmate attacks.

In May 2014, a teenaged inmate was found hanging from an iron ventilator grille in a toilet. He had been held on charges of kidnapping and raping a girl. Jail officials claimed that he had died by suicide, but the post-mortem – which showed at least nine injuries – concluded that the fifteen-year-old had been tortured and then strangulated. It was only when his family gathered en masse to protest – blocking the highway, disrupting traffic and attracting the attention of the media – that the police even agreed to open an investigation.[4]

It was then confirmed that the boy had been found being intimate with the girl. Her family, to protect their daughter's honour, had claimed that she had been raped. Then, to protect their honour, they had paid the jailer and some of his men to kill the boy.[5]

The Yadav brothers knew to keep to themselves, but every twist in their case made the newspapers – and the warden taunted them by reading the reports out loud for everyone to hear. Very quickly the brothers came to be known as the infamous criminals behind 'the Budaun double gang rape and murder'. This was despite the fact that it had now been established that the girls had not been raped. Agency officials, of course, also knew that Pappu's brothers weren't with him in the orchard that night.

To stay out of sight and inconspicuous, as much as was possible, Avdesh and Urvesh volunteered in the jail kitchen.

Their father came to see them, but they had never had much to say to each other. Yes, yes, Pappu was innocent, the older two nodded along as their father mumbled about the misfortune his small boy had stumbled into.

But if it weren't for him would they be here in the first place? 'I have a child,' Avdesh said. Urvesh would miss his tenth-class finals – again. The brief meeting ended on a sour note. Even when they did things right, everything went wrong. He couldn't have prevented this, protested Veere. 'As if boys tell their father anything.'

Pappu wasn't with his brothers. Veere had insisted that his youngest son was fifteen. He couldn't prove it, but the police couldn't disprove it at the time; so they kept Pappu separate, with the other juveniles. When Veere went to meet him, his son looked embarrassed to be publicly caught out over a matter of sex. 'I don't know anything,' he said. 'I am innocent.'

Elsewhere in the district jail, visits between the former head constable, Gangwar, and his wife were more conversational. She brought tiered steel containers packed with home-cooked food and listened as he complained – the entire mess involved other people's children, he said. This one's daughters, that one's sons. And what of his children, who was asking after them?

Like most Indian fathers, Gangwar was obsessed with his oldest son, the one who would carry on his name into future generations. The one who would look after him in his old age. All his children were wonderful. Even the girls, by the grace of the gods, were sharp, he always did say. But what about Manoj, he now asked his wife. Was Manoj eating well? Was Manoj sleeping?

Manoj had wanted to study business. When his father was arrested, he was in Delhi, where he was about to sit an entrance exam for a prestigious college. He had skipped it to come home to his family. Gangwar held himself responsible and made it a point to pray out loud every day, begging the gods for forgiveness and for his freedom.

His fellow inmates were impressed. 'Daddu,' they begged, 'grandfather, pray for us.' They were innocent too, they said.

Gangwar concluded that his mistake, the sole reason why he was even here, was because he had accompanied Pappu out of the village. The sight of him with the Yadav boy angered the Shakyas, he said, and they had implicated him as punishment.

'If I hadn't taken him, I wouldn't be here today,' he said.

But it wasn't chance that had placed Gangwar on the motorcycle that morning. As second in rank only to his boss, he would have been the natural choice to visit the orchard at the first opportunity. And he would have been asked along if only he hadn't been incapacitated by drink. Then, after the girls were found, he would have received a dressing-down from his superiors. He would have been transferred, just like the other officers had, but he wouldn't be called a rapist and a murderer. And he wouldn't be sitting here in jail.

Now his pension was in jeopardy, and for someone who had two wives – one of whom he had never got round to divorcing – and five children, this was something to worry about.

As it was, Gangwar couldn't afford a lawyer.

At first, he wondered if he and his former colleague, who was in the same jail, could split the cost. After all, they were in this together.

Then he learned, through the grapevine, that Sarvesh had already hired a lawyer. His man was a member of the city's wealthy new middle class. He wore western-style suits and a flashy gold chain and he drove a Japanese car with a personalised licence plate ('Mathur's'). Lawyer and client looked unnervingly alike, with the same closed fist of a face. But the lawyer was said to charge 10,000 rupees for a single appearance, and Sarvesh was a former constable who had earned 27,000 rupees a month.

When Gangwar learned of the arrangement, he sighed. He might have lied for his friend, but Sarvesh had made it clear that they weren't close. If someone asked how his former colleague could afford such expensive representation, Gangwar would tell the truth. And the other police officers would back him up.

Sarvesh, alleged Gangwar, and the CBI later confirmed, didn't keep track of the sand mafia's comings and goings for the sake of the law. And he didn't befriend the Yadav family just because they belonged to the same caste. He kept an eye on the mafia so he could demand bribes in exchange for his silence.

Sarvesh was the most corrupt police officer in the chowki, and he had used the Yadav house as a lookout.

The Case of the Missing Phones

The rains had been expected on 1 June, but they were already a fortnight behind schedule. The temperature climbed steadily. The air was as dense as wool. The rivers that irrigated land, in which people washed dishes, clothes, cattle and themselves were crusting up. In the villages, children walked long distances with their goats and buffaloes looking for water. In towns, many people turned to submersible pumps to dig water from the ground. Even expensive private schools told parents to keep children home unless they were willing to have them go to the toilet in the open. The pumps, fans, coolers and air-conditioners stretched the supply of power.

The temperature hit 48.3 degrees Celsius.

Farmers feared that a drought was inevitable.

Then came the blackouts, which set off the riots.

Thousands of enraged people stormed a power substation near Lucknow, holding workers hostage for eighteen hours before the police showed up, exhausted from settling skirmishes elsewhere. Other substations were also set on fire.[1]

A working paper released by Harvard Business School that year showed a correlation between high temperatures and low rainfall in India and the risk of violent crimes and conflict.[2] As tempers skyrocketed, a petition to the High

Court in Allahabad alleged that the only areas in Uttar Pradesh with uninterrupted power were constituencies of politicians such as Prime Minister Narendra Modi, Chief Minister Akhilesh Yadav and members of Yadav's ruling party.[3] 'Residents have been particularly angry about the power cuts after receiving reliable supplies throughout the Indian elections, which ended on 16 May,' reported a paper.[4]

When sticky winds finally started to circulate, a collective sigh of relief filled the air. Typically, the rains arrived with fanfare, tumbling in heavy grey sheets for at least two months. If the agency wanted to exhume the bodies, now was the time.

One morning, investigators came to the courtyard of the Shakya house to enquire about the whereabouts of some phones. The first was the black and gold handset, which was the phone Padma had taken with her to the fields the night she disappeared. Although it was switched on when she left the house, by the time distraught family members started to call, it had been switched off. The second handset contained the recording of the call between Lalli and Pappu. This handset belonged to Lalli's father Sohan Lal. After Lalli had used it, on the day she disappeared, she returned it to her father. Later that night, he had played the recording for numerous villagers. Several of them had told the agency about the recording, and the CBI naturally wanted to hear it for themselves.

Sohan Lal said that no such phones existed.

In fact, not only did he know where they were, he had engineered the disappearance of Padma's phone that morning in the orchard, all those days ago. The investigators already knew this from a policewoman who had been on the scene.

The idea came to Sohan Lal as he gazed up at his niece.

'Who knows what's in the phone,' he said to a relative. 'Good or bad, it's better to remove it. Whatever recordings and messages are on there should be deleted.'

The relative was Padma's oldest maternal uncle, Ram Chander, who lived in the village of Nabiganj. He and his four brothers had worked hard to maintain a relationship with their niece. In recent months their home had become a refuge for the teenager. But he understood what Sohan Lal was saying and agreed. Honour was at stake – his, hers, theirs. The elderly man slipped his hand into his niece's kameez and retrieved the phone.

Standing by, watching, was Padma's father Jeevan Lal. There were plenty of other eyewitnesses to this removal of evidence. 'The villagers said that the phone contained conversations between Pappu and Padma,' remembered one bystander.

Sohan Lal apparently wasn't familiar with GPS, or how technology embedded in the phone made its coordinates easily available. He was sure that if the phone was hidden, it could not be found. He asked Padma's uncle to take it home with him. Nabiganj village was two hours away, no one would think to look for it there.

The battery was dead, and when the phone was plugged in to charge, 'messages poured in,' Ram Chander's eighteen-year-old son, Ram Avtar later recalled. The five or six new messages all expressed concern for Padma's whereabouts. 'Padma, we're trying to reach you,' was a typical example. Ram Avtar didn't recognise the numbers offhand, but it was almost certain, given the content, that they belonged to relatives. Even so, he deleted them, just as Sohan Lal had asked. 'I wanted to protect Padma's family from scandal,' he explained.

By the next day Sohan Lal had changed his mind. The phone was better off with him, where he could keep an eye on it. He had taken Padma and Lalli's slippers from the base of the tree – to keep them safe from the crowd, he later said – and perhaps, he now told his brothers, he should have also taken the phone. He brought it home and stuck it in some cow dung piled up in a corner of the courtyard.

Investigators didn't want to confront Sohan Lal just yet, so they went to Nabiganj to meet Padma's uncles first. They threatened to arrest them if they didn't tell the truth. The horrified men cursed Sohan Lal. He had sent wolves to their door! The investigators softened their tone. The phone was a potential clue to the identity of their niece's killer. Didn't they want to know who had done it? They wanted those men behind bars, didn't they?

After the investigators left, one of the brothers phoned Sohan Lal. It was 20 June, around a week into the investigation.

'We're in trouble because of you,' Kanhaiya Lal said. 'If you don't hand over the phone to the CBI by tomorrow morning, we will cut off all relations with your family.'

In a community that was as closely bound as theirs, this was the gravest threat one could make.

Sohan Lal agreed to do as he was told, but then pushed the matter out of his mind. He had bigger worries at the moment. Some villagers were now telling the reporters who roamed Katra in search of a fresh angle that the girls' deaths may have been an honour killing. These men said 'girls shouldn't use phones' and 'good girls don't talk to boys' and that those who did brought dishonour to the village. 'If they had been my girls,' said one man in a boastful voice, 'I would have shot them dead.'

Padma's uncles in Nabiganj were aware of the pressure that Sohan Lal was under – he was famous. Everyone knew who he was. They had an opinion about what had happened to his girls. The only way he could make his case was through the media – and, they had heard, he spoke to whoever walked through the door even though he wasn't always convinced that they were who they claimed. On more than one occasion, he had asked reporters if they were working undercover for the CBI.

Still, they refused to be fobbed off.

Kanhaiya Lal phoned Lalli's father again, and this time he made it clear that the brothers were wondering if there was some other reason he was refusing to give up the phone.

'We won't stand by you if you hide the truth,' he said. 'And if you've done something wrong, be sure you will be punished.' Kanhaiya Lal wasn't talking about criminal justice. He meant that the gods would punish Sohan Lal.

The investigators also kept up the pressure. They told the brothers that the police were running a background check on Sohan Lal and some family members to see if they had a criminal record. (They didn't.)

Then one night, agency men picked up Ram Chander, the uncle who had removed the phone from Padma's kameez, and drove him to Katra village. They had concluded that the only way to get the truth was through a face-to-face confrontation. Now, they stood in the courtyard of the Shakya house as everyone watched – family members, friends and neighbours.

'He made me do it,' Ram Chander said.

'Nahin ji,' Sohan Lal shot back. 'Jhoot.' No sir, all lies.

'You made me return it the next day!'

'Theek hai, maybe it's somewhere in the house.'

It was the middle of the night. He brought his hands together and swore to personally scour the house in the morning, but the investigators refused to be put off again. The phone was evidence of something that Sohan Lal wanted to keep hidden. Shukla, the investigating officer, believed that given the opportunity, Lalli's father would destroy it. He instructed his team to search the house. They looked and looked, but when they passed the pile of cow dung, they crinkled their noses and quickly sidestepped.

The Truth About the Phone

Sohan Lal stuck his hand into the cow dung. He pulled out the phone that Padma was carrying with her at the time of her death. He wiped it clean, and then struck it on the ground repeatedly to disgorge its contents. He broke the battery, the keypad and steel frame. The manufacturer's label peeled off. All the many pieces now fitted into the palms of his hands. He slipped them into a polythene bag and quietly knotted it.

The handset was in 'flakes', said a report from the Forensic Science Laboratory in the western state of Gujarat. Sohan Lal had also handed over his phone, the one with the recording between Lalli and Pappu. This phone was physically intact but missing the original memory card, without which it was impossible to hear the recorded call.

Although he admitted to tampering with the phones, Sohan Lal at first refused to say why. He did say that the phone he had newly bought was always meant for Padma. 'She asked me to,' he said. 'She could read and write a little, and most of the calls that came were for her anyway.'

This was not a satisfactory explanation, as far as Shukla was concerned. Girls in the village used phones, but they did not own them. And Sohan Lal was hardly progressive. If his niece was getting calls, he would have been annoyed.

Now, as before, members of Sohan Lal's own family came forward to contradict him, perhaps concerned that his stubbornness was hurting the investigation. One of them was Sohan Lal's eldest son, Virender, who told investigators that his father had 'smashed the phone' because he was angry that it had been used to 'contact the girls and meet them'.

Shukla believed that Sohan Lal had bought the phone to spy on Padma, possibly intending to confront her. He had destroyed it to get rid of any evidence that linked her to Pappu, therefore putting an end to the matter. When he had called for an investigation by the CBI, this was not one of the things he had imagined would come to light.

Looking for confirmation about his theory, Shukla then sent some men to Keshav Communications. On 26 June, Keshav presented them with a bill of sale in the name of a fifty-one-year-old woman named Vidyawati. The investigators were taken aback. Who was this?

Keshav looked embarrassed. He had copied some details from another customer's identity card, he said, but only to help Sohan Lal. The old man wasn't carrying ID. Keshav had assumed he didn't have any. That wasn't true, the officers told him. Sohan Lal had a voting card that he got three years ago.

Keshav shrugged. In his experience, most people didn't break the law because they were criminals; they broke the law because they thought they could get away with it, just as he had thought that he could.

No lies now, investigators said. What kind of phone was it?

Sohan Lal had asked to see phones with a good battery life, Keshav replied. There was nothing unusual about the request. It wasn't like the village had many power sockets.

What else?

Keshav swallowed hard. He had never interacted with a police officer before. And these investigators scrutinised him in disbelieving silence. It was clear they thought him the lying sort. Keshav didn't want more trouble. Once again, he thought about his dead father, his widowed mother, the uncle to whom he was in debt and so on, until his forehead burned. He started talking very fast. 'I was half-minded,' he later recalled, terrified that the CBI would arrest him for fraud.

Keshav talked so much that he lost track of what he was saying. At one point, he felt his mouth moving but couldn't hear the words coming out. But of everything he said there was just one thing that really interested the CBI.

'Sohan Lal wanted a phone that could record calls at length.'

'She Is All I Have'

Ram Sakhi was only a teenager when she was dispatched to marry. She was eighteen, maybe nineteen – a bit on the older side – but the match was a good one even though she didn't know it, having never seen her future husband's face.

What his name was even, it didn't matter, because she wouldn't call him anything but the father of her children.

The groom, Jeevan Lal, owned some land and a house. He didn't drink. He had no debt, and no known history of criminal activity. He was stringy but healthy, with high cheekbones, a neatly pruned moustache and protruding ears. He was soft-spoken and seemed gentle in his ways, which made him stand out in these parts where machismo was a necessary show of strength and belonging.

Over time, the differences between their families started to emerge. Ram Sakhi was illiterate, but her brothers could write their names in two languages, Hindi and English. Jeevan Lal identified himself with a thumbprint. As the years accumulated, Ram Sakhi's brothers travelled. One went to Punjab, to work on a farm, another made a living on construction sites in Haryana. Jeevan Lal stayed home. New experiences meant new ways, and the brothers built a toilet in their house. But even when her belly was as full as a sack of watermelons, they bitterly recalled, their sister had to roam the fields for a place to squat.

Ram Sakhi had a daughter, Padma, who was dearly loved – but girls were a prelude to better things. The second child would be a boy, everyone said, and if not, then the third. But the couple never made it that far, for just as Ram Sakhi was about to give birth a second time she fell ill. As his wife lay confined to her bed in a village without doctors, and with neither cars nor phones, Jeevan Lal worriedly cracked his knuckles. When the baby was ready to be born, he rushed his wife to hospital, where she died. He didn't know how – he couldn't understand the doctors, he said.

The baby died too.

He had been a longed-for boy, and the loss struck Jeevan Lal like a physical blow to his heart. His mother moved in to cook for him and two-year-old Padma. Jeevan Lal went mechanically back and forth from the fields. His family was certain he would never again smile.

Ram Sakhi's brothers had always got along with Jeevan Lal, but the death of their sister created a predictable distance, they said. 'We wanted a relationship with our niece,' Kanhaiya Lal, the youngest brother, recalled. 'But the relationship with the others felt like it was over.'

Although they continued to refer to Jeevan Lal as their bahnoi, brother-in-law, they didn't like visiting him any more.

He was still in his twenties, and he married again. His new wife was well suited to him. She said very little; in part because she was traditionally bound to keep her face concealed and with it her opinions too. The silences were comfortable. They got along, the rest of the family observed with a sigh of relief.

As the youngest of the daughters-in-law, Sunita Devi occupied the low end of the totem pole, bringing up the rear after the men, her mother-in-law and the older daughters-in-law. She was above the children, but as the boys grew, their gender would propel them higher up the family hierarchy and their wishes would supersede hers. She was aware of her place. She huddled and bent as she tended to the fire, the buffaloes, the pots and pans. If she wanted something from the others, she whispered in her husband's ear, and he advocated on her behalf.

It was soon clear that theirs was a partnership, as much as was possible given the circumstances. Perhaps grateful for this second chance at life, Jeevan Lal took his new wife's side in all matters.

Ram Sakhi's brothers worried that their niece would be neglected in favour of the new wife's biological children. They asked if Padma could stay with them. Jeevan Lal, understandably, refused. 'She is my reason for living,' he said.

Over the years the brothers heard rumours. Padma called her stepmother 'mummy', but Sunita Devi wasn't bringing her up. The entirety of the task still fell to Padma's grandmother. Sunita Devi didn't even cook for the child. Jeevan Lal was forced to come out and explain. 'My mother and daughter eat food such as fish,' he said. 'But my wife is a pure vegetarian.' By touching fish she could pollute herself.

The household was also affected by a more private turmoil. Jeevan Lal and Sunita Devi were trying for children, but Sunita Devi repeatedly suffered miscarriages. The village doctors didn't have medical degrees and were jokingly referred to by those who spoke some English as 'temporary' – meaning they would have to do for now – but Sunita Devi went to them anyway. She also went to herbalists, whose concoctions sometimes killed patients. And to actual doctors, in Budaun and beyond. She took anything anyone would give her. Her aching heart, her tired body, the eyes of everyone on her – now she barely spoke at all.

The uncles then enrolled Padma in a school in their village, hoping to convince her father to give her up. But although she attended some classes, Jeevan Lal soon came back for her. A friend she made at the time later recalled that while Padma spoke fondly of her grandmother, she never mentioned having a stepmother.

When Padma completed class eight in 2013, her father said she should stay home from now on. There was no secondary school in the village. This was true, but because it was also true that some families sent their girls to schools outside the village, her uncles concluded that Jeevan Lal wanted to marry Padma off.

They again approached him. 'We told him to wait,' one said. 'Let her study, let her grow up.' There were half a dozen school-going children in their family. Their niece would be happy if she lived with them. The brothers would send her to secondary school and pay for it besides. Jeevan Lal again refused.

'We are not in a position,' he said firmly.

Jeevan Lal would later say that it was his reluctance to educate his daughter further that had caused tension in the family. But Padma had told cousin Manju that she didn't enjoy school. The teachers at Saraswati Gyan Mandir practised the usual rote method with emphasis on repetition rather than learning. Corporal punishment was standard. Padma wasn't always attentive, and her attitude was reflected in her results. Her eighth-class English teacher called her a 'medium' girl. She wasn't his best, and she wasn't the worst.

By the spring of 2014, relations between Padma and her stepmother, and consequently her father too, had become worse. When she came to visit her uncles in March it was without a leaving date. The latest fight, they heard, was a 'roti paani' argument with Sunita Devi over how long Padma had taken to serve a meal. These fights, over seemingly trivial things, had by now become so routine that the brothers didn't pay them much heed. Anyway, they didn't even know what to believe.

When she was with them, there was nothing Padma wouldn't do. She was so conscientious that when a cousin fell ill, it was the teenager – of everyone present – who took it upon herself to look after the sick girl. As much as she scrubbed dishes, she also enjoyed a game of Ludo with the other children. She embroidered quietly when the adults talked. The last thing she had made them was a parrot with a chunky green belly and a furry red beak. After dinner, when members of the thirty-strong joint family competed against one another in singing games, Padma was the most enthusiastic performer of all. In their midst, she radiated joy.

A perfect guest. A lovely child. A good girl.

A fortnight passed.

Holi, a joyful festival that was celebrated with family, came and went.

Then an exasperated Jeevan Lal showed up on the back of a motorcycle to retrieve his daughter.

The brothers were unclear about the nature of Padma's alleged infractions, but it was a father's right, they felt, to discipline her. On the other hand, it was apparent that the environment in Katra was toxic.

Again, they asked to keep her. Again, Jeevan Lal refused. 'She is all I have,' he said.

'There Is No Need to Go Here and There'

In Katra, there were more fights. The reason, ostensibly, was the friendship between Padma and Lalli. 'You roam around together all day,' Jeevan Lal scolded. 'Why don't you focus on your responsibilities?'

'I don't want you going to other people's houses,' he said another time. 'Be it my brother's or anyone else's. Stay at home. There is no need to go here and there.'

The tensions took some villagers aback. It was normal practice to encourage girls to develop friendships within the family. That way they wouldn't seek out others for company. And Padma and Lalli were first cousins who lived next door to each other. It was their parents who had made them graze their animals together. The fact that Padma's parents were expressing agitation – whereas Lalli's weren't, as yet – didn't surprise anyone. Padma was older. She had arrived at that place of no return, marriageable age. The rumours then escalated, and Sunita Devi was forced to defend herself. 'When I saw Padma doing something wrong, or when she left the house without permission, then yes, I would scold her,' she said.

'She didn't love Padma,' observed a family friend. 'That's why Padma mostly stayed away.'

Their last fight took place in May, a fortnight before the girls went missing. 'You don't work,' Jeevan Lal had shouted.

He'd had enough. His daughter was no longer to sit with her cousin or to set foot outside with her. A distraught Padma threw some clothes into a bag and ran into the bazaar, intending to find a ride to her uncles'. Her grandmother hobbled after her. They sat by the roadside. In the village, this was a spectacle.

A woman named Vishaka, who happened to be idling outside her house, was struck by the expression on the wisp of a girl. 'She looked so sad,' she said. No cars were headed in their direction. Vishaka grew concerned. What would people say?

'Come inside,' she begged.

'They've made my life hell,' Padma wept. Her father called her names. Her stepmother accused her of all kinds of things.

Vishaka's husband walked in with hay for the buffaloes. He insisted on calling Jeevan Lal right away. 'Your daughter wants to go to her uncle's house, by herself. Should I stop her or let her go?'

'Don't let her go!' Jeevan Lal exclaimed. He was in the fields. 'I'll be right there.'

At first Jeevan Lal blamed his mother. 'She carries tales and gets the women fighting among each other.' But to the couple standing before him it was obvious that the old lady wasn't to blame.

He had told his daughter to stop going to his brother's house, Jeevan Lal said, but she wouldn't listen. 'This girl roams around all day. What can I do but scold her?'

Another villager now walked in to pick up some boxes of country liquor, which he stored in the house for a small fee. Padma hasn't eaten in several days, the man heard her grandmother say. She used the words 'illicit relations' to describe the accusations that Padma's stepmother had levelled against the teenager. The villager was alarmed. In Katra, there was no polite way to describe unmarried girls who were sexually active.

With the arrival of the newcomer, it was virtually ensured that the matter would become public. He would tell his boss at the liquor shop, and their customers too. A matter of sex was always a scandal.

Vishaka and her husband would talk as well, bringing it up in phone calls to their daughters who were married in villages far away, and certainly while talking to their sons over dinner later that evening.

And so the news would circulate. It would serve as an indictment of Jeevan Lal's parenting skills and Sunita Devi's failure to avoid becoming the stereotypical cruel stepmother. Everyone would wonder how things had been allowed to come to this. They had *one* child!

Girls had to be kept in control, for their sake, for the sake of society, people would say. After all, one bad fish can dirty the whole pond. What was happening in the Shakya household wouldn't just be judged a failure of parenting, but of citizenship.

The newcomer grew angry. 'If you can't control her,' he shouted, 'marry her off.'

The squabbles between parents and child dragged on. They soured the days, throwing up new challenges at an already taxing time. Jeevan Lal's eighteen-year-old niece was to be married soon, and the groom's list of dowry demands included pots and pans, a cupboard and a cycle. Then there were the saris, sandals and face powder that the bride must take with her so that her in-laws couldn't

accuse her of being a burden from the get-go. As many
as a hundred people were invited to attend. Six large cars
would ferry them back and forth. The expense was sure to
be enormous, and all the Shakya brothers were expected
to contribute.

There was no question of taking on the burden of
another wedding. But it was clear to Jeevan Lal that his
child could no longer sit at home.

The best place to look for a groom was a wedding. A few
days later, at a wedding in another village, Jeevan Lal
scoured the crowd of invitees for a potential son-in-law.
He visited two more villages but didn't care for any of the
boys he was introduced to. They met the basic criteria –
they were Hindu and they belonged to the same caste,
and the same sub-caste, which meant that they did the
same kind of work as the Shakya men and ate the same
kind of food as the Shakya women cooked, celebrated
the same festivals, and shared the same social values and
judgements, all of which would minimise the risks that
were already sewn into an agreement that was expected
to last a lifetime even though it was between complete
strangers.

But like any father, Jeevan Lal wanted more for his
child, his only daughter, the one who carried the imprint
of the woman he had loved. He wanted a good boy.

Two days after he went looking, his daughter was dead.

'Did You Kill Padma and Lalli?'

With the major Shakya family interventions finally laid bare, the investigation now picked up pace. Then, in mid-June, the CBI team took a call that was rather strange.

They sent the five suspects for a polygraph, a lie detector test which remains so controversial that any statements that emerge from it are not admissible as evidence at the trial stage – this is true as much for India as it is in many parts of the world.

Dr Asha Srivastava was an experienced forensic scientist who had worked at the agency's Central Forensic Science Laboratory in Delhi for more than two decades. She ran the Forensic Psychology Division and was responsible for conducting polygraph tests, voice analysis and psychological assessments.

The previous year, in 2013, she was invited by the Mumbai police to examine the suspects in India's latest high-profile rape case.[1] The Shakti Mills gang rape, as it came to be known, took place in August, eight months after the Delhi bus rape. The victim was a twenty-two-year-old photojournalist with a city magazine. She was with a colleague, looking to take photographs for an essay on abandoned buildings.

Although Shakti Mills, a former cotton mill, was derelict, it was located in downtown Mumbai, in an area that was thronging with office workers. Around an hour before sunset, two men approached the journalists and offered to show them around. They left them alone to take photographs, but then returned with a third man, who said, 'Our boss has seen you, and you have to come with us now.' Later, he thrust a broken beer bottle at the woman. 'You don't know what a bastard I am,' he said. 'You're not the first girl I've raped.'[2]

Mumbai had a certain reputation for women's safety, relative to the rest of India, and the headline case shocked people. The police, acting swiftly, arrested all five suspects within days. They lived in slums near the mill. One culprit's mother later told a paper, 'Obviously, the fault is the girl's. Why did she have to go to that jungle? It's her fault, too. Also, she was wearing skimpy clothes.'[3]

Srivastava's job was to talk to the men involved in the Shakti Mills gang rape to understand their motives, to predict their risk of future violence, and to share this information with the court in order to help with sentencing. After spending time with them, she became convinced that this wasn't the first time they had raped someone. They had carefully selected the mill for its location, she said, as a place to easily ambush women, and once they achieved success, they repeated the strategy over and over. 'Brain-wise they were very sharp,' she concluded.

When an eighteen-year-old telephone operator came forward to accuse three of the men of having raped her in the same location, Srivastava's observations were shown to be correct. The men had also raped a scavenger, a sex worker and a transvestite. In all, the police later concluded, they had raped at least ten people in a span of five or six months.[4] The rapists had referred to their victims as 'prey' and recorded the crimes on their phones to blackmail them into silence.

One of the culprits told the police that after the first two rapes weren't reported, they had been 'emboldened' to commit more.[5] 'They often lurked in the mills in the evenings and laid traps for unsuspecting women,' said an officer.[6]

In early 2014, the court declared all five men guilty. The new rape laws punished repeat offenders with the death sentence, and three of the five men received this sentence.

Srivastava was catching up with her backlog of cases when she was asked to join the investigation in Katra. The CBI wanted her to run polygraph tests on the five suspects, as well as to offer her assessment on their states of mind.

On 24 June, she sat down alongside an associate to explain the process to Pappu Yadav. Two expandable tubes would be attached to his chest and abdomen, she said, to record perspiration. A blood pressure monitor would note his systolic and diastolic blood pressure and pulse rate, and electrodes, on his ring finger and forefinger, would measure his response to a questionnaire that had been formulated by the investigating officer. Pappu could only answer yes or no and he would have twenty-five seconds to recover between questions. Further tests would take the form of a more flexible question and answer session.

'Did Padma call you on the day of the incident?'

'Yes,' Pappu replied.

'Is it true that on the day of the incident you got into a shoving match with Nazru?'

'Yes.'

'Is it true that after this shoving match with Nazru you ran away from the spot?'

'Yes.'

'On the day of the incident did Nazru take the girls away?'

'Yes.'

'Did you kill Padma and Lalli?'

'No.'

Pappu maintained good eye contact, Srivastava said. Having examined his responses to the lie detector test, she concluded that he was telling the truth.

She was wrong. At least one of these answers, as Pappu himself would later admit, was a lie.

When his eldest brother Avdesh was tested, the question of whether he'd participated in the alleged rape and murder of the teenagers was put to him in several ways. Did he assist his brother in kidnapping Padma and Lalli, raping them and hanging them? Did he help the police kill them? Did he know who killed them? Did he rape them? Did he kill them?

No, Avdesh said. No, no, no.

He was being truthful, Srivastava concluded. And he was open and relaxed, until he was asked about his 'brother's activities'.

'Whenever his brother Pappu's name comes, he breaks eye contact in frustration stating that because of him, they all are suffering.'

The other men also acquitted themselves in Srivastava's eyes. They claimed their innocence and she found them to be truthful. Just one answer, by former Constable Sarvesh, resisted interpretation.

The question was straightforward.

'Do you know who killed Padma and Lalli?'

He had answered no, Srivastava later recalled, but she had found it hard to say whether he was telling the truth.

'Perhaps he was nervous,' she shrugged.

'Machines Don't Lie'

Scientific and legal organisations have disputed the reliability of the polygraph machine since it was invented in Berkeley, California in 1921.

Among specialists, there's almost unanimous agreement that it is at best a stress test. The test catches symptoms of fear – an increase in heart rate, blood pressure, sweating and breathing – and interprets these as indicative of deception. It was entirely possible for an innocent person to react negatively to being interrogated, and for a practised liar to do well under scrutiny. 'Polygraph tests can be easily beaten,' one expert told the BBC in 2013. 'You don't have to be a trained spy or a sociopath. You just have to understand how to recognise the control questions and augment reactions to them with techniques such as biting the side of your tongue.'[1]

Srivastava disagreed. 'Machines don't lie,' she said, echoing a common phrase in the CBI. 'Human physiology is the same, hardened criminal or not. It's very difficult to manipulate a polygraph test. As long as an expert conducts the test, 100 per cent results will come. The results will be 100 per cent accurate.'

But although India's foremost investigative agency believed that lie detector tests were reliable – 100 per cent of the time – they only used the results when it suited them.

In the Aarushi case, the tests had established that the teenager's parents were telling the truth when they denied having anything to do with her murder. The CBI nevertheless – wrongly, as it turned out – pursued the theory that they were guilty.

The agency, clarified a former top CBI officer, actually used the test for 'direction'. 'If someone is wobbling, if his heart rate goes up when I ask difficult questions, then he becomes a suspect,' he said. 'But this by itself doesn't condemn him as the accused. I have to find additional evidence.'

In fact, lie detector tests served another purpose for the agency, and this became clear when the results of the polygraphs were leaked to the media.

As far as most people were concerned, certainly outside the village, the case was open and shut. The Yadav brothers had raped and then killed the girls with the collusion of the police. All the CBI had to do, these people said, was file a chargesheet listing the charges against the suspects and the laws they had breached – then the case could go to trial. But the CBI knew that the facts so far didn't back this popular theory. And the way they saw it, they were faced with not just one obvious challenge, which was to learn what had happened, but a second, more delicate one.

If they became convinced that Pappu Yadav was innocent, they would then have to find a way to convince the media and the public. This wasn't part of their job, but it would make it easier to get on with things. While many people admired the agency, there were others who publicly disparaged them for making mistakes or allowing themselves to be manipulated by politicians. The word 'botched' was so often repeated on cable news channels in relation to agency news stories that even investigators who didn't speak fluent English were familiar with it.

The CBI could show that the post-mortem was riddled with errors, as was so often the case. That the girls had not been raped, as Dr Tripathi had by now concluded. And that Dr Gupta, who had led the post-mortem, said that they had died by their own hands.

They could also show that Nazru had repeatedly lied about what he had seen. Although they believed that he had come across Pappu in the fields with the girls, as far as what happened next, it was his word against Pappu's. Furthermore, Nazru had not then seen the two policemen in the fields who now stood accused of rape and murder, or for that matter Pappu's brothers, and neither had anyone else. These people were being accused of crimes of extreme violence, but the evidence pointed to nothing more than a meeting between a teenaged boy and two teenaged girls who had sought privacy.

Would it make a difference?

The theory of what had happened to Padma and Lalli had been repeated over and over for weeks now. It was everywhere one looked, on TV, online and in newspapers, in many languages. The theory was so well established that it would be virtually impossible to dislodge. By leaking the lie detector test results, the CBI hoped to plant the idea of Pappu's innocence as a tiny seed in the public imagination – whether or not they believed the science behind it was immaterial.

'Have You Ever Been in Love?'

'Have you ever been to Bombay?' Srivastava, the forensic scientist, asked Lalli's father.

It was 7 July; two weeks after the five suspects had taken lie detector tests. Sohan Lal had undergone the same preliminaries as they had but he didn't completely grasp what was happening.

The doctor-lady attached medical equipment to him, he later said, of the sort they used to diagnose a fever. (He was possibly comparing the pneumograph, which measures breathing patterns, to a stethoscope.) She ordered him to breathe in and out. And then she asked him odd questions and insisted on only yes or no answers.

Why was he asked whether he'd been to Bombay? What did that have to do with the death of his child?

'No sir,' he replied, not sure what to call Srivastava.

When she said to him, 'Have you ever been in love?' Sohan Lal gave up. He worked hard to keep a roof over his family's head. He kept his wife and children fed and clothed, he paid for school and for weddings. Honour and duty alone were the guiding lights of his life.

'No sir,' he replied, truthfully.

The first set of questions related to the case were ones to which the agency already knew the answers.

'Is it true, on being requested by the CBI to hand over the phone Padma used, that you instead broke it into small pieces?'

'Yes.'

Did you destroy the phone's SIM card?

'Yes.'

'Is it true that the girls were killed over a land dispute?'

'No.'

So far, so clear. Then the polygraph recorded a lie.

The question Sohan Lal was asked was whether he was far away when he heard the news of the girls going missing.

'Yes,' he said.

And he was, as witnesses and call records would later show.

The test had recorded this falsely as a lie.

After the polygraph ended, the psychological assessment began. Sohan Lal was asked a question about Padma's phone and encouraged to respond in his own words. He admitted to having broken it. The 'details in the phone … might have hurt the honour of the family,' he said. 'Girls are honour of family.'

The voice recording of his daughter Lalli speaking to Pappu established that the teenagers knew each other, Srivastava said. 'If the girls were alive, what step would you have taken for the honour of the family?'

'We would have killed them,' he replied.

Nazru came in that same day. The outcome of his various tests was a predictable disaster.

During his behavioural test, Nazru claimed that while he was able to recognise Pappu, he couldn't tell who the others were. Pressed for details, he started 'swallowing and had dry lips, asked for water'. 'He was pretending to be emotional,' Srivastava noted, 'but timing and duration of emotional gestures and emotions are off ... The display of emotion is delayed, stays for a few seconds and then stops suddenly.'

Again, he changed his story. Asked whether he saw Pappu taking the girls away, he said no, he had not.

Nazru made quite the impression. Five years, and dozens of cases later, it was him Srivastava remembered most clearly of all the people she had studied during that time. He was literally shivering as he sat before her, she recalled. He refused to make eye contact. He wasn't scared, she said, he was being manipulative.

After he admitted to having been paid off by the Shakyas, he became so distraught that he started shouting.

Srivastava remembered his words.

'I will return the money! I will return the money!'

Then he attempted to make a run for it.

DROWNED

The sky cracked open, soaking the thirsty earth and reviving everything to joyful life. As village children leapt into the flowing rivers for a celebratory swim, the regional Met director spoke of heavy to moderate rainfall but warned of 'full force' starting 11 July. The medical board from the All India Institute of Medical Sciences in New Delhi scheduled the exhumation of the bodies for 20 July – nearly eight weeks after the children were first found.

The doctors from Delhi asked for around-the-clock personal security while they were in Uttar Pradesh. An agency description of the shambolic state of the post-mortem house had rightly put them off, but rather than suggest an alternative, such as a hospital room, they wanted to conduct the exam on the banks of the river. They asked for an enclosure to be set up with a table, plastic sheets, masks, gowns, gloves and gumboots. They also asked for an assistant, specifically Lala Ram: 'The sweeper of Budaun Mortuary who has helped the doctors in conducting post-mortem should be available, along with all the tools for opening all the cavities of the bodies, including head.'

The CBI had rubbished Lala Ram's work on the post-mortem. He had used a 'butcher's knife' they said, in a report. The knife, which Lala Ram had purchased from an ordinary shop in the bazaar, was indeed a kitchen knife for chopping meat. That the doctors still picked him and his tools suggested that what was standard procedure in a backward place like Budaun, was also standard procedure in Delhi.

Now, Lala Ram gathered an apron and a fresh pair of gloves and prepared to leave his staff quarters in the early hours of 20 July, a Sunday. He had been ordered to arrive before sunrise to avoid alerting the media.

On Saturday, the promised heavy rainfall commenced its lashing. The power clapped out and people rooted for torches, candles and lamp oil. The streets soon turned into roiling swamps.

A cluster of police officers stationed on the banks of the river, where the bodies were buried, informed their superiors that the water level was rising rapidly. It was already a foot above the graves. By the time television crews arrived, the graves were no longer even accessible by foot. A man who ventured in was submerged waist-deep.

When agency SUVs rolled in with the doctors from Delhi, all they could do was watch the drama from high up the river's bank. The Shakya brothers stood nearby. 'I went to the CBI with folded hands,' Sohan Lal later recalled. 'I said, "Please take out the bodies quickly." ' He couldn't believe that investigators had taken on the Ganga, the mightiest and holiest river in India, with the expectation that they would win.

The agency then requested help from the state government's flood department to start pumping out the water around the graves. As they awaited a response they rounded up fifty villagers, put them in a boat and dispatched them to find the graves. They chucked in sandbags to help keep some of the water out. Outlandish talk started to circulate: Bring in divers! Construct a bridge!

At 7 p.m., the graves were sunken, eight feet deep. Then the pumps ran out of diesel. There were obviously no divers, so five good swimmers stripped down to their underwear and hurled themselves into the swirling, mud-brown foam.

'Was this a game?' Sohan Lal thought.

A police officer instructed his men to stick a crimson-coloured flag in one of the sandbags, to be safe. Otherwise, when the water receded, they would be unable to tell the graves of the girls from the hundreds of others located up and down the riverbank.

Asked when he thought the examination might happen, the head of the medical board, Dr Adarsh Kumar, in his crisp, collared shirt, responded casually. 'Maybe in the month of September or so.' Four months after the girls had died.[1]

As Shukla, the investigating officer, glumly scanned the disaster zone, reporters in hearing distance placed the blame squarely on his team. 'Budaun Botch-Up,' they declared, using that favourite word again. The CBI was 'publicly shamed' for its 'lazy attitude' in arranging the exhumation.[2] 'DROWNED!' blared a news channel.[3] The flooding had 'possibly [ended] all chances of a fair investigation'.

In fact, it wasn't the agency that was to blame, but the medical board they had put in place. Correspondence between the two showed that the medical board was set up on 23 June. The team convened for the first time four days later but broke up without agreeing on when to visit the graves. That was left for their next meeting, which they scheduled for more than three weeks later, to accommodate vacation plans.

Then one of the board members backed out and a replacement had to be found.

In July, Shukla faxed the doctors, urging them to make up their minds. 'Field reports as well as media reports indicate that due to increased water level in the River Ganga, the place where the bodies of the two victims have been buried may get submerged very soon.' He asked the doctors to hold an 'emergency meeting' to pick a date. They had settled on 20 July.

There was no question of retrieving the bodies now, which meant there would be no second post-mortem.

The only option that was left, the agency concluded, was for the doctors to watch the original post-mortem videos. This was also how Dr Ghyasuddin Khan at the Forensic Science Laboratory in Lucknow had given his opinion on how Padma and Lalli had died. He had determined that they were smothered and his conclusion – which differed from the post-mortem results – was one reason why the exhumation was considered necessary in the first place.

For context, the medical board was taken to Katra. The air was crisp, the smell was wet goats. The doctors picked their way cautiously through the fields where they were shown the tree on which the girls were found. Watching from a distance, their feet planted in the sodden earth, the Shakya villagers shook their head in amazement. In the monsoons, Gangaji's waters swelled to such a height that she could be seen from every terrace in the village. You would think that the city folk would have come better prepared.

The CBI officers then took the medical board to the post-mortem house, presumably so they could understand the agency's doubts over the exam results. They were given photographs, transcripts and all the forensic and medical reports that had come in so far.

Even once the board had everything they needed, they still couldn't make time to meet. One meeting was cancelled because a team member was called away on an urgent assignment. Another was postponed for mysterious reasons, or it 'could not be materialised' – to use the board's language.

'Pl. keep following up,' a desperate Shukla wrote to his deputies, delegating the onerous task of prodding the doctors. He reminded them that the agency had ninety days to file a chargesheet against the suspects.

If the CBI didn't file a chargesheet within this time, the five men would be entitled to bail.

Results and Rumours

DNA analysis could take months, given the backlog that laboratories struggled under, but after a non-profit filed a public interest litigation, the High Court in Allahabad, which had jurisdiction over the whole state, started to monitor Shukla's investigation. They asked for regular updates – and the investigating officer felt pressure to show results.

He fired off letters to the Centre for DNA Fingerprinting and Diagnostics (CDFD) in Hyderabad, in Telengana state, describing the case as one of national importance. He urged the scientists to prioritise his requests. 'The case involves sensitive issues which need to be investigated without any delay,' he wrote in June. 'It is therefore requested that the aforesaid exhibits may be processed on an urgent basis and a report provided to this office at the earliest.'

A few days later he asked that the scientists preserve the 'dust/soil' on the girls' clothes. The post-mortem doctors had failed to note the condition of the salwar kameezes Padma and Lalli were wearing, and Shukla wanted to avoid the repetition of seemingly small, but potentially consequential mistakes. In another letter he reminded the CDFD, 'The report is still awaited.'

The items for analysis included the girls' underwear, kameezes, salwars and dupattas, as well as rings, hairbands and nose pins.

Some of these items did not yield DNA suitable for analysis. This was hardly surprising, given how the bodies had been treated. It's very likely that they were contaminated at collection or en route to testing. It could also mean that the sample size was small. Other objects, however, did yield DNA profiles that could be compared with the genetic material extracted from the five suspects.

The list of items collected from the suspects, on the other hand, was dismayingly incomplete. A bundle of Pappu's clothes contained a white shirt with a red spot and his underwear 'with somewhat white spots'. But where were the trousers he'd slipped on to accompany the police to the chowki in the early hours of 28 May? It was very likely the same pair he had worn for his meeting with the girls. And he almost certainly wore footwear when he went out at night to a field that was usually infested with snakes.

His eldest brother, Avdesh, was undoubtedly wearing more than just underwear and a shirt.

It was the state police that had collected samples from the suspects. They took blood, nail and hair samples as well as penile swabs from each of the Yadav brothers. They only took blood samples from the two police suspects – they would probably argue that since all cells in the body contain the same DNA this really didn't matter. Even so, it's difficult to understand why they didn't submit every item of clothing that the five men had worn on the night of 27 May and the morning of 28 May.

The DNA results from the clothing, samples and swabs of the five suspects showed no female DNA. Then, rather miraculously, given how Lala Ram had handled the girls' bodies, the vaginal slides he had taken of the girls showed two separate sets of female DNA. The DNA from Padma's slide corresponded with the DNA extracted from her dupatta. Lalli's DNA found a match on her salwar. There was no male DNA present in any of the tested samples that belonged to the girls.

The post-mortem doctors had told the agency that their original assessment about the girls having been raped was wrong. The DNA evidence now supported this fact.

'Big news!'

'A twist!'

'A U-turn!'

'The latest forensic tests do not establish the presence of the five accused at the scene of crime, and in fact the needle of suspicion at this point is towards the victims' family. The family, of course, unhappy with this says they will go back to the same tree and hang themselves to death if justice is not served.'[1]

Just as agency investigators had suspected, this latest breaking news drew an incredulous reaction. The idea that the girls were raped didn't need to be proved. This, on the other hand, was unbelievable to many people who had followed the case on the news. It was also unacceptable to the girls' family members. 'Pappu admitted to being with the girls,' Sohan Lal told a reporter.

He wondered if the CBI had sent someone else's clothes for DNA testing. 'They could have been anybody's. I have no proof that they were my daughter and her cousin's clothes.'[2] The strand of hair and the stained leaves from the orchard hadn't revealed any useful information either, which Sohan Lal also found odd.

It was difficult to know how much Lalli's father believed what he said. Did he believe the girls were raped, despite what the evidence showed? And if so, did he want the five men punished for it, or did he want *someone* punished for the fact that his children were dead? And did these five men most closely fit the profile of the sort of goondas, thugs, who would do such a thing? His own actions provided a clue.

The morning that Padma and Lalli were found, Nazru had confided in his friend: 'Sohan and Jeevan tell me to say one thing, then they say another. First they told me to say that the Yadav brothers kidnapped the girls, then they said it was their father and Constable Sarvesh who did it. They're just saying and doing anything, and I don't know who to listen to any more. I'm going mad!'

And that same day Sohan Lal told a friend of his, 'Nazru saw three or four men. He couldn't identify them, so why not just say they were the Yadav brothers? They probably were.'

And anyone looking to side with him agreed.

Lalli's father was well established with television viewers as a sympathetic and believable figure. When he said, 'I'll fight for justice until my last breath' – and then went further still, saying, 'I'm willing to lay down my life' – he was every Indian who had struggled with every fibre of his being to be treated justly. Even scientific fact couldn't dislodge what people *felt*, seemingly in their bones. And it was easy to point to earlier acts of grave malfeasance – by police officers, even the prime minister[3] – to show that in India anything was possible, and nothing was what it seemed.

'If the CBI was from outside the state,' Sohan Lal said, getting confused, 'the investigation would have had integrity. They were under pressure from the state government.'

This wasn't true. The investigating officer, his supervisor, and almost the entire team *was* from out of state. If the agency's independence was ever compromised in the past, it wasn't from proximity to state governments, who had no control over them, but, as the Supreme Court had declared in 2013,[4] by coercion from the centre.

Shukla, the investigating officer, may have known how things went. He had earlier worked a case in which border security forces were accused of shooting dead more than fifty-five people and burning down hundreds of houses and shops as collective punishment for the murder of one of their men by a separatist terror outfit. Senior Indian officials had admitted to the rampage, calling it 'shameful'[5] but Shukla had closed the case without making any arrests.

The killings had taken place in the northern region of Jammu and Kashmir, home to a long-running independence movement that had resulted in the deaths of more than 70,000 people since the 1980s. The army, which was permanently posted there, was in constant conflict with civilians. Two highly controversial laws gave soldiers the unchecked power to arrest, shoot and even kill civilians without facing disciplinary action. Investigators of the CBI were repeatedly unsuccessful in taking army officers to court.

This particular crime took place in the 1990s, when violence was at its peak, and the forces – perhaps with the support of the central government – appear to have used the pretext of a court martial to get the CBI to close the case without making any arrests.

The deaths in Katra were an entirely different matter. Chief Minister Akhilesh Yadav had no influence over the CBI. The prime minister may have, but Narendra Modi had no reason to protect Yadavs. His antagonism towards Akhilesh, who belonged to a different party with a conflicting ideology, was well known. They had spent the entirety of the recently concluded general election trading barbs. Uttar Pradesh, said Modi, was infamous for 'atrocities against women'.[6]

But there was fact, and there was feeling. And the Shakyas felt that the CBI had failed them, perhaps because they had failed to point the finger at anyone at all. The brothers circulated the rumour that the agency had accepted a bribe from people sympathetic to the Yadavs to fix the case.

Like the rumour that the girls were raped, the rumour that investigating officers were corrupt was entirely believable. The story gained traction when details of the supervising officer's past started to circulate in the village.

The Rogue Officer

Most people knew fifty-four-year-old Anil Girdhari Lal Kaul from the Aarushi Talwar case. It was Kaul's investigation that led the teenager's parents to be sentenced to life imprisonment. He alleged that they had murdered their child and the domestic help after finding them in an 'objectionable position'[1] – this was a euphemism for sex.

In 2017, a higher court overturned the conviction.[2] It emerged that Kaul had tampered with evidence to entrap the parents.[3] In 2014, however, the Talwars were still in jail and it appeared as though the headline-making case that had obsessed the nation was solved. In theory, Kaul was successful, which might explain why he was in Katra.

The agency followed a policy of participatory supervision, which meant that the supervisory officer actively participated in the investigation. Shukla was the investigating officer – this was *his* case – but his boss was right there beside him, or rather, in front of him, striding up and down the village with one hand tucked in his pocket as the other imperiously beckoned people forward for interviews. He scrutinised them carefully, and those who dared match his gaze saw tufts of white hair, narrow eyes and a double chin embedded in folds of skin that the blazing sun had roasted the colour of an aubergine. Kaul's reading glasses dangled from a chain around his substantial neck. He carried several pens in the breast pocket of his billowing shirt. And whereas his English was fluent, when he heckled the people he was interviewing – which was often, the villagers said – it was always in Hindi, a language that afforded more colourful possibilities. After he was done, he walked briskly away, as though to signal that he was a man of many responsibilities.

It was during the course of some interviews that the Shakya family got a taste of Kaul's methods. His behaviour compounded their distrust of the CBI.

Investigators had interrogated Pappu Yadav numerous times. He was even brought back to Katra village and made to retrace his steps on the night the girls went missing. It was still Nazru's word against his on the matter of what exactly had happened, and on one occasion Pappu went out of his way to tell investigators that Padma had complained to him about Nazru. 'Like he wanted to have sex with her.'

On the night of 27 May, Pappu said, when Nazru came upon Pappu and the girls, he demanded that the girls have sex with him. When they refused, he dragged them away by force.

Investigators had already established that Nazru was spying on the girls. At first, they thought he had planned to blackmail them. Then they wondered if he'd wanted to go further. They knew the girls hadn't been raped the night they went missing, but had Nazru *attempted* to rape them? Then they heard the rumours about him being 'neither completely male, nor completely female' – they were taken aback.

Kaul summoned Nazru to the field office and demanded that he submit himself to a medical examination. The young man gave his consent, but it's unlikely he did so willingly. It was Dr Rajiv Gupta, who had led the post-mortem, who asked Nazru to pull down his trousers right there. He looked the tobacco farmer up and down and concluded that he had 'a congenital deformity'.

Dr Gupta couldn't later recall the problem, though he was sure it had a 'catchy name', but he had told Kaul that it was impossible for Nazru to have intercourse with a woman. With that, Kaul lost interest in the idea of Nazru as a suspect. If he hadn't attempted to rape the girls, he believed, Nazru had no reason to kill them to ensure their silence.

Although he was no longer a suspect, Nazru was still an eyewitness, and still altering his story every time he was interviewed. One day, Kaul allegedly grew so furious with him that he grabbed him, held him down, and ordered a junior officer to beat him. Nazru claimed that Kaul had him beaten on two further occasions.

When the allegations were put to Shukla, the investigating officer, he dismissed them as false. 'I wouldn't have allowed such behaviour,' he said. 'Not even a slap. We don't believe in criminal force.' Shukla let it slip that similar allegations had been made against Kaul before. 'Knowing his temperament,' he said, 'I did not allow him to interfere. When he attempted to do so there were altercations.' And, he said, there were so many eyes on the Katra case, that even Kaul would have held back from expressing himself in his customary ways.

Then a second person accused Kaul of assault. This was Sohan Lal's ten-year-old son, Parvesh. The sturdy, stong-featured boy was admired for his quick intelligence. He was studying in a private school. Like everyone else in his family he spoke Braj Bhasha and Hindi, but, unlike them, he had also mastered some English.

Parvesh said that Kaul showed him a picture.

Where was this, the officer demanded?

The low-quality image taken on Sohan Lal's mobile phone showed Parvesh nestled high up in a tree.

The Shakyas had steadfastly maintained that the tree on which the girls were found was too high for them to climb. The foothold stood at nearly three feet, and while Padma was exactly five feet tall, Lalli was short that figure by three inches. Other people in the village disputed this. They said that village children frequently climbed the trees in the orchard, with the taller ones boosting littler ones. The tree on which Padma and Lalli were found, said Ramnath, who owned the mango orchard, was one that 'even an eleven- or twelve-year-old could easily climb'.

Investigators had tested this theory by getting two women of around the same height and build as the girls to climb the tree. They did so with ease.

Kaul, it seems, was collecting proof to advance this argument. He wanted to show that children younger and smaller than Lalli could climb the tree. Someone such as her little brother, for example.

In fact, the orchard was a wildly popular hang-out for the village children. It was their playground. They climbed up and down the trees like they were using stairs. If Parvesh had been asked nicely he would have said so. He would have said that climbing trees was a childhood habit for all the girls and boys in his family, including for his sister Lalli and his cousin Padma.

But Parvesh couldn't remember where the picture was taken. Rather than leaving it there, Kaul started to taunt him. Then, said Parvesh, the beefy investigator, who was

more than four decades older, leaned over and slapped
him. Sohan Lal, who was sitting right there, was stunned,
but felt helpless to intervene. Kaul slapped Parvesh five or
six times across the face. He then kicked the little boy in
the ribs with the toe of his leather shoe. 'You were in the
fields the night your sister went missing,' he shouted.

'Who says so?' replied a shocked Parvesh, picking
himself up from the floor.

'No one said so. I saw you.'

'You saw me? When did you show up? And if I was in
the fields, what could I have done? I'm a child!'

'Where did you find this boy?' Kaul turned to Sohan
Lal. 'Rich people have sons like this.'

The backhanded compliment was lost on parent and
child who left the CBI field office feeling revolted at the
behaviour of this powerful man.

Years later, when Parvesh was asked if he remembered
his sister he sighed, 'I was only a child.' When he was
asked if he remembered Kaul, his face tightened.

'The things he said pinched our hearts.'

Friends, Not Strangers

One day in July, Padma's father was watering the crops. Lalli's father was with Nazru, knee-deep in the upturned earth of his plot. Sunita Devi was washing dishes and Siya Devi was lying on the charpoy. Investigators gathered them to share the news. The call records had come in.

The records showed an exchange of 377 calls between Pappu's phone and one of the Shakya phones. The calls covered a period of six months. A further 48 calls were exchanged between Pappu's phone and a second Shakya phone.

The phone records helped to establish a timeline of events, especially when corroborated with eyewitness accounts. Pappu received a call from Lalli at 5.58 a.m. on the day she would disappear. He called back at 6.01 a.m. These times match the account of the relative, Prem Singh, who saw Lalli talking into Sohan Lal's phone that morning. Lalli then returned the phone to her father who carried it with him to the oil distillation machine.

According to family members, the girls left home for the fields around 9 p.m. The Yadav women said that it was around this time that Pappu went out. They assumed he planned to spend the night at his cousin's. The girls dialled Pappu several times, most likely to alert him of their arrival and exact whereabouts in the fields.

They called him at 9.04, 9.05, 9.16 and then at 9.18 p.m.
At 9.18 p.m. Pappu called back.

The teenagers met and shortly afterwards Nazru
discovered them. Nazru may have followed Padma and
Lalli to the meeting spot, but it's just as likely that he was
waiting for them at the same place he had seen them with
Pappu earlier. According to both men a scuffle ensued.
Nazru said that he was threatened with a gun, forcing
him to retreat. He made straight for Jeevan Lal's animal
shelter on the edge of the fields. 'Khet mein admi hai!' he
shouted. There are thieves in your field.

Jeevan Lal raced to the fields with Nazru, phoning his
brother Ram Babu on the way. It was 9.29 p.m. Ram Babu
responded instantly. 'Thieves in the tobacco! Thieves in
the tobacco!'

Over in Jati, Pappu walked into his cousin Raju's hut
complaining of having suffered a stomach upset from
something he had eaten at the fair. He'd been to the fields,
Pappu said. It was around 9.30 p.m., Raju later recalled.
The youngsters shared some fruit and Raju, at least, fell
asleep.

No further calls were made from Padma's phone, which
had been switched off after that last call to Pappu, and
presumably after Nazru's exit. The handset was switched
on again at 11.41 p.m., giving it enough time to grab
data from seven calls that were made by worried family
members. After a few seconds, the phone was switched off
again, as call records established.

The next time it would be switched on the girls would
be dead. The phone would be in another village in the
hands of Padma's cousin who deleted the messages on
the behest of Sohan Lal, who was concerned they would
damage the family's honour.

By a quarter to ten on the night of 27 May, many of the Shakyas were at home. They were confused and afraid. Already, two Shakya brothers had gone in search of thieves and their wives had come running to tell them that the girls were missing. After Nazru identified Pappu as the culprit, Lalli's mother, Siya Devi, ran home. Jeevan Lal called Sohan Lal, but his brother's phone had died; so further calls were made to Harbans, the cousin.

Thereafter, a group of men attempted to look for the girls. Sohan Lal arranged for transport and was back in Katra at 11.16 p.m. He joined the search party. The mystery motorcycle made an appearance. The voice recording, heard by multiple witnesses, established that the girls knew the boy in the hamlet next door.

A similar set of data helped to account for the movement of the five suspects, but only to a partial extent. The first call that Pappu received on 27 May was from Lalli. Thereafter, his phone was in use seventeen times. The last call he received that day was at 9.23 p.m., when he should have been on his way to his cousin Raju's shack. It lasted a second, so perhaps it was a misdial. Call records didn't register a number.

What is clear is that Pappu didn't speak to his brother Avdesh or the two police suspects at any time on 27 May. His brother Urvesh didn't have a phone, but Avdesh did. The eldest Yadav boy was in the hamlet, cutting tobacco plants for a neighbour alongside his wife. Although he received four calls that day, none of them were from people who would be later associated with the case.

However, two days earlier, on 25 May, Avdesh had phoned Constable Sarvesh at 12 p.m. The call lasted fifty-two seconds. It would be impossible to verify the nature of the call, but according to Avdesh he was the officer's lookout. Whenever he saw activity seemingly connected to the mining of sand, he made sure to inform his friend in the chowki.

Avdesh next heard from the officer on the morning of 28 May at 3.04 a.m. According to the chowki policemen, the villagers of Katra had approached them between 2 and 2.30 a.m. Keeping in mind that the officers dallied, first in responding to the cries of help, and then in getting ready, it's possible to speculate that the call was meant to forewarn the Yadavs that the police were on their way.

At 5.01 a.m., it was Avdesh's turn to dial the officer. 'We are hearing,' he said sketchily, 'that the girls have been found in the orchard.' Avdesh dialled Sarvesh a second time that morning, at 7.37 a.m. By then the constable had left Katra, taking Pappu with him to the police station in Ushait.

After investigators had delivered the information about the call records to the Shakyas, they left the village, and the family returned to work. It was now early evening. A hot breeze was blowing. A bright-red dirt-caked tractor revved its way through the fields. The potatoes are good this year, someone said as he walked passed Sohan Lal and Jeevan Lal. The brothers nodded. Yes, it was true. The potatoes were good.

August passed in heat and rain. The orchard was picked clean of fruit. The investigation continued.

In September, Sohan Lal's brother, Ram Babu, officially retracted his false eyewitness testimony in which he had claimed to have seen Pappu and some men take the girls.

That month, the suspects were set to be released on bail. The investigators might have asked the court for more time, but they didn't. 'The CBI is not filing a chargesheet presently against the five accused who are in custody because forensic tests have ruled out sexual assault,' said a CBI spokesperson. 'However, we have not given a clean chit to anyone. Though rape has been ruled out, murder has not. We are investigating the matter.'[1]

In the hamlet of Jati, Pappu's father, who had by now returned home, was unclear about how to proceed. He had hired a lawyer for his sons, but when he didn't pay the man, the lawyer blocked his calls. 'Yes, someone read out to me the CBI's announcement yesterday,' Veere told a reporter. 'But I do not know how to go about the bail application and I will have to sell one of the two buffaloes I own for money.'[2]

The first to receive bail, on 1 September, were the policemen. Former Head Constable Gangwar went back to the flat that came with his job – even though he had been fired – hoping his former bosses would forget to have him evicted. He stayed indoors virtually all day long to avoid being seen and even refrained from using the air cooler – the loud noise might attract attention. His former colleague Sarvesh went home to his family's farm in Etah district and when reporters phoned he swore at them, called them fucking scum and hung up.

On 4 September, it was the turn of the Yadav brothers to be presented in court.[3] They weren't in handcuffs, because there weren't enough handcuffs to go around. They were secured with a length of rope, like cattle. Pappu was in trackpants, hair close-shaven, feet bare. His cheekbones poked out of his face like chips of concrete.

Once out, the brothers went back to work on the other side of the river, tending to their watermelons. Their father still beckoned them to join him outside on the charpoy some evenings, but now they refused to oblige.

Pappu and Nazru Face to Face

On the morning of 10 October, Anil Girdhari Lal
Kaul died of a heart attack. An obituary in the papers
described the supervising officer on the Katra case as 'a
noble gentleman and an honest officer, full of zest for life,
committed to his profession of serving the country'.[1]

'How could he have died?' Sohan Lal wondered,
grinning from ear to ear. 'He told me he was God.'

A few days later, investigators were back for Pappu. They
picked him up in Jati and took him to their field office.

It was time to fill in the blanks.

They had met in the fields grazing animals, Pappu told
them. He was with his buffaloes, he claimed, they with
their goats. They didn't tell him their real names. The one
who called herself Rajni was, he now knew, actually named
Padma. The younger one called herself Rina. 'Padma said
she wanted to be friends. Their grandmother was sitting
close by. I was so scared I barely spoke.' They happened to
meet at the same spot a few days later, and this time the
girls gave him a mobile number. They would give him a
missed call, they said, and then, and only then, was he to
call them back.

They started meeting regularly in the fields. They teased
him about his shyness. Then they had sex, he and Padma.
Lalli was the lookout. One time, he claimed, Lalli asked

if they could try. Then Padma told him he would have to choose. He chose Padma.

On the morning of 27 May, he said, Lalli gave him a missed call. He called her back. He asked her where she was, and whether she would visit the fair. They bantered, agreeing to meet later.

That night, it was Padma's turn to call, to invite him to the fields, near the family plots. He was wearing trousers and a vest and carrying money, which he handed over. 'We embraced and got ready to have sex. Then the younger girl said she could hear someone approach. By then Padma and I were sitting on the ground. We immediately stood up. I pulled up my trousers and Padma also made herself presentable.'

'Get out of here!' she said.

It was too late.

'Nazru slapped me twice or thrice and threw me to the ground. We scuffled for a bit. I saw Lalli run. I don't know where Padma went. Then Nazru flashed his torch on my face and took my name. "Pappu!" In that time, I disentangled myself and ran away. I went to my cousin's where I fell asleep.'

He didn't know whether the girls went back with Nazru or not, he admitted. 'The last time I saw them alive was when Nazru threw me down.'

Padma had asked him to marry her, he said.

'That day, she asked if I loved her. I said "yes".'

A teenaged vegetable vendor named Pintoo Shakya came forward to say that on the night of 27 May he was walking through the fields to go to the toilet when, somewhere between the Shakya plots, at a distance of about forty paces, he saw a figure picking himself up from the ground as though he'd just been in a fight.

'Is it you, Rajiv?' the man said.

'Not Rajiv, Pintoo.'

'Aah,' Nazru replied. He scrambled up and ran off in the direction of the village.

Rajiv Kumar was Nazru's friend, the man who had seen the girls talking on the phone and had complained about it.

Then another villager said that at around 9.30 p.m. the sound of running footsteps had alerted his dog, who started to bark.

'My mother checked to see who it was, and it was Nazru.'

And so, it became clear beyond any doubt that an encounter of some sort involving Nazru had indeed taken place. But Nazru had said that some men had kidnapped the girls.

To sort out the contradictory statements, investigators fell back on a technique called amna samna, face to face. Pappu and Nazru were brought together at the agency's field office and made to sit, quite literally, face to face. They would go through their stories before agency officers and the proceedings would be recorded on video. There would also be a neutral witness present to prevent either of the two men from later misrepresenting the meeting in their respective communities.

The witness was Neksu Lal. He was Sohan Lal's uncle, and therefore, not technically neutral at all. One of his sons, Yogendra, had helped Sohan Lal buy Padma a phone. Another son, Prem Singh, had overheard Lalli talking on the phone with Pappu. He himself had helped look for the girls. But Neksu Lal was first and foremost a prosperous landlord with a large house, three toilets, two

tractors and one SUV. He did business with the villagers
of both Katra and Jati and was respected across caste lines.

Sohan Lal and Jeevan Lal were also present.

As the camera whirred, Pappu once again described the
events of the night the girls disappeared. He was alone
when he had come to meet them, he said.

This time, Nazru acknowledged that it was indeed the
case. 'I saw a light near the [Shakya family] plots and
tiptoed towards it,' Nazru said. 'I saw a boy and Padma.
Neither of them was wearing the lower half of their
clothing. I got there, grabbed the boy and gave him a few
slaps. I threw him to the ground. I shined the torch on
his face and when I saw who it was, I cried, "Pappu!" But
then he freed himself and ran towards his house. I turned
and ran towards Jeevan Lal's house. I don't know where
the girls went.'

There weren't any other men with Pappu, he admitted.
He'd made that up. And he'd also made up the part about
the gun.

'Why did you run?' the investigators asked.

'I was afraid that the girls would accuse me of
something.'

'What?'

'I don't know what was on their mind. That's why I was
afraid and ran away. I'd caught them red-handed with
Pappu. Naked. I was afraid they would accuse me of rape
to save him.'

He'd lied to Padma's father, Jeevan Lal, about having seen
thieves, he said, because he felt he had to say something
to get him to come to the fields, but without implicating
himself. Jeevan Lal must see what the girls were up to,
otherwise they could accuse him of wrongdoing. But
when the first search party saw nothing, and the girls still

hadn't returned home, Nazru believed that the girls were afraid of what he might have told their family.

'They were in no position to return home,' he said.

Then it was Pappu's turn to speak.

'I lied,' he admitted. Nazru didn't demand that the girls have sex with him. He didn't shout at them. And he didn't drag them away.

'So where did the girls go?'

'I don't know,' he said.

He hadn't bothered to turn back and see what happened to them.

'Girls Are Honour of Family'

On 21 October, the medical board submitted its report to the CBI. The post-mortem had declared that the girls had died by hanging, but a statement by the Forensic Science Laboratory in Lucknow had disputed this. This latest report, which was based primarily on the video recordings of the post-mortem, was meant to settle the matter.

There was no evidence of struggle prior to death, the board said. There wasn't a single injury on the bodies, other than the ligature marks. There were no internal injuries. The girls were not sexually assaulted prior to their deaths, which they concluded occurred between midnight on 27 May and 4 a.m. on 28 May.

At midnight the search party was looking for the girls in the fields. At 2.30 a.m. they were at the chowki. At 4 a.m. they were arguing with the police over where the girls were.

As to the cause of death, the board responded in medical terms. 'The skin under ligature mark was flattened and parchmentised in appearance, tongue was protruded, and faecal matter was present around perineal region; these findings are suggestive of ante-mortem hanging. In view of the above observations, medical board is of the considered opinion that manner of death was suicidal.'

Padma and Lalli, they said, had taken their own lives.

The Shakyas rejected the report.

'Why would they commit suicide?' Lalli's father asked the people around him. 'Tell me. Give me one reason.'

The villagers didn't respond to his face, but they knew the answer as well as he did. 'Girls are honour of family,' Sohan Lal had told the forensic scientist Dr Asha Srivastava. It had been over for Padma the moment she was found with a boy, her salwar at her ankles. And for Lalli too, by association.

Padma had been removed from school to be married, but no size of dowry could have now secured her a husband. The neighbours who had welcomed her arrival as a baby, who had watched her learn how to walk, who had admired her fine embroidery, would have refused to let their girls near her, or Lalli. The village men would refuse to do business with their fathers, the women would gossip about their mothers. The dishonour would be insurmountable by this generation of Shakyas at the very least.

The question, the villagers declared when the Shakya brothers' backs were turned, wasn't why Padma and Lalli had taken their lives. It was how they could have not.

Dr Adarsh Kumar, who led the board, agreed. He believed that the girls ran away and hid themselves, and that when they saw the villagers looking frantically for them 'searchlights everywhere … for three, four hours … they were so much afraid'. They were sure that the search party, even though it comprised their own fathers, uncles and cousins 'would kill them if they found them'.

Sohan Lal had said as much to Dr Srivastava. 'If the girls were alive, what step would you have taken for the honour of the family?' she had asked him. 'We would have killed them,' he had replied.

It was impossible to know if Sohan Lal had meant what he said or if it was a knee-jerk reaction to honouring social codes. The villagers didn't think he was that sort of man. But the dark sentiment was hardly uncommon in the area.

Some members of the Shakya clan believed that the family was to blame for the deaths. This was at least according to Lalitha, who was married to the Shakyas' cousin Yogendra Singh. First, they had allowed the girls to use phones. Then, she said, they had failed to provide them toilets.

'If the girls had a toilet at home they would have had no reason to go out,' she said. 'If they did, family members could challenge them – "what for are you going out?"' Her father-in-law Neksu Lal had built three toilets, she said, and she never went anywhere.

Then the Shakyas had given the girls permission to visit the mela, a place that her father-in-law, the most respected man in the village, prohibited her, even at her age, from stepping foot in. What was a mela but a dhakka mukki, a scrum, of men? Neksu Lal had built a large courtyard. When the women wanted to stretch their legs that's as far as they went. When they craved shopping, Neksu Lal stuck his head out of the door and motioned for the shopkeepers sitting in the lane to bring over their wares for the women to browse through.

But it wasn't anyone's place to say such things, for it would implicate the Shakya family, and the village too. After the girls went missing the Shakya men had privileged honour over everything else, but they hadn't done anything that many of their neighbours wouldn't do in the same circumstances.

So, instead, the villagers said that whatever happened was terrible, and who knew who the culprit really was, but

one thing was clear – the girls should not have died. And
with this uniting sentiment they were able to comfort the
family, and themselves also.

November brought Diwali, the Festival of Lights, and
some villagers celebrated with new clothes and sweets.
Boys burst crackers in the fields. The Shakyas opened
their doors and windows and lit a few diyas. The flickering
golden light in their small earthen bowls symbolised the
dispelling of darkness and the victory of good over evil.

Then came winter. Fog filled the village like smoke. In
the fields, farmers wrapped in blankets hunched over piles
of rubbish to which they had set a flame. Sohan Lal was
often among them, in a striped sweater and a white scarf,
his fingers swollen blue and grey with the cold. Women
walked quickly to and from their buffaloes. Children in
monkey caps napped in animal shelters, for they were
packed warm with livestock and hay. Everyone now
carried a torch.

Then came the winter rain, falling in icy ropes. The
schools were shut, the roads impassable. The villagers
calculated their stores of fodder, grain, lentils and oil.
The case had gripped Katra for months, discussed up and
down, but the cold was merciless, and every man had a
family to feed.

On 12 December, the agency closed the case with a final
report it filed at the Court of the Special Judge in Budaun,
which had been set up under a new child protection law.[1]
The report repeated the agency's findings that the children
had taken their own lives. The agency enclosed forty-two
medical and forensic reports and interviews with over 200
people.

In Jati, Pappu's older brother said that the Yadavs had
told the truth from the first day on. 'We have nothing to

hide,' Avdesh told a reporter, while sitting on the charpoy outside his house. His mother, who was at his feet, looked grim. 'It is by God's grace that this CBI investigation has freed us,' Avdesh went on. 'Even if we had sold our land we wouldn't have enough money to fight the case and prove our innocence.'

The Shakya family rejected this report as well, but for an entirely justifiable reason.

Although the CBI had interviewed Pappu, at least ten times by their own count, they didn't act on one of the most crucial pieces of information that he gave them. The nineteen-year-old had admitted to repeatedly having sex with Padma – four times, he said – and to having attempted sex with Lalli. The previous year the age of consent had been increased from sixteen to eighteen by the Criminal Law (Amendment) Act, 2013,[2] which had been passed in response to the Delhi bus rape.[3]

Padma was sixteen, Lalli was fourteen, which meant that Pappu – by his own admission, and irrespective of consent – was guilty of statutory rape. He could also be charged with child sexual abuse.

Instead, in their final report, investigators attacked the Shakya family. They concluded by saying that since the family had filed a false police complaint they had broken the law and committed criminal conspiracy. They were the ones who should be investigated.

The family responded with a protest petition, which is a legal remedy that registers concerns over the quality of a police investigation and requests redressal. They were determined that Pappu should be punished – and it was perhaps because of this that their petition claimed, incorrectly, that on the night of 27 May when Pappu was brought to the police chowki, he had confessed to having raped and murdered the girls. As multiple Shakya villagers present at the time would attest, Pappu had said no such thing.

The next year, in October, the court concluded that some of the CBI's key findings were correct. All the evidence showed that Padma and Lalli had died by suicide. However, declared the judge, Pappu would be arrested and must stand trial for kidnapping, criminal assault and penetrative sexual assault of a minor.

Shukla, the investigating officer, tried to justify his decision not to arrest Pappu. The boy hadn't kidnapped the girls, he said. If anything, they had called *him* to the fields. As to the matter of rape, 'Indian law doesn't accept a confession to a police officer. The confession must be made to a magistrate.'

Asked whether he had thought to take Pappu before a magistrate, he replied, 'Nahin.'

No.

Pappu in Jail, the Shakyas in Court

In Katra village, Nazru was back to his old ways. The police officer deputised to keep watch over him complained that the young man was 'running around needlessly at night. It's so hard to control him. He seeks out trouble.' When the officer warned Nazru that he couldn't just take off without informing him, Nazru didn't appear to understand. 'Ask him a question and he'll give you the most upside-down answer imaginable,' the officer groaned.

The villagers had turned against him. What need had there been to spy on the girls. Padma's parents were about to get her married. Soon she would have gone away. Instead, Nazru had to make a point. To make himself feel big, he had scared the small girls so much that they couldn't come home.

On 26 January 2016, Pappu Yadav was arrested.

The Shakya family used his arrest to file a petition in the Allahabad High Court against the four other men. If Pappu had committed a crime, they argued, he had done so with the help of his brothers and two police officers. The villagers of Katra didn't understand why the family thought they would win this case, when the court in Budaun had already accepted the men's innocence.

But Sohan Lal had a secret.

Nazru had recently approached him in confidence. This time he was certain of what he had seen, he said. And what he had seen were some men dragging away Padma and Lalli. He was sure of it. 'I won't change my testimony till the day I die,' he promised.

'We have an eyewitness,' Sohan Lal, newly invigorated, told the villagers.

Epilogue

BIRTH

It was 2016. The girls had been dead for two years.

Asked how he was, Padma's father Jeevan Lal said, 'Theek hi to hain.' I'm just about okay.

And Lalli's mother Siya Devi said, 'I am as I am.'

Or she would say that although she cooked and cleaned – for after all, she had other children – she would no longer go to the fields to help with the harvest, or graze the buffaloes, or meet the women. She could do what needed to be done, but it was too much to expect that she could be who she once was. 'My hands and feet don't really move as they should,' she said.

Padma's stepmother Sunita Devi said, 'it's been so long' or 'what is there to say?' or even 'it's hard to remember them' – and in a corner, her stooped-over mother-in-law might agree that time had passed. But she never said that the memory of her granddaughters was waning. 'I'm not dying,' she wept, as tears slid down her face, 'but I am not living.'

All around them, people had moved on. Little cousin Manju, now fourteen years old, had learned more about loss. Her mother had died of cancer. Manju was still in school, hoping to stay there, but her father was doubtful. 'I'm just a tailor,' he had told her.

Tragedy had also visited Kanhaiya Lal, Padma's maternal uncle, who lived in Nabiganj village. He had lost a baby boy. The doctors, he said, couldn't diagnose the cause of death.

Somwati, sixteen when she strolled through the fair with the girls, was now a married woman. She lived in a village in Gujarat with her husband who worked in a cotton field. Rekha, the other friend who had met the girls at the fair, now lived some villages away. Her in-laws didn't like her to talk about Padma and Lalli; perhaps they were concerned about bringing home bad luck. 'I didn't see them that day,' Rekha could be heard telling people. 'I barely even knew them.'

One of Lalli's classmates now went to a private school and would possibly graduate, because her brother also studied there. They would walk to and fro together, which made her parents think she was safe. But Lalli's other friends, all sixteen, were sewing wall hangings and decorating handmade fans for family members to remember them by. Soon they would be married. Then they would belong to their husbands and would need permission to visit home.

The sun broke through that spring, when Padma's stepmother gave birth to her first child. It had taken years and years, but delivered on a bed in a private hospital, the timing – like the baby – was perfect. They named her Saraswati after the goddess of knowledge and music, arts and nature, but since she was too little to comfortably wear such a grand name, for now she was Kajol. They slipped bangles on her wrists and lined her brown eyes with kajol. They anointed her with concoctions to stay safe and well.

With Kajol curled up under a piece of cloth on a shaded charpoy – snoozy, warm and delicious with that new baby smell – it was impossible for anyone in the family, even Siya Devi, to keep the smile from reaching their eyes.

Many new parents experienced immediate, boundless love for their babies – but if some wondered whether sorrow or guilt over Padma's death would force Jeevan Lal to be cautious with his heart, to give less than his full self, they were mistaken. He thrummed with joy at the sight of his baby. His voice was liquid gold.

'She is the gods' grace,' he beamed.

There was a new set of officers in the chowki. They weren't any better trained than the last, but they didn't drink during work hours. And they responded promptly to complaints. When a villager came running to say that a wedding guest was misbehaving with girls, the officers plucked the boy from the dancing crowd and cooled his head with some slaps.

Their enthusiasm inspired the villagers to contribute bricks, cement and free labour to build the chowki a toilet. Akhilesh Yadav's government sent around a brightly polished jeep so the men would no longer have to use their motorcycles to get around. Six hours away, in Delhi, Vijay Kumar Shukla was the newly garlanded recipient of the President's Police Medal for Distinguished Service. The annual honour, which was bestowed on only six officers in 2016, was awarded to him for his work in Katra.

Virender, Sohan Lal's eldest son, was twenty-one and a farmer now. He had given up his factory job in Noida to support his father, whose shrunken frame was testimony to the toll the deaths had taken. Sohan Lal had trouble with the legalese in the cases he was fighting, so Virender, who could read and write, accompanied him to meet lawyers. He stepped forward to greet the politicians who still, sometimes, came to the village. He wondered if he might become a politician. All said, they had helped him. He developed a reputation as a man with a promising future, and the proposals started to come in.

Weddings meant babies, and soon the house would be unable to comfortably hold them all in its embrace. Jeevan Lal started to build a new room for the family.

Just as well, for the next year, Sunita Devi gave birth to a second child. They named her Anjali, 'divine offering'.

Although the Shakyas wouldn't know it, around this time a woman in the hamlet next door also had a baby.

Basanta, Avdesh's wife, named her second daughter Kamini, beautiful. As before, the young mother still spent most of her time by herself, except that now there was one child fastened to her breast, and another to her waist.

Pappu's mother Jhalla Devi still poured her energy into maintaining the buffaloes. His father, Veere, was always across the river. Urvesh was even now trying to graduate tenth-class. In fact, they were all almost exactly where they had been before the events of that night, except that their business, and they, were now widely known. For people like them, who believed that survival lay in being inconspicuous, this was a severe punishment.

The older brothers blamed the youngest for having been wrongfully accused of rape and murder. Their lives had been dismantled. And not one politician, they said, not even one of their own, had come to see them, never mind offer them assistance of any sort. Although they didn't speak English, they still used the word 'media trial'. *This* is what it meant to be poor, they said, low caste and above all, Yadav.

The family took some comfort in the fact that no one in their hamlet had believed the accusations. To be a Yadav was to be easy prey, they had all agreed. Chalo, they said, whereas this time the police, politicians and media was with that lot, one day, they will be with us.

As for Pappu, he was again out on bail.

But the boy who had loved to roam around, chase girls and act 'naughty' was all but gone. The new Pappu kept to himself and focused on work, neighbours said.

Whether by purpose or coincidence, Pappu's family slowly started to fill their backyard. First the buffalo shelter was expanded, and then Veere allowed some other Yadavs to build shacks there. Now, it was no longer possible to stroll easily into the Katra fields. It was difficult even to see the orchard.

Rebirth

It was three years after the girls had died, after Ram Babu, Sohan Lal's brother, had accepted a proposal on behalf of one of his boys, that they heard about the twins. The twins lived in a village named Nagla Khamani, an hour's driving distance from Katra.

One day, when the twins' mother's milk dried up, they were given buffalo milk. The strongly flavoured froth was unpalatable to the breastfed children and soon they were shitting all over the courtyard, driving their poor mother quite mad so that unable to help herself she cried, 'where have you come from to torment me?'

'We've come from Katra,' they replied in unison.

An astounded Raj Rani summoned her husband, and he told some men in the fields, and then it was only a matter of time before the news reached the Shakya family. The Shakyas didn't believe for a minute that the twins' mother might be a fantasist.

Family patriarch Sohan Lal took it upon himself to go to the village on the pretext of inviting Raj Rani and her husband, neither of whom he had met before, to the wedding – but really he had gone to meet the girls.

The twins had soft black hair, poker-straight fringes and enormous eyes. They were truly identical, he marvelled.

Where one went, the other followed. When they saw him, he said, one of them cried, 'Papa!'

On the day of the Shakya wedding, the family was overwrought, but no one more so than Lalli's mother, Siya Devi. She was yet to visit her daughter's grave. Someone had told her that it was now covered with rubbish and impossible to distinguish from the others. But none of that mattered any more.

If it were true!

But what if it were true?

The children had other parents.

When Raj Rani entered the courtyard of the Shakya house, she smiled around at everyone and put her children down. They ran here and there with a vivid excitement that seemed to the Shakyas as proof that they were delighted to be home. They pointed at wall hangings that Padma and Lalli had made, then gestured at themselves as though to say, 'I made that!'

When they touched their ears, family members wondered if the thorns they had seen embedded in the dead girls' clothing were hurting the living children. And when they responded fussily to being picked up, it was clear that they were afraid they would be taken back to the orchard, the place where they had died.

'Our children have been reborn!' rejoiced Sohan Lal.

Siya Devi waited for the twins to leave.

Then she cried.

Love, Hope, Vote

Now, it was the day before the fourth anniversary of Padma and Lalli's death. In the courtyard of the Shakya house, Lalli's mother placed the leftovers from lunch in a bowl and covered it with a piece of cloth. Then she started washing the dishes. When they were done, she spread them in a row to dry in the sun.

Next door, her niece Kajol let out a hungry cry.

'Mama, roti.'

'There are no more rotis,' Sunita Devi replied.

'Mama, roti!' the toddler said, tears flowing down her face.

'What did I just tell you?'

'Mama ...'

'Drink this,' Sunita Devi said, offering the child some water.

Siya Devi looked away.

She hadn't seen the twins since the wedding, but she thought about them often. Her child wasn't buried in sand, or drifting in the orchard like some in the village said. The girls had been reborn. They were alive!

Siya Devi would like to visit them. They were growing up so fast. They were sure to be laughing and chatting non-stop.

But would she visit them?

'My child has been born again,' she told herself. She examined her hands. The long fingers, the tough brown skin, the lines on her palms. Heart. Life. What a life. Full of hardship and heartbreak. But love also, a life full of love.

She hid her face in her sari.

'Will they give her to me? Will they give her to me? No, she is now their child.'

Outside, the village was bustling with life, for the harvest was under way. Once again the clouds boiled with heat. A hot, dry wind crackled through the standing crops. The sun had bleached the landscape and everyone who occupied it. Cyclists carried baskets of chickens. Pale horses pulled loads of sugar cane, mint and garlic. As farm animals barked and baaed, dusty-faced children chased a kite through the orchard.

The tree they mostly avoided was festooned with a piece of white cloth, a man's vest perhaps. They hadn't been mischievous, the children swore, a monkey had raided someone's washing line.

The wheat and tobacco was gone, sold, leaving behind ruptures in the earth. But the disappointingly low rates this season had left the Shakya farmers talking dispiritedly among themselves as they worked on the taro and mint. Garlic was going for 500 rupees and tobacco for 900. Counting back from the money they had spent on irrigation, fertiliser, manpower and transport to the wholesaler, it didn't seem worth it.

Away from the chatter, keeping to himself, was a diligent labourer in a lungi, a goatee partially obscuring his face. Nazru's father had died, which meant one less mouth to feed, but life was still unspeakably hard. This harvest he had again attached himself to the Shakyas, working for his cousins. It was with Sohan Lal and Jeevan Lal that he passed the fourth death anniversary of Padma and Lalli. As music from the mela wafted into the orchard, Nazru hummed quietly to himself. Sometime later, his friend Rajiv Kumar would join him for their daily catch-up.

The Shakya farmers had now moved on to politics. The new chief minister, Yogi Adityanath of the Hindu nationalist Bharatiya Janata Party, was initially a source of humour – for he was besotted with cows and extolled the beneficial effects of bovine urine – but the cleric faced criminal charges for attempted murder and rioting.[1] He was said to be 'India's most divisive and abusive politician'.[2]

'The thing is,' Sohan Lal said, 'Akhilesh Yadav wasn't all that bad, I'll say it to his face. He worked hard for the farmers and for the poor. It was goondas, thugs, who claimed to speak for him, that made him look bad.'

The refreshing attitude of the new chowki policemen aside, it didn't seem to Sohan Lal that anything good had come out of the deaths. If the success of a protest was measured by what happened afterwards, then the Shakyas' protest had only achieved short-term gains. By keeping the children's bodies in the tree, the family attracted a great deal of attention, police, politicians and, thereafter, three investigations – but each one had left them disappointed. They were given some money, and a non-profit built a few toilets, but many of the villagers used the closed-door latrines to safeguard their harvest. Even the Shakyas, who did use their toilet, let one or two of the goats inside on very hot days.

The two court cases, the one in which Pappu was accused of rape, and the other, in which the Shakya family had accused all five men of rape and murder, would likely continue for years, decades even. By the time the courts delivered their judgments, if they ever did, Jeevan Lal's daughters would very likely be as old as their sister Padma had once been.

Sohan Lal had finally accepted that Padma and Pappu had what he called a 'love affair'. Padma had taken her own life, he agreed. But he didn't understand why his daughter Lalli had taken hers.

Whatever it was he planned to see the cases through. It was a matter of honour, after all, and what message would it send to back out now.

And, if the newspapers were accurate, crimes against women across India continued unabated. It was impossible to know just how bad it was because the National Crime Records Bureau, for the first time since 1953, had failed to publish its annual crime report.[3] The move was widely seen as a part of a government effort to suppress negative data.[4] That summer a poll released by the Thompson Reuters Foundation declared that India was the most dangerous place in the world for women.[5] Six years after the Delhi bus rape, women in India were at a greater risk of sexual violence and human trafficking than women in war-torn Afghanistan and Syria.[6]

A lot of the bad news these days involved the prime minister. Narendra Modi had come to power promising achhe din, good days, but these days were worse than ever before. The economy had slowed to a crawl[7] and employment was at its lowest in forty-five years.[8]

The government had even reneged on a promise to build the required number of rape crisis centres. After initially agreeing to build one centre in every district, it now proposed to build only one in every state. Or, rather than 660 centres nationwide, there would be 36.[9] Given the size

of some states, such as Uttar Pradesh, and the population
density, such a step made no sense at all. According to
a report, the Prime Minister's Office 'remarked that the
police are sensitive enough and that there is no need for
such centres'.[10] Meanwhile, the Nirbhaya Fund, a ten
billion rupee corpus created by the previous government
to bolster women's safety initiatives lay almost entirely
unused.[11] Activists alleged that the funds were being
diverted elsewhere. Atrocities against women, they said,
had witnessed 'a spike under the BJP dispensation'.[12]

The prime minister was even accused of using the CBI
to harass opponents, and the agency's reputation was at its
lowest ebb.[13] But Modi's own colleagues were committing
crimes. One Bharatiya Janata Party politician had raped a
young woman in Uttar Pradesh. When she told him she
would go to the police, he threatened to kill her father
and four-year-old brother. She complained to the police
anyhow, on thirty-three different occasions, until the
politician's brother and some aides beat her father – in
front of the police. He died a few days later in custody.
Finally, in despair, the girl marched to the chief minister's
residence and threatened to set herself on fire.[14]

What was there to do, the Shakyas said, but to keep
voting for people like them. Such people, though they
may be rich now, had gone hungry once. Only such
people would know the lengths the Shakyas went to keep
that gnawing feeling away.

Keep voting, keep hoping.

Hope was a hard thing to hold on to in times such
as these, as slippery as the snakes that frequented the
village fields.

Why, just the other day, near the capital city of the state
no less, a girl who had gone missing was found hanging
in a tree.[15]

Author's Note

I didn't know the Delhi bus rape victim, but like many Indian women, when she died in the winter of 2012, I felt as though I had lost someone. I had lived in Delhi until my mid-twenties, first as a student and later as a journalist. An exciting period full of dreams and opportunities was tarnished by the behaviour of men. It seemed to me that it was only a matter of time before the filthy comments and hard pinches would escalate. The friends who had already been assaulted, on streets and on public transport, advised me to carry chilli powder. One opened her handbag to reveal a kitchen knife.

Although Delhi was notoriously unsafe, stories about sexual assault didn't often make the news. This changed with the bus rape because of the particularly shocking nature of the crime, and also because of the victim herself – at only twenty-three the medical student had already achieved what so many of her peers dream of. In a country that systematically keeps women back, the porter's daughter from Uttar Pradesh had surged forward.

The victim's death introduced an unprecedented cultural shift – for one thing, the subject of sexual assault entered the national conversation. The outpouring of sentiment encouraged the media to cover similar incidents and they did so with such diligence that soon Delhi came to be known as the rape capital of the world. A culture of violence had always existed, but even I found myself wondering what was going on. Who were these men carrying out all these rapes, and why wasn't anyone stopping them? I decided to find out, and to gather my findings in a book-length study of rape in India.

In May 2014, the Katra case made headlines. I first heard about it on Twitter, where the deeply disturbing image of the hanging children was circulated with reports that they had been raped and murdered by dominant-caste men. The case was compared, for sheer depravity, with the Delhi bus rape. In fact, it became the highest profile sexual assault case since the incident in the national capital and this was why I decided to make it the centrepiece of my study. In accordance with the same Indian law that did not permit the media to name the Delhi bus rape victim, I chose to call the girls Padma and Lalli.

In the spring of 2015, one year after the children were found, I left London, where I was now living, for my old home, Delhi. I drove to Katra directly from the airport, a journey that took over six hours.

Creating a record meant returning to it, and after several years of the back and forth, I realised that the story I now had was very different from the one I had initially heard.

I had spent months interviewing the Shakya family, but I had also combed Katra. Then I visited the villages in the immediate vicinity, and later went further still. Uttar Pradesh is the size of a large country – it's been compared to Brazil – and there were days when I could conduct just one interview. This slowed my pace considerably and a reporting exercise that should have been completed in perhaps two years, ended up taking four.

But what I had come to learn was this – that while the Delhi bus rape had shown just how deadly public places were for women, the story of Padma and Lalli revealed something more terrible still – that an Indian woman's first challenge was surviving her own home.

To reconstruct the events in this book, I interviewed more than a hundred people. All of these interviews were recorded on tape, some also on video. A small number of interviews were captured in handwritten notes because of the subject's reluctance to be recorded. The material I gathered between 2015 and 2018 forms the foundation of *The Good Girls*.

I supplemented this material with hundreds of records and investigation files that the CBI submitted to the court. The files contained interview transcripts, forensic results, crime scene investigation reports, minutes of meetings, letters, memos and more totalling 3,272 pages.

When quotation marks are used, or when I ascribe a statement to someone's thoughts, the source is either the person, a witness, or a transcript. In addition, I worked with a factchecker and consulted with a lawyer. I speak Hindi fluently, but used the assistance of a translator for interviews that contained Braj Bhasha.

It is often the case that a recurring visit from a journalist signifies to some sources that the journalist will prioritise their version of the story. But I wanted to give readers an objective view of the girls' lives and the events surrounding their deaths. I didn't want to present just one or two people's opinion, however sympathetic or compelling they may have been. And I wanted to interview as many people as possible. To ensure there was no misunderstanding I made it a point to say as much to the Shakya family. I extended a similar courtesy to the Yadavs, the police and investigators.

Here, now, are some examples of how I reconstructed the more vivid scenes in the book. The episode in the police chowki, during which Pappu is beaten by Sub-Inspector Ram Vilas, was based on interviews I recorded with Ram Vilas, as well as his former colleagues Chattrapal Singh Gangwar, Raghunandan Singh and Satinder Pal Singh. There were numerous other people present besides, and I interviewed many of them, including the Shakya brothers – Sohan Lal, Jeevan Lal and Ram Babu, their relatives Nazru, Neksu Lal, Yogendra Singh and Prem Singh, and Pappu's brothers Avdesh and Urvesh Yadav.

The scene in the Katra fields on the day that the girls were found was also based on recorded interviews – among the individuals involved, the Shakya family and members of their clan, politicians like Sinod Kumar Shakya, his aide Shareef Ahmed Ansari, and officers Ganga Singh, Mukesh Kumar Saxena and Maan Singh Chauhan.

Again, I was able to reconstruct the post-mortem scene by speaking to those who were present at the time – Dr Rajiv Gupta, who led the exam, his associate Dr Avdhesh Kumar, the hospital pharmacist A. K. Singh, and of course, Lala Ram. The CBI, in its investigation files, had said that Lala Ram had examined the girls with a 'butcher's knife'. The post-mortem, the agency said, 'was conducted in a despicable condition in the absence of proper light, autopsy instruments and water supply'. This sounded like an exaggeration to me, and so I requested permission to watch Lala Ram at work.

One morning in 2015 when I was visiting Budaun, Lala Ram phoned and said that I should hurry up and come

over to the post-mortem house. A young man had been
pulled under the wheels of his own tractor and the police
had brought his body over for an exam. As I watched,
Lala Ram stripped down to his undershirt, and started
examining the body in the back garden of the post-mortem
house. The instruments he used were indeed butcher's
knives – he told me so – and as he sliced and scooped, he
washed the excess blood by dipping the knives in a pail of
water that he had filled from the tap in the garden. I sat
through the entire post-mortem and then watched as Lala
Ram washed his instruments, his hands and feet under
the garden tap.

To draw a portrait of the girls – their daily life, their
pastimes, their joys and frustrations – I spoke to their
parents, older siblings Virender and Phoolan Devi, friends
such as Rekha, and cousin Manju who lives in Noida.
Padma's maternal uncles in Nabiganj were a vital source of
information. They loved their niece and were devastated
by her death.

It was inevitable, given the attention around the case,
and also the many highly publicised mistakes, that not
everyone would want to speak to me. Dr Pushpa Pant
Tripathi declined to be interviewed. And when I phoned
former constable Sarvesh Yadav he called me various
unprintable names and threatened me, warning me never
to phone him again. A second request made on a later
trip, this time through Constable Raghunandan, received
the same response.

As for Pappu, I went to his house every time I visited
the little hamlet where he lived, but he was never there.
His family insisted that he was around. Then, one day
I found myself in what remains of Badam Nagla, where
I interviewed Veere's older brother. A man came up to

me and asked who I was. He had a peaked face, a shock of very black hair and he was small, like a boy. I told him my name and asked him his, but he didn't reply. 'Are you Pappu?' I said. 'No,' he replied and walked off, and I never saw him again.

The CBI and the Shakya family didn't see eye to eye, and when I first read out transcripts of the family's interviews with the agency back to them, they claimed that they had been deliberately misquoted. I was alarmed. Then I started to see a pattern.

Sohan Lal told me that he hadn't hidden and then destroyed evidence and that the CBI was lying by claiming that he had. Shortly afterwards, Sohan Lal's brother, Ram Babu, admitted to me that the CBI version was indeed correct. Ram Babu laughed sheepishly as he said this, perhaps because he knew that this behaviour had undermined the family's position and their claim that they wanted the case solved. Padma's maternal uncles told me about the roles they had played in the mystery, thus corroborating what the CBI had said.

Thereafter, every time the family claimed that the agency had either misquoted them in transcripts or outright lied, I sought a trustworthy witness from their own clan to clarify the matter.

As for Nazru, when I met him last, in 2018, I asked him whether he regretted changing his story so many times. He claimed that he had done no such thing. 'You first said that you saw thieves,' I reminded him. He grew agitated. 'But they were thieves!' he said.

This is a story about women in modern India. But it's also about what it means to be poor. India is changing; some say it is rapidly modernising. Yet for the poor, who have always suffered the most, India hasn't changed all that much. In villages like Katra, just a few hours outside the national capital, people now have phones, but they don't have toilets. Women have some education, but they are forbidden from working. Fear of social ostracism and mob justice forces people to waive their rights. They are held back and, sometimes, they keep others back too. No one is in a position to reach their full potential.

The situation is only getting worse. According to numerous surveys, more women than men reported losing their jobs during the Covid-19 pandemic, more women expressed anxiety over their future and more women were set to perform unpaid care work. The BBC reported a rise in child marriage and trafficking.

The promised change must start now. People need clean drinking water and nourishing food, safe housing and toilets. They need education, employment and empowerment. And their children need, and deserve, the right to hopes and dreams.

Sonia Faleiro
London, 2020

Notes

AN ACCUSATION IS MADE

1 forbade unmarried women from using phones: indiatoday. in/india/north/story/up-panchayat-bans-love-marriages-bars-women-from-using-mobile-phones-109131-2012-07-12
2 married within their caste: thehindu.com/data/just-5-per-cent-of-indian-marriages-are-intercaste/article6591502.ece
3 Twenty-eight cases were reported in the country: pib.gov.in/PressReleaseIframePage.aspx?PRID=1540824; hindustantimes. com/india-news/792-spike-in-honour-killing-cases-up-tops-the-list-govt-in-parliament/story-xoIfcFpfAljYi15yQtPoYP. html
4 accused of killing his daughter: Jim Yardley, 'In India, Castes, Honour and Killings Intertwine', *New York Times*, 10 July 2010, nytimes.com/2010/07/10/world/asia/10honor.html

UNSPEAKABLE THINGS

1 clothes, cooking pots and even cash: dnaindia.com/india/report-mulayam-caught-bribing-voters-1238446
2 World Bank report: http://documents.worldbank.org/curated/en/187721467995647501/pdf/105884-BRI-P157572-ADD-SERIES-India-state-briefs-PUBLIC-UttarPradesh-Proverty. pdf

3 people ate grass to survive: ndtv.com/india-news/in-drought-
   hit-uttar-pradesh-the-poor-are-eating-rotis-made-of-
   grass-1252317
4 statues of herself: bbc.co.uk/news/world-asia-india-17254658
5 'That's why ... young generation leading the party':
   caravanmagazine.in/reportage/everybodys-brother-akhilesh-
   yadav
6 a third of the politicians ... had a criminal record: adrindia.
   org/content/lok-sabha-elections-2014-analysis-criminal-
   background-financial-education-gender-and-other
7 this figure amounted to over half: rediff.com/news/report/
   fifty-four-pc-of-akhilesh-yadavs-cabinet-has-a-criminal-
   record/20120413.htm
8 the rule of criminals: blogs.wsj.com/indiarealtime/2012/03/20/
   samajwadi-partys-goonda-raj-appears-alive-and-well/

THE FAIR COMES TO THE VILLAGE

1 'Rama's faithful wife!': The *Ramayana* and the *Mahabharata*
   condensed into English verse by Romesh C. Dutt (J. M. Dent,
   1917), oll.libertyfund.org/titles/1778

THIEVES IN THE TOBACCO

1 deaths from gun violence in India: indiaspend.com/cover-story/
   uttar-pradesh-awash-in-illegal-guns-shooting-deaths-80762

WHERE ARE THEY?

1 Uttar Pradesh was the murder capital of India: hindustantimes.
   com/lucknow/up-is-the-murder-capital-of-india/story-
   YXx35AZhrSvnXXHehbSNYP.html

EVERY EIGHT MINUTES

1 just as likely to kill: www.bbc.co.uk/news/world-south-asia-
   12696470

2 'Why do you people have so many children': nytimes.
  com/2007/01/07/world/asia/07india.html
3 Ibid.
4 The gruesome details made headlines: ndtv.com/india-news/
  nithari-rape-and-murder-case-moninder-singh-pandher-
  surender-koli-sentenced-to-death-1728506
5 FIRs ... in less than 60 per cent of such cases: tribuneindia.
  com/news/sunday-special/kaleidoscope/wanted-most-wanted-
  search-for-kids/105492.html
6 an epidemic of missing and exploited children: hrw.org/
  world-report/2014/country-chapters/india
7 12,361 people were kidnapped and abducted in Uttar
  Pradesh: ncrb.gov.in/sites/default/files/crime_in_india_table_
  additional_table_chapter_reports/Chapter%2023_2014.pdf
8 one child went missing every eight minutes: straitstimes.com/
  asia/south-asia/india-nobel-winner-in-new-campaign-for-
  abused-and-trafficked-children
9 'a result of abuse' ... this was likely 'rampant': Sonia Faleiro,
  'Why Do So Many Indian Children Go Missing?', *New York
  Times*, 20 November 2017, nytimes.com/2017/11/19/opinion/
  missing-children-india.html

A FINGER IS POINTED

1 the document required to start an investigation: childrights.
  in/2013/07/fir-in-all-cases-of-missing-children.html

THE POSTER CHILD FOR A NEW INDIA

1 'she would cry if you didn't let her go to school': spiegel.de/
  international/world/exploring-the-lives-of-the-rape-victim-
  and-suspects-in-india-a-879187.html
2 https://www.nytimes.com/2020/03/19/world/asia/india-bus-
  rape-convicts-hanged.html

A REPORTER'S BIG BREAK

1 It included five Indian and Indian-origin women: indianexpress.com/article/business/business-others/sbis-arundhati-bhattacharya-icicis-chanda-kochhar-among-forbes-most-powerful-women/

2 eight Indians made the cut: ndtv.com/photos/business/fortunes-list-of-most-powerful-women-in-asia-pacific-has-8-indians-18511#photo-238490

3 coverage of rural India ... 0.23 per cent of the news: https://cpj.org/reports/2016/08/dangerous-pursuit-india-corruption-journalists-killed-impunity-Foreword-Sainath/

4 fewer nutrients than were required to stay healthy: Ellen Barry and Harsha Vadlamani, 'After Farmers Commit Suicide, Debts Fall on Families in India', *New York Times*, 23 February 2014. nytimes.com/2014/02/23/world/asia/after-farmers-commit-suicide-debts-fall-on-families-in-india.html

5 the poor ... 4.1 per cent of national wealth: livemint.com/Money/VL5yuBxydKzZHMetfC97HL/Richest-1-own-53-of-Indias-wealth.html

THE FIRST POLITICIAN ARRIVES

1 'He ran into my house': archive.indianexpress.com/news/cong-leader-in-dock-for--sheltering--wanted-man/1012833/

2 contaminated by more than a hundred people: youtube.com/watch?v=IvnTluEriQs

THE MATTER SHOULD BE SETTLED

1 striking rule-breaking motorcyclists: timesofindia.indiatimes.com/city/meerut/outgoing-meerut-sp-caught-in-video-beating-commuters-protesters-at-demolition/articleshow/63886903.cms

2 a state-run mortuary: edition.cnn.com/2009/WORLD/asiapcf/05/25/india.skulls/?iref=nextin

3 Now, please leave me alone: timesofindia.indiatimes.com/
city/agra/Five-years-after-gay-AMU-profs-death-lover-
breaks-silence-on-affair/articleshow/50224046.cms

SOMEONE TO SOLVE THEIR PROBLEMS

1 they too viewed secularism as inimical: nytimes.
com/2019/12/20/world/asia/india-muslims-citizenship.html;
ft.com/content/8e5bf5a2-1c34-11ea-97df-cc63de1d73f4

2 'thinker, poet & a social reformer': twitter.com/narendramodi/
status/471512748119957504?lang=en

3 'encouraged further violence': hrw.org/world-report/2019/
country-chapters/india#d91ede

4 a Dalit boy was lynched: indianexpress.com/article/india/
crime/dalit-youth-killed-for-talking-to-upper-caste-girl-in-
pune/

5 another was set on fire: theguardian.com/world/2014/oct/19/
lynching-boy-underlines-curse-caste-still-blights-india

6 accused of being a witch: news.trust.org/item/
20140813124950-sxqal

7 a disproportionate amount of this time settling
scores: economictimes.indiatimes.com/news/politics-
and-nation/sp-bsp-slugfest-getting-worse-by-the-day/
articleshow/3229721.cms

8 The going rate … 'roughly $250,000': wikileaks.org/plusd/
cables/08NEWDELHI2783_a.html

9 She denied the claims: ndtv.com/wikileak/assange-belongs-
in-mental-asylum-says-angry-mayawati-466799

10 low literacy … especially among women: rchiips.org/nfhs/
FCTS/UP/UP_Factsheet_149_Budaun.pdf

11 Dataganj was electrified in 1960: Balwant Singh, *Gazetteer
of India, Uttar Pradesh* (Govt. of Uttar Pradesh, Dept. of
District Gazetteers, 1986)

12 total assets worth 9 lakh rupees: myneta.info/up2007/
candidate.php?candidate_id=59

13 now worth 3 crore rupees: myneta.info/compare_profile.
    php?group_id=eRi9a25Kv2APZQSeuJQ8
14 'Someone to solve their problems': rediff.com/election/2002/
    feb/20_upr_prem_spe_1.htm

THE POLITICIAN'S AIDE

 1 fired from rooftops and mobbed a train: sciencespo.fr/
    mass-violence-war-massacre-resistance/en/document/
    hindu-muslim-communal-riots-india-ii-1986-2011
 2 78 per cent of the population ... was Hindu: census2011.
    co.in/census/district/520-budaun.html

CABLE WARS IN THE KATRA FIELDS

 1 5 per cent of the state force: bprd.nic.in/WriteReadData/
    userfiles/file/201607121235174125303FinalDATABOOKSM
    ALL2015.pdf
 2 photograph on Facebook: lens.blogs.nytimes.com/2014/
    07/24/a-india-photo-hanging-reflection/
 3 who else is responsible: aajtak.intoday.in/video/sisters-
    gangraped-and-killed-in-uttar-pradesh-budaun-three-police-
    --officers-suspend--1-765991.html
 4 drugged, raped, then dumped: indianexpress.com/article/
    india/india-others/dalits-flee-haryana-village-after-four-
    women-raped-seek-justice-in-delhi/
 5 'alarmist music and a sound track': caravanmagazine.in/
    vantage/times-now-processes-embarrassing-debacles
 6 'People couldn't stop watching it': openthemagazine.com/
    article/india/the-world-according-to-india-tv

A SWEEPER AND A 'WEAKER' DOCTOR

 1 250; at the most, 325: propublica.org/getinvolved/how-to-
    investigate-coroners-and-medical-examiners/

THE POST-MORTEM

1 guidelines for doctors: https://main.mohfw.gov.in/reports/
guidelines-and-protocols-medico-legal-care-survivors-victims-
sexual-violence

2 response to the 2012 Delhi bus rape: scroll.in/pulse/851783/
health-centres-are-still-failing-rape-survivors-three-years-after-
guidelines-on-unbiased-treatment

FAREWELL PADMA LALLI

1 200 tonnes of half-burnt human flesh: ft.com/content/
dadfae24-b23e-11e4-b380-00144feab7de

THE WORST PLACE IN THE WORLD

1 'Conspiracy by a Caste': Gardiner Harris and Hari Kumar,
'Rapes in India Fuel Charges of Conspiracy by a Caste',
New York Times, 29 May 2014, nytimes.com/2014/05/30/
world/asia/in-india-rape-and-murder-allegations-of-a-caste-
conspiracy.html

2 'extremely graphic images': huffingtonpost.co.uk/2014/05/29/
gang-rape-teen-india_n_5411634.html

3 'did not have access to a toilet': hindustantimes.com/india/
un-chief-ban-ki-moon-slams-Budaun-gang-rapes/story-
EhFYtPbgFpFNhQnpjD6BtJ.html

4 the worst place ... to be a woman: in.reuters.com/article/g20-
women/canada-best-g20-country-to-be-a-woman-india-worst-
idINDEE85C00420120613

5 Ibid.

6 The police stood nearby and watched: youtube.com/
watch?v=k7fApfVIyhg

7 'The same politicians who make laws against child
labour': youtube.com/watch?v=k7fApfVIyhg/; indiatoday.in/
india/north/story/mayawati-Budaun-visit-children-working-
helipad-samajwadi-party-195259-2014-06-01

8 'They tried to defame the girls and protect the culprits': youtube.
com/watch?v=3CFsz4DlRVk

9 only 'jungle raj': ibid.

10 https://www.ndtv.com/video/news/news/badaun-gang-rape-am-i-not-a-citizen-of-india-father-of-girl-asks-samajwadi-mp-323851

11 police officer to citizen ratio: livemint.com/news/india/indias-police-force-among-the-world-s-weakest-1560925355383.html

12 the police functioned at 48.1 per cent of its capacity: commoncause.in/uploadimage/page/Status_of_Policing_in_India_Report_2019_by_Common_Cause_and_CSDS.pdf

13 A recruitment drive was announced: ibid.

14 1 per cent ... on training new recruits: ibid.

15 7,338 cases of kidnapping and abduction: ncrb.gov.in/sites/default/files/crime_in_india_table_additional_table_chapter_reports/Chapter%205_2014.pdf

16 'marriage' accounted for about 40 per cent: blogs.wsj.com/indiarealtime/2015/08/20/abduction-of-women-for-marriage-is-on-the-rise-in-india/

17 a teenager ... was gang-raped: timesofindia.indiatimes.com/india/Girl-gang-raped-in-UPs-Azamgarh-district/articleshow/35777331.cms

18 found dangling in a tree: indianexpress.com/article/india/india-others/another-woman-found-hanging-from-tree-in-up-gangrape-suspected/

19 the body of yet another teenaged girl: Malavika Vyawahare, 'Another Case of Hanging in Indian State', *New York Times*, 12 June 2014, nytimes.com/2014/06/13/world/asia/in-india-another-woman-is-hanged-from-tree.html

THE WOMEN WHO CHANGED INDIA

1 In 2012 ... nearly 25,000 rapes: ncrb.gov.in/sites/default/files/crime_in_india_table_additional_table_chapter_reports/Chapter%205_2014.pdf

2 long trials and low conviction rates: epw.in/engage/article/deep-social-bias-marks-indias-response-rape

3 79 per cent of women ... didn't tell anyone: rchiips.org/nfhs/NFHS-4Reports/India.pdf

4 99.1 per cent cases of sexual violence were not reported: livemint.
   com/Politics/AV3sIKoEBAGZozALMX8THK/99-cases-of-
   sexual-assaults-go-unreported-govt-data-shows.html
5 made her story more compelling: cjr.org/analysis/india_rape_
   journalism.php
6 'the case was unstoppable': ibid.
7 These included rape, murder: ncrb.gov.in/sites/default/files/
   crime_in_india_table_additional_table_chapter_reports/
   Chapter%206_2014.pdf
8 'Emotion is a critical factor': npr.org/sections/goatsands
   oda/2017/01/13/509650251/study-what-was-the-impact-of-
   the-iconic-photo-of-the-syrian-boy
9 'imagine security personnel as a perpetrator': www.livemint.
   com/Politics/oUV23rXo2Z3zdJdB8qV8IK/Anatomy-of-
   rape-protests-in-India.html
10 'also a tissue of lies': indiankanoon.org/doc/1092711/
11 four law professors ... wrote a letter of protest: pldindia.org/
   wp-content/uploads/2013/03/Open-Letter-to-CJI-in-the-
   Mathura-Rape-Case.pdf
12 'the Court shall presume that she did not consent':
   indiankanoon.org/doc/1586025/
13 'her name was Jyoti Singh': theguardian.com/world/2017/
   feb/16/jyoti-singh-parents-call-for-honorary-museum-
   nirbhaya-to-use-her-real-name
14 'judges were ... changed five times': bbc.co.uk/news/
   world-asia-india-39265653

THE ZERO TOLERANCE POLICY

1 net worth was estimated at 15.6 million USD: ndtv.com/
   india-news/mayawatis-assets-worth-111-crores-she-has-380-
   carats-of-diamonds-471455
2 'We want justice': mewatch.sg/en/series/undercover-asia-s2/
   ep7/321996
3 Akhilesh ... didn't make the drive down: indiatoday.in/india/
   north/story/Budaun-rape-murder-whats-keeping-akhilesh-
   away-from-victims-kin-195450-2014-06-02

4 'Boys will be boys': indianexpress.com/article/india/politics/
mulayam-singh-yadav-questions-death-penalty-for-rape-
says-boys-make-mistakes/

5 'You're safe, right?': youtube.com/watch?v=oXZ7YeLni1c/;
ndtv.com/india-news/you-are-safe-arent-you-defiant-
akhilesh-on-being-questioned-over-law-order-564718

6 'look inwards and seek answers': timesofindia.indiatimes.
com/india/Narendra-Modi-pained-by-Budaun-rape-techie-
killing-in-Pune/articleshow/36412050.cms

7 'When you vote, do not forget this': indiatoday.in/elections/
story/delhi-polls-modi-attacks-congress-on-graft-security-of-
women-219290-2013-12-01

8 A majority ... had no confidence in the police: news.
gallup.com/poll/168956/indian-election-highlights-women-
personal-safety-concerns.aspx

9 strengthened for 'effective implementation': indiatoday.
in/india/north/story/narendra-modi-government-
violence-against-women-criminal-justice-system-
bjp-196312-2014-06-09

10 'stop their sons before they take the wrong path': bbc.co.uk/
news/world-asia-india-28799397

11 https://economictimes.indiatimes.com/news/politics-and-
nation/narendra-modi-hits-out-at-delhi-govt-over-security-
of-women-issue/articleshow/26707377.cms?from=mdr

A BROKEN SYSTEM EXPOSED

1 accused of gang rape, murder and criminal conspiracy:
hindustantimes.com/india/Budaun-gang-rape-   case-
5-main-accused-arrested-two-still-at-large/story-
cL8sbIqBKTlYfNALUpP54L.html

2 a broken system was being fixed: ndtv.com/india-news/66-
ias-42-ips-officers-transferred-in-uttar-pradesh-after-spate-
of-rapes-576203

3 'not saying that this is the motive': ibid.

4 give women the right ... to inherit: in 2017, the Supreme
Court clarified that the amended position of law applied to
daughters, irrespective of whether they were born before or

after 5 September 2005 (i.e. the date on which the amended law came into effect). egazette.nic.in/WriteReadData/200 5/E_45_2012_114.pdf

5 only 13 per cent of women ... inherited: s24756.pcdn.co/ wp-content/uploads/hsaa-study-report.pdf

6 fast-track courts: bbc.co.uk/news/world-asia-india-20944633

7 https://digitalcommons.law.yale.edu/cgi/viewcontent.cgi?ref erer=&httpsredir=1&article=1137&context=yhrdlj

8 enduring ... six trials: washingtonpost.com/world/ asia_pacific/an-indian-gang-rape-victim-went-to-court-for-11-years-but-her-ordeal-continues/2016/08/15/c92075ce-5757-4073-b8c2-b0dc42f54ed0_story.html?postshare=2371471 326459064&tid=ss_mail

9 judge-population ratio: lawcommissionofindia.nic.in/101-169/Report120.pdf

10 31.28 million cases pending: timesofindia.indiatimes.com/ india/Courts-will-take-320-years-to-clear-backlog-cases-Justice-Rao/articleshow/5651782.cms

11 320 years to clear the backlog: ibid.

12 allegations ... that SITs were vulnerable to political influence: caravanmagazine.in/vantage/postings-cops-bureaucrats-sit-members-godhra-2002-investigation

13 Yadav officers headed nearly 60 per cent of police stations: timesofindia.indiatimes.com/india/Yadavisation-of-UP-cops-behind-anarchy/articleshow/36165826.cms

SEPARATE MILK FROM WATER

1 'I *want* the CBI': youtube.com/watch?v=JDYGO506VNw

2 Special Police Establishment: cbi.gov.in/history.php

3 legal power to investigate: legislative.gov.in/sites/default/files/ A1946-25.pdf

4 state-of-the-art building: india.blogs.nytimes.com/2011/11/09/ inside-the-c-b-i-well-the-building-anyway/

5 registered with the Anti-Corruption Division: *Routledge Handbook of Corruption in Asia*, edited by Ting Gong, Ian Scott (Routledge, 2017)

6 It could probe 700 cases a year: livemint.com/
Politics/1LYhKM5HPoaBFxmQH3VvGN/CBI-may-
collapse-due-to-lack-of-staff-Anil-Sinha.html

7 'everyone wants every case to go to the CBI': old.tehelka.
com/some-call-us-congress-bureau-of-investigation-but-also-
ask-for-a-cbi-inquiry-ap-singh/

8 60 per cent more work than it was equipped to handle:
timesofindia.indiatimes.com/india/CBI-arrested-only-nine-
persons-in-anti-graft-cases-in-2014/articleshow/38928682.
cms; ndtv.com/india-news/cbi-may-collapse-due-to-lack-of-
manpower-says-its-chief-anil-sinha-1399701

9 it was at 69 per cent: economictimes.indiatimes.com/news/
politics-and-nation/conviction-rate-of-cbi-dipped-in-last-3-
years-govt/articleshow/58148427.cms

10 1,000 posts left unfilled: persmin.gov.in/AnnualReport/
AR2015_2016(Eng).pdf

11 the agency would 'collapse and fail': ndtv.com/india-news/
cbi-may-collapse-due-to-lack-of-manpower-says-its-chief-
anil-sinha-1399701

12 if the agency wanted to prosecute a government official:
economictimes.indiatimes.com/news/politics-and-
nation/not-easy-for-cbi-to-be-independent-agency/
articleshow/19980389.cms

13 a scam that involved coal field leases: Neha Thirani Bagri,
'India's Top Court Revokes Coal Leases', New York Times,
25 September 2014, nytimes.com/2014/09/25/business/
international/indias-supreme-court-revokes-hundreds-of-
coal-concessions.html

14 'The heart of the report was changed': timesofindia.indiatimes.
com/india/CBI-a-caged-parrot-heart-of-Coalgate-report-
changed-Supreme-Court/articleshow/19952260.cms

15 corruption charges against ... their own former
director: livemint.com/Politics/mspqgmEEizhIFGplsoiFqM/
CBI-files-FIR-against-Ranjit-Sinha-in-a-coal-scam-case.html

16 the force was subject to political influence: in.reuters.com/
   article/cbi-supreme-court-parrot-coal/a-caged-parrot-
   supreme-court-describes-cbi-idINDEE94901W20130510
17 theagency'sconvictionrateincorruptioncases:hindustantimes.
   com/delhi-news/cbi-conviction-rate-stands-at-a-lowly-4-
   reveals-study/story-wfZ2GgFUuGIeH4M9SAwIjM.html
18 'the cycle continues': in.reuters.com/article/cbi-supreme-
   court-parrot-coal/a-caged-parrot-supreme-court-describes-
   cbi-idINDEE94901W20130510

PURITY AND POLLUTION

1 'production-line abattoirs': timesofindia.indiatimes.com/
   india/Forensic-expert-seeks-end-to-abattoir-style-post-
   mortems/articleshow/45959581.cms
2 Hindu pandits ... took up vigil: timesofindia.indiatimes.
   com/city/kolkata/175-year-old-dissection-papers-unearthed/
   articleshow/7272410.cms

'HABITUAL OF SEXUAL INTERCOURSE'

1 Scarlett Keeling: news.bbc.co.uk/1/hi/england/devon/
   7426821.stm
2 some internal organs ... hadn't been put back: news.bbc.
   co.uk/1/hi/england/devon/8067134.stm
3 jail plus hard labour: theguardian.com/world/2019/jul/19/
   man-sentenced-to-10-years-hard-labour-over-death-of-
   scarlett-keeling
4 'others must come to know of her conduct': indiankanoon.
   org/docfragment/76278/?formInput=%22habituated%20
   to%20sex%22%20%20sortby%3A%20leastrecent
5 An affirmative report ... was not proof of consent: thehindu.
   com/news/national/No-two-finger-test-for-rape-SC/
   article12141055.ece
6 'to tell if someone has had vaginal intercourse': https://www.
   nytimes.com/2019/11/07/health/ti-daughter-virginity-test.
   html?searchResultPosition=2

A MOTHER GOES 'MAD'

1 if his boys were guilty ... they *should* be punished: youtube. com/watch?v=Gr2rG5trGw4

VISITORS TO THE JAIL

1 less care ... is taken of girls than of boys: archive.org/stream/ in.ernet.dli.2015.48010/2015.48010.Budaun---A-Gazetteer_ djvu.txt
2 released 300 convicts: ibid.
3 squeezed in three times the number: timesofindia.indiatimes. com/city/bareilly/-100-inmates-from-district-jails-to-be-shifted-to-bareilly-central-jail/articleshow/64324511.cms
4 the police ... agreed to open an investigation: timesofindia. indiatimes.com/articleshow/35625314.cms?utm_ source=contentofinterest&utm_medium=text&utm_ campaign=cppst
5 paid the jailer and some of his men to kill the boy: timesofindia. indiatimes.com/city/lucknow/Rape-accused-murdered-in-Budaun-jail-report-says/articleshow/35612681.cms

THE CASE OF THE MISSING PHONES

1 Other substations were also set on fire: scotsman.com/ news/world/anger-boils-indian-power-cuts-fuel-heat-misery-1534751
2 a correlation between high temperatures ... and the risk of violent crimes: hbs.edu/faculty/Publication%20Files/14-067_45092fee-b164-4662-894b-5d28471fa69b.pdf
3 constituencies of politicians: scotsman.com/news/world/ anger-boils-indian-power-cuts-fuel-heat-misery-1534751
4 'Residents have been particularly angry': ibid.

'DID YOU KILL PADMA AND LALLI?'

1 India's latest high-profile rape case: timesofindia. indiatimes.com/city/mumbai/Two-forensic-labs-from-

outside-state-called-upon-to-collect-fresh-evidence/
articleshow/22083726.cms

2 'not the first girl I've raped': Ellen Barry and Mansi Choksi,
'Gang Rape, Routine and Invisible', *New York Times*, 27
October 2013, nytimes.com/2013/10/27/world/asia/gang-rape-
in-india-routine-and-invisible.html

3 'she was wearing skimpy clothes': ibid.

4 raped at least ten people: timesofindia.indiatimes.com/
city/mumbai/Shakti-Mills-gang-rape-accused-assaulted-10-
women-in-6-months/articleshow/22273845.cms

5 'emboldened' to commit more: ibid.

6 'traps for unsuspecting women': timesofindia.indiatimes.com/
articleshow/22273845.cms?utm_source=contentofinterest&utm_
medium=text&utm_campaign=cppst

'MACHINES DON'T LIE'

1 'how to recognise the control questions': bbc.com/news/
magazine-22467640

DROWNED

1 Four months after the girls had died: youtube.com/watch?v=
3ygizX5AAQE

2 'lazy attitude': youtube.com/watch?v=Y-p5KWhEoOU

3 'DROWNED!': youtube.com/watch?v=whTAjoLojAU

RESULTS AND RUMOURS

1 'they will … hang themselves to death': ndtv.com/video/
news/the-buck-stops-here/watch-complete-u-turn-in-
Budaun-case-335409

2 'I have no proof': indianexpress.com/article/india/india-others/
girls-family-to-challenge-cbi-conclusion-in-court/

3 earlier acts of grave malfeasance: nytimes.com/2019/01/30/
opinion/india-arms-deal-corruption-modi.html

4 as the Supreme Court had declared: reuters.
com/article/india-politics-cbi-coalgate/

government-meddled-in-cbi-probe-says-supreme-court-idIN
DEE9470DZ20130508?irpc=932

5 admitted to the rampage: independent.co.uk/news/world/
outcry-in-delhi-over-kashmir-massacre-1477194.html

6 'atrocities against women': indianexpress.com/article/
india/india-others/in-up-modi-takes-on-mulayam-says-sp-
misleading-people-under-veil-of-secularism/

THE ROGUE OFFICER

1 an 'objectionable position': timesofindia.indiatimes.com/city/
delhi/Aarushi-and-Hemraj-were-in-objectionable-position-
CBI/articleshow/19698674.cms

2 a higher court overturned the conviction: hindustantimes.
com/india-news/aarushi-hemraj-murder-case-rajesh-nupur-
talwar-walk-free/story-VM79MJ2cDNA67OGJltIZsN.html

3 Kaul had tampered with evidence: firstpost.com/india/
aarushi-murder-case-allahabad-hc-judgment-answers-how-
cbi-tampered-perjured-itself-and-wrecked-trial-against-
talwars-4164221.html

FRIENDS, NOT STRANGERS

1 'We are investigating the matter': indianexpress.com/article/
india/india-others/girls-family-to-challenge-cbi-conclusion-
in-court/

2 'how to go about the bail application': ibid.

3 the turn of the Yadav brothers: www.bbc.co.uk/news/
world-asia-india-29062228

PAPPU AND NAZRU FACE TO FACE

1 'an honest officer': statetimes.in/epaper/uploads/2014/10/19/2.
pdf

'GIRLS ARE HONOUR OF FAMILY'

1 https://www.indiacode.nic.in/bitstream/123456789 /2079/1/201232.pdf#search=Protection% 20of%20Children%20 from%20Sexual%20Offences%20Act

2 the age of consent had been increased: iitk.ac.in/wc/data/ TheCriminalLaw.pdf

3 in response to the Delhi bus rape: iitk.ac.in/wc/data/ TheCriminalLaw.pdf; bbc.co.uk/news/world-asia-india-21950197

LOVE, HOPE, VOTE

1 criminal charges for attempted murder and rioting: bbc. co.uk/news/world-asia-india-39403778

2 'whip up anti-Muslim hysteria': ibid.

3 failed to publish its annual crime report: timesofindia. indiatimes.com/city/surat/ncrb-fails-to-publish-crime-in-india-report-even-after-year/articleshow/67445165.cms

4 effort to suppress negative data: newsclick.in/ NCRB-DATA-Crime-India

5 most dangerous place in the world for women: poll2018.trust. org/stories/item/?id=e52a1260-260c-47e0-94fc-a636b1956da7

6 at a greater risk of sexual violence: poll2018.trust.org/ country/?id=india

7 The economy had slowed to a crawl: ft.com/content/ c697cf60-1813-11ea-9ee4-11f260415385

8 unemployment was at its highest: reuters.com/article/ us-india-economy-jobs/indian-jobless-rate-at-multi-decade-high-report-says-in-blow-to-modi-idUSKCN1PP0FX

9 https://www.dnaindia.com/india/report-modi-government-says-no-to-rape-crisis-centres-in-every-district-2063977

10 https://www.dnaindia.com/india/report-modi-government-says-no-to-rape-crisis-centres-in-every-district-2063977

11 https://timesofindia.indiatimes.com/india/nearly-90-of-nirbhaya-fund-lying-unused-govt-data/ articleshow/72421059.cms

12 https://www.business-standard.com/article/pti-stories/
    atrocities-on-womenhave-spiked-under-bjp-govt-women-
    organisations-119031400951_1.html
13 the agency's reputation was at its lowest ebb: huffingtonpost.
    in/2018/10/25/modi-doval-manipulating-and-misusing-cvc-
    and-cbi-says-ex-bjp-leader-yashwant-sinha_a_23571426/;
    huffingtonpost.in/2018/10/24/modi-govt-affecting-
    independence-of-cbi-ousted-director-alok-verma-tells-
    supreme-court_a_23570596/
14 threatenedtosetherselfonfire:nytimes.com/2019/07/31/world/
    asia/unnao-india-rape-case.html?searchResultPosition=2
15 a girl ... was found hanging in a tree: hindustantimes.com/
    india-news/six-year-old-girl-found-hanging-from-tree-on-
    outskirts-of-lucknow/story-svO8B11hDnoWmUoxFHfj4N.
    html

Bibliography

Agrawal, Ravi, *India Connected* (Oxford University Press, 2018)

Andolan, Bachpan Bachao, *Missing Children of India: A Pioneering Study* (Vitasta Publishing, 2012)

Aron, Sunita, *Akhilesh Yadav: Winds of Change* (Westland, 2013)

Banerjee, Abhijit V., and Duflo, Esther, *Poor Economics: A Radical Rethinking of the Way to Fight Global Poverty* (Penguin Random House India, 2011)

Bose, Ajoy, *Behenji: A Political Biography of Mayawati* (Penguin India, 2009)

Byapari, Manoranjan, *Interrogating my Chandal Life: An Autobiography of a Dalit* (Sage Samya, 2018)

Coffey, Diane and Spears, Dean, *Where India Goes: Abandoned Toilets, Stunted Development and the Costs of Caste* (Harper Litmus, 2017)

Devy, GN, *The Crisis Within: On Knowledge and Education in India* (Aleph Book Company, 2017)

Doniger, Wendy, *The Hindus: An Alternative History* (Speaking Tiger, 2015)

Drèze, Jean and Sen, Amartya, *An Uncertain Glory: India and its Contradictions* (Allen Lane, 2013)

Eck, Diana L., *India: A Sacred Geography* (Random House, 2012)

Gidla, Sujatha, *Ants Among Elephants: An Untouchable Family and the Making of Modern India* (Harper Collins, 2017)

Jauregui, Beatrice, *Provisional Authority: Police, Order, and Security in India* (The Orient Blackswan, 2017)

Jeffrey, Robin and Doron, Assa, *Cell Phone Nation: How Mobile Phones have Revolutionized Business, Politics and Ordinary Life in India* (Hachette India, 2015)

Joseph, Josy, *A Feast of Vultures: The Hidden Business of Democracy in India* (Harper Collins India, 2016)

Kumar, Ravish, *The Free Voice: On Democracy, Culture and the Nation* (Speaking Tiger, 2019)

McDermid, Val, *Forensics: The Anatomy of Crime* (Profile Books, 2015)

Nehru, Jawaharlal, *An Autobiography* (Oxford University Press, 1936)

Oldenburg, Veena Talwar, *Dowry Murder: Revisiting a Cultural Whodunnit* (Penguin Books India, 2010)

Saini, Angela, *Geek Nation: How Indian Science is Taking Over the World* (Hodder Paperbacks, 2012)

Sen, Amartya, *The Country of First Boys* (Oxford University Press India, 2015)

Sen, Amartya, 'Millions of Missing Women', *New York Review of Books*, 20 December 1990

Sen, Avirook, *Aarushi* (Penguin Books India, 2015)

Sen, Mala, *Death by Fire: Sati, Dowry Death and Female Infanticide in Modern India* (Phoenix, 2002)

Sen, Mala, *India's Bandit Queen: The True Story of Phoolan Devi* (Pandora, 1995)

Acknowledgements

Thank you: Eduardo Faleiro and Muriel Faleiro, Shaila Faleiro and Nirmala Faleiro, Raoul Makkar and Samara Makkar.

Negar Akhavi, Anne Alden, Anshul Avijit, Manica Singh Avijit, Bipin Pradip Aspatwar, Vikas Bajaj, Abhijit Banerjee, Sidharth Bhatia, Fatima Bhutto, Fanny Cabrera, Julia Churchill, Chandrahas Choudhury, Tom Daniel, Sujeet Singh Deo, Elisabeth Dodds, Jean Drèze, Stephan Faris, Sarah Faulding, McKenzie Funk, Rajni George, Monica Gandhi, Vanessa Gezari, Marc Herman, Samar Halarnkar, Mira Kamdar, Adrian Levy, Phil McKnight, Katherine Kodama, Mary Mount, Pankaj Mishra, Sunil Menon, Shalini Menon, Richa Nigam, Vik Sharma, Arunava Sinha, Michael Shilman, Mary Shilman, Ruchika Soi, Rajesh Sharma, Amit Varma, Jasmine ShahVarma, Priyanka Vadra and Astrid Van Weyenberg.

For generously sharing information, thank you Soutik Biswas, Jason Burke, Shashank Bengali, James Crabtree, Shoaib Daniyal, Naresh Fernandes, P. Kerim Friedman, Annie Gowen, Sarah Hafeez, Rustom Irani, Hari Kumar, Gargi Rawat, Daisy Rockwell, Betwa Sharma, Shashwati Talukdar and Abhishek Waghmare. For transcription and translation, thank you Bhaskar Tripathi.

For early reads, and so much more, thank you Rahul Bhatia, Isaac Chotiner and Angela Saini.

For everything you do, thank you Nikita Lalwani.

Tracy Bohan is the agent of my dreams, and I'm also very grateful to Jin Auh and everyone at the Wylie Agency.

I'm indebted to my brilliant editor Alexandra Pringle who encouraged me to use my voice. In India, Meru Gokhale, Manasi Subramaniam and Shiny Das were steadfast in their support. In the US, I was very lucky to have Elisabeth Schmitz on my team. I also owe profound thanks to Faiza Sultan Khan and Saba Ahmed for making this manuscript better and stronger. And I'm grateful to Angelique Tran Van Sang, Allegra Le Fanu, Lauren Whybrow, Yvonne Cha, Anne Collins and Amanda Betts, and their many superb colleagues at Bloomsbury UK, Grove Atlantic, Penguin Random House India and Penguin Random House Canada.

Over the years I've been lucky to work with excellent editors. I'd particularly like to thank Ravi Agrawal, Rosie Blau, Emily Cooke, John Freeman, Yuka Igarashi, Bobbie Johnson, Joe Kent, Rachel Poser, Kit Rachlis, Parul Sehgal, Sasha Polakow-Suransky, Sankarshan Thakur, Altaf Tyrewala and Simon Willis. I'm also thankful for the support of Tom Hundley and the Pulitzer Centre, as well as to The Investigative Fund.

Thank you Ulrik McKnight, Indira Freya McKnight and Zoey Faleiro McKnight: I'm so lucky to call you mine.

This book is dedicated to the memory of Dr Rakesh Mishra, an exceptional scholar and beloved friend.

A Note on the Author

Sonia Faleiro is the author of *Beautiful Thing: Inside the Secret World of Bombay's Dance Bars*, which was named a book of the year by the *Guardian, Observer, Sunday Times, Economist* and *Time Out*, and a novella, *The Girl*. She is a co-founder of Deca, a global cooperative of award-winning journalists. Her writing and photographs appear in the *New York Times, Financial Times, Granta, 1843 and Harper's*. She lives in London.

A Note on the Type

The text of this book is set Adobe Garamond. It is one of several versions of Garamond based on the designs of Claude Garamond. It is thought that Garamond based his font on Bembo, cut in 1495 by Francesco Griffo in collaboration with the Italian printer Aldus Manutius. Garamond types were first used in books printed in Paris around 1532. Many of the present-day versions of this type are based on the *Typi Academiae* of Jean Jannon cut in Sedan in 1615.

Claude Garamond was born in Paris in 1480. He learned how to cut type from his father and by the age of fifteen he was able to fashion steel punches the size of a pica with great precision. At the age of sixty he was commissioned by King Francis I to design a Greek alphabet, and for this he was given the honourable title of royal type founder. He died in 1561.